From Learning to Love

Centennial Psychology Series
Charles D. Spielberger, *General Editor*

Anne Anastasi   *Contributions to Differential Psychology*
John J. Atkinson   *Personality, Motivation, and Action*
Raymond B. Cattell   *Structured Personality Learning Theory*
William K. Estes   *Models of Learning, Memory, and Choice*
Hans J. Eysenck   *Personality, Genetics and Behavior*
Harry F. Harlow   *From Learning to Love*
Irving L. Janis   *Stress, Attitudes and Decisions*
David C. McClelland   *Motives, Personality, and Society*
Neal Miller   *Bridges between Laboratory and Clinic*
Brenda Milner   *Brain Function and Cognition*
O. Hobart Mowrer   *Leaves from Many Seasons*
Charles E. Osgood   *Language, Meaning, and Culture*
Julian B. Rotter   *The Development and Applications of Social Learning Theory*
Seymour B. Sarason   *Psychology and Social Action*
Benton J. Underwood   *Studies in Learning and Memory*

From Learning to Love

The Selected Papers
of H. F. Harlow

Edited by Clara Mears Harlow

PRAEGER

New York
Westport, Connecticut
London

Library of Congress Cataloging-in-Publication Data

Harlow, Harry Frederick, 1905–
    From learning to love.

    (Centennial psychology series)
    Includes index.
    1. Primates—Behavior. 2. Love—Psychological
aspects. 3. Learning in animals. I. Harlow, Clara Mears
II. Title. III. Series.
[QL737.P9H25 1986]   599.8′0451   86-15120
ISBN 0-275-92224-3 (alk. paper)

Library of Congress Catalog Card Number: 86-15120
ISBN: 0-275-92224-3

First published in 1986

Praeger Publishers, 521 Fifth Avenue, New York, NY 10175
A division of Greenwood Press, Inc.

Printed in the United States of America

The paper used in this book complies with the Permanent
Paper Standard issued by the National Information Standards
Organization (Z39.48-1984).

10 9 8 7 6 5 4 3 2 1

Contents

List of Figures

List of Tables

Editor's Introduction

The founding of Wilhelm Wundt's laboratory at Leipzig in 1879 is widely acclaimed as the landmark event that provided the initial impetus for the development of psychology as an experimental science. To commemorate scientific psychology's one-hundredth anniversary, Praeger Publishers commissioned the Centennial Psychology Series. The general goals of the Series are to present, in both historical and contemporary perspective, the most important papers of distinguished contributors to psychological theory and research.

As psychology enters its second century, the Centennial Series proposes to examine the foundation on which scientific psychology is built. Each volume provides a unique opportunity for the reader to witness the emerging theoretical insights of eminent psychologists whose seminal work has served to define and shape their respective fields, and to share with them the excitement associated with the discovery of new scientific knowledge.

The selection of the authors for this Series was an extremely difficult task. Indexes of scientific citations and rosters of the recipients of prestigious awards for research contributions were examined. Nominations were invited from leading authorities in various fields of psychology. The opinions of experienced teachers of psychology and recent graduates of doctoral programs were solicited. There was, in addition, a self-selection factor: A few of the distinguished senior psychologists invited to participate in the Series were not able to do so, most often because of demanding professional commitments or ill health.

Each Series author was invited to develop a volume comprising five major parts: (1) an original introductory chapter; (2) previously published articles and original papers; (3) a concluding chapter; (4) a brief autobiography; and (5) a complete bibliography of the author's publications. The main content of each volume consists of articles and papers especially selected for this Series by the author. These papers trace the historical development of the author's work over a period of forty to fifty years. Each volume also provides a cogent presentation of the author's current research and theoretical viewpoints.

In their introductory chapters, the Series authors were asked to describe the intellectual climate that prevailed at the beginning of their scientific careers, and to examine the evolution of the ideas that led them from one study to another. They were also invited to comment on significant factors—both scientific and personal—that stimulated and motivated them to embark on their research programs and to consider special opportunities or constraints that influenced their work, including experimental failures and blind alleys only rarely reported in the literature.

In order to preserve the historical record, most of the articles reprinted in these volumes have been reproduced exactly as they appeared when they were first published. In some cases, however, the authors have abridged their original papers (but not altered the content), so that redundant materials could be eliminated and more papers could be included. In the concluding chapters, authors were asked to comment on their selected papers, to describe representative studies on which they are currently working, and to evaluate the status of their research. Perhaps the most difficult task faced by Series authors was in selecting a limited number of papers considered most representative of their life work from the complete bibliography that appears at the end of the Volume.

The Centennial Psychology Series is especially designed for courses on the history of psychology. Individual volumes are well-suited for use as supplementary texts in those areas of the discipline to which the authors have been major contributors. Students of psychology and related disciplines, as well as authorities in specialized fields, will find that each Series volume provides penetrating insight into the work of a significant contributor to the behavioral sciences. The Series also affords a unique perspective on psychological research as a living process.

HARLOW'S CONTRIBUTION

Although general guidelines were suggested for each Centennial Volume, authors were encouraged to adapt the Series format to meet their individual needs. The papers reprinted in this Volume were selected by Professor Harry F. Harlow in the spring of 1981, and received in the Praeger editorial offices by mid-summer of that year. The responsibility for completing the Volume after Professor Harlow's death was assumed by Dr. Clara Mears Harlow.

After graduating from Stanford University in 1930, Harry Frederick Harlow was appointed Assistant Professor of Psychology at the University of Wisconsin, and remained there throughout his highly productive career until retirement. He was named George Cary Comstock Research Professor of Psychology in 1955, and was Editor of the *Journal of Comparative and Physiological Psychology* for more than 20 years. A member of numerous professional and scientific societies, he was elected to the National Research Council and the National Academy of Sciences, and served as President of the American Psychological Association in 1957–58, the Midwestern Psychological Association and the APA Division of Experimental Psychology.

In her introduction, Clara Mears Harlow highlights the personal characteristics and formative experiences that shaped the evolution of

Harry Harlow's scientific research. She also shares her sensitive insights into the unique creative genius, the extraordinary powers of observation and remarkable resourcefulness that guided Harry Harlow's scientific work throughout his highly productive career, spanning a period of more than 50 years. The significance of Harlow's impact on the social and behavioral sciences, especially on comparative and physiological psychology, can be readily seen in the papers that are reprinted in this Volume.

The Society of Experimental Psychologists awarded Harlow the Warren Medal in 1956 and he received the APA Distinguished Scientific Contributions Award in 1960. Although presented a quarter century ago, the citation for the Distinguished Contributions Award (American Psychologist, 1960, p. 790) provides a succinct summary of Harlow's remarkable personal qualities and most significant scientific contributions:

> For his indefatigable curiosity which has opened up new areas of research in animal behavior and has helped greatly to keep comparative psychology near the center of the psychological stage. Throughout the years his vivid imagination has led to the analysis of many stimulus relationships, the exploratory and manipulatory motives, and the all-but-ubiquitous learning sets. Recently the age-old problem of love has been revitalized by his persistent concern for the facts of motivation. It is, indeed, his unswerving devotion to fact, observation, and experiment that has given his contribution an integrity of inestimable value to scientific psychology.

ACKNOWLEDGEMENTS

The interest and enthusiasm of all with whom we have consulted concerning the establishment of the Centennial Psychology Series have been most gratifying. I am especially grateful to Professors Anne Anastasi, Hans J. Eysenck, and Irving L. Janis for their many helpful comments and suggestions and their early agreement to contribute to the Series. The completion of this Volume would not have been possible without the original contributions and dedicated editorial work of Dr. Clara Mears Harlow. We are also indebted to Mrs. Helen A. LeRoy, Harry Harlow's Executive Secretary, for her assistance in locating the original art work and preparing Professor Harlow's reprinted papers for publication. For invaluable advice and consultation in the conception and planning of the Series, and his dedicated and effective work in making the Series a reality, I am deeply indebted to Dr. George Zimmar, Psychology Editor for Praeger Publishers.

Charles D. Spielberger

The Evolution of Harlow Research

Clara Mears Harlow

Harry Harlow was not always famous, but he had a long-standing reputation for being unique. He was, to start, unique in having a fine job of his choice awaiting him at the University of Wisconsin in 1930, the first full year of the Great Depression. In the fall of the year he arrived, he joined the staff of the Department of Psychology, fresh from earning his doctoral degree, his second degree from Stanford University.

Upon arrival in Madison he was immediately treated to a series of experiences which added up to the third degree.

Harlow first located the faculty club he planned to make his temporary residence. He crossed the lobby to the reception desk and asked, "Do you have a room reservation for Dr. Harry Harlow of the psychology department?"

"Why, yes," was the answer. "Do you happen to know when he will arrive?"

Harlow went to his room, unpacked one bag, and then ventured forth to begin his acquaintance with the campus. He joined the swelling ranks of persons trudging up the sidewalks on both sides of the long, wide, grassy slope known as "The Hill."

The sidewalks were lined with a series of University buildings. Harry turned toward two young men next to him and said, "Pardon me, but can you tell me which of the buildings is Bascom Hall?"

"Sorry, but we can't help you," they replied. "We're freshmen too."

Bascom Hall proved to be an imposing edifice straight ahead at the top of the hill, and Harry, not very self-confident but unabashed, even located his office on the lower floor. The door was open—at least the door knew that he was coming. He sat down at his desk. Just at that moment a fairly tall young man with a Lincolnesque face poked his head into the doorway. He looked straight at Harry Harlow and said "Don't tell me he isn't here yet. I absolutely must get started, and I've been waiting to see him to know what to do. Haven't you any idea when he is coming?"

Recently I came across an excerpt from the beginning of an unfinished, unpublished autobiography of Harry Harlow, which follows:

> My student associations at Stanford during graduate school represented the finest collection of animate I.Q.'s that Terman ever assembled since his studies on genius. Within the group there were Homer Weaver, Barbara Burks, Dick Husband, E. Lowell Kelley, Don Marquis, L. P. Herrington, Ted and Floyd Ruch, Ray Carpenter, and Roger Barker. As a farewell gesture before leaving Stanford, we changed Bob Sears' major from English to Psychology, and he remained an honorary member of the group even after he went to Yale. To complete the picture, he eventually changed from being a goldfish experimenter to a child development theorist.
>
> I almost failed to become a member of this distinguished group because I had been a timid child and had been a timid graduate student. Dr. Terman called me into his office and told me he thought I was a bright young man, but that I was so timid that I would never be able to speak in public. He indicated that they expected to place me in a California junior college, and, with every Wisconsin winter, I wish to God they had. Unfortunately, the junior college had standards which required some education courses which I had not taken, and, as a result, I was condemned to get a Ph.D.

Harry Harlow was still shy when I became acquainted with him, but the only time I ever knew him to be really modest about his own accomplishments was when referring to his fellow graduate students at Stanford.

OVERVIEW OF HARLOW RESEARCH

In the early 1930s psychology was still an infant. Had Harlow by then already made his studies of the affectional systems, he might well have said that psychology was still suffering the pangs and problems of mother separation after being weaned from its philosophical parent.

Harlow's research and the number of his publications grew steadily along with the entire field of psychology. There were pioneer studies to determine basic principles of behavior and better strategies for its exploration. He covered and uncovered significant aspects of the localization of functions in the cortex and studied in depth the evolution and development of learning, motivation, and the affectional systems in the primate. His vistas broadened to include the pathological effects of some rearing conditions and the interrelationships between love, aggression, and fear.

Harlow explored enough behavioral areas to have occupied the lives of several ordinary mortals, but then the results, too, would probably have been ordinary.

By the end of the fifty years, Harlow's publications numbered over 320. Had one not known of the caliber of the Harlow research, one might have suspected productivity for its own sake, but Harlow himself had an apt description of an example of just that. This was a recipe for converting one article into three. The first article portrays the discovery of a wild boy of Africa, giving some details of his location and condition. The next article, a year later, gives an account of his capture and return to civilization. The last and third of the series sadly apologizes for the writer's slight mistake and offers a retraction: the boy was not quite wild after all, but there was a tempting suggestion that a boy in India might have more promise.

For the volume of selected papers, the number of articles required reduction to about twenty. The selection would have been a Herculean task, but fortunately the choice was made by Harry Harlow himself, in the spring of 1981. By that time Harlow had already made miracles his prerogative.

The following selections are as representative of all the different stages of Harlow research as was possible within the limitations of space. One of the purposes of this introduction is to briefly fill in a few of the missing links which show how one important field of exploration led inexorably to the next series of experiments. Harlow (251)* described the process: "A basic maxim of scientific investigation is that research directed toward providing an answer for a particular question will generate a host of new problems awaiting resolution. Rarely is scientific inquiry germinated and subsequently resolved in a vacuum."

WHAT MADE HARLOW HARLOW?

The other purpose, of equal importance, in this introduction is more complex, probably because it involves primate behavior. What is there about Harlow's background or his general makeup that resulted in the ability to create such exciting, unique, and yet realistic experiments? These were experiments which changed or redirected many phases of the science of psychology. With the contributions of such researchers as Wollff and Fantz, Harlow also turned the incompetent infant into a fascinating individual. I am not sure that even Harry Harlow could answer these questions, but his response would not be dull.

*Numbers refer to complete bibliography in this volume.

Anyone who knew Harry Harlow knew that he was unique. At his lectures the students were alert to prevent their missing some new twist of thought. Even if they sometimes forgot to take notes, they often remembered the content better than at other classes well notarized.

Some family background facts may bring a glimmer of insight into the Harlow accomplishments. Harry's family was a closely knit, extended family, claiming a nearby paternal grandmother and two married but childless aunts. Not everyone grows up with three surrogate mothers plus a biological mother and then proceeds to make the surrogate mother famous. One aunt moved to Oregon when Harry was an infant, but she returned for frequent visits, just to see her beloved nephews. This Aunt Nellie had an imagination different from, but at least equal to, Harlow's own. She created life-sized actor-figures and produced theatricals for the neighborhood children in a backyard theater.

Harry's father kept the family from monotony by periodically changing his occupation from farming to real estate to general stores. He also was the only man known to refuse an offer to run the first Ford Agency in his city.

Harry was the next to the youngest of four bright boys. The brothers found their closest friendships within the family as they grew. They played most of the games which were well-known at the time, and when they were bored, they invented their own. The two older brothers set the pace and made the rules. In order to be included in the group, Harry learned that he must be alert, listen, be aware of what he was saying, and be able to substantiate his words. Years later, these traits were to be long-term assets.

All four brothers pursued graduate studies after obtaining their bachelor's degrees, all at Stanford University except the eldest, who earned his M.D. at Portland, Oregon. During this time, Harry spent his first year at Reed College before entering Stanford.

Harry Harlow completed his doctorate at Stanford just prior to coming to the University of Wisconsin, Madison. When being interviewed for the new position, he had been informed that his primary responsibilities would be to direct the Psychology Animal Laboratory, as well as to teach some classes and seminars.

Being a comparative psychologist in the first half of the twentieth century denoted having more than a speaking acquaintance with rats. Rats were the subjects for experiments in practically every psychology laboratory in the United States and in the world. Harry Harlow had used rats as the subjects for his dissertation on the social facilitation of eating. He had run rats for the studies of Professor Walter Miles at Stanford. When he arrived in Madison in September 1930, he was anxious to see his laboratory. He sought Dr. V. A. C. Henmon, the chairman of the Department of Psychology.

A SCIENTIST WITHOUT A LABORATORY

Dr. Henmon was a kindly man who had postponed breaking bad news to the new member of the department. Now he had to inform Harry Harlow that the animal laboratory had been condemned and torn down last spring. A comparative psychologist, in Harlow's language, was a psychologist without compare, but a comparative psychologist without a laboratory was like a doctor without patients.

The University officials had been searching for a new laboratory or even a new but temporary location. They continued to do so. They tried to find any room that would hold Dr. Harlow, a few students, and quite a few mice or rats. They were becoming discouraged. On the last try, they chose a room in the basement of Bascom Hall, just below the office of the dean of men. In the thirties in Wisconsin, air conditioning was just a new term, not one related in any way to education. As summer approached, the aroma rose with heat, and the dean of men sent out an ultimatum: "The aroma wafting up from below was not good for solving the problems of either the dean or the students."

Your present author started her graduate studies at the University of Wisconsin Department of Psychology the same month and year that Dr. Harlow started his teaching. I was a graduate assistant in the Department of Educational Psychology because that was the only position open.

Dr. Harlow entered my life almost as soon as I entered the University. My first course under him was in my first semester: The psychology of the emotions, and I quickly discovered the fascination of his lectures. The next semester I signed up for physiological psychology. I didn't know it at the time, but that was Harlow's course for weeding out borderline students.

I was also enrolled in a Harlow evening seminar. When I began making As in physiological psychology, Harry Harlow began escorting me home. In the course of our walks, we found that we both shared an interest in playing bridge, as well as an interest in psychology. This seemingly irrelevant fact played a part in altering the course of Harlow's research.

Dr. and Mrs. Henmon also enjoyed bridge, and a once-a-week invitation to play at their home ensued. One evening Mrs. Henmon and I were winning against the men. Mrs. Henmon was very pleased, and suddenly she said, "Now, Harry Harlow, I want you to stop worrying about your laboratory. They will find you a good one. The problem will be solved, but, meanwhile, why don't you go over to the Vilas Park Zoo and test the monkeys in the monkey house there? They are smart monkeys. I know because I watch them most every day."

Mrs. Henmon was a Vilas; her family had endowed the city of

Madison with both Vilas Park and the zoo. The next day Mrs. Henmon and Harry Harlow went to the zoo. Harlow met the director who personally introduced him to every monkey there, from the gibbon to the baboons. Some years later, Harlow described the gibbon as the dumbest of the monkeys, and the only one who was monogamous.

The director of the zoo was very pleased that his monkeys were prospective contributors to the research of the University of Wisconsin. The town and gown formed a partnership that extended far past the acquisition of a new psychology primate laboratory.

The zoo provided a preparatory laboratory. What proved to be its most significant contribution was introducing the monkey as the subject of Harlow research throughout his professional career. The shift from rats to rhesus brought the experimental subjects countless evolutionary periods closer to the behavior of the human primate.

The monkey, and especially the rhesus monkey, gave clear evidence of being able to replicate many human behaviors. This fact was of the utmost importance since it solidified and established the formula used by Harlow in his experiments: if human behavior could be replicated in the monkey, the results of the study would generalize to human behavior.

After the first testing of the monkey, Harlow never wished to test another rat.

THEORETICAL CONFUSION

Once learning theories began to stabilize, the term "trial and error" came to denote a simple learning process. From the 1920s through the 1950s, the term might just as well have been applied to many of the psychological theories themselves.

Harry Harlow had a prodigious memory, and whether or not it was photographic does not really matter. He was very familiar with many of the outstanding theorists, among whom were Watson, Freud, Lashley, Tolman, Miller, Hull, and Spence. If he were not familiar with the theorists, he was still sure to be familiar with their theories.

In an unpublished American Psychological Association (APA) lecture Harlow said of Watson, "Watson favorably considered, at one time or another, every psychological concept that had ever been conceived, and then, over a period of time, he reversed almost every concept he had ever considered." For example, in his 1914 *Introduction to Comparative Psychology*, Watson described instincts eloquently as "complicated, concatenated behaviors unfolding serially to appropriate stimulation"; Watson listed and defended eleven instincts. Beginning in the 1920s, however, Watson gained a reputation as one of the men who erased and eradicated instinct theory.

An additional area fostering conflicting concepts was the cortex, including its functions and capabilities. At that time the cortex was just about as uncharted as was the moon and, like the moon, was accessible only from outer space. Not too long before this period, the non-science of phrenology was widely accepted. A variety of behaviors were specifically located according to the contours of the skull. The bump of knowledge sat primly at the top and very center of the head, roughly where, in the future, the motor activity of the big toe was to be somewhat more scientifically located.

Scientists interested in exploring the cortex held a wide variety of views, from Lashley's theory of equipotentiality of the entire cortex to many and varied approaches to localization of functions. Harry Harlow chose to enter the arena. It was his first major field of research. He joined a number of neurologists and physiological psychologists in attempting to master the mysteries of the primate cortex.

BACKGROUND TESTS FOR CORTICAL RESEARCH

The monkey house at the zoo had no spatial or equipment facilities that even a starting scientific laboratory required, but it was an ideal place to begin to build a meaningful battery of learning tests for an intensive investigation of the cortex.

Harlow was a pioneer in the development of the monkey learning tests for research on the cortex. The primary monkey-effective test at the beginning of the primate studies at the zoo was the delayed reaction test, which was useful in many ways. Harlow was able to locate the learning ability of the rhesus in relation to that of the animals above or below it in the phyletic scale. He gave the more complicated of the delayed response tests to primates ranging from the lemur to the orangutan. String tests which required selective manipulation of the strings were also extremely useful, after norms had been established, to determine loss or retention of motor-sensory abilities.

Harlow did not, at this time, champion any specific, hard-and-fast theory of behavior, as did many of his contemporaries. Being thoroughly cognizant of the theories, however, he felt strongly that in the majority of cases the theories were not complex enough to represent or to describe primate behavior, whether human or subhuman.

Although Harlow did not settle for any overall theory of behavior, he did frequently single out one aspect or part of a theory to analyze and to challenge. Sometimes the monkeys solved the problems first, all by themselves.

Harlow and his students were working on a test situation designed to question the belief held by some behaviorists that in order to solve delayed reaction problems, the subjects must maintain bodily and/or visual orientation toward the object under which the experimenter had placed the reward.

The first subjects tested in this experiment were two Hamadryas baboons named Tristan and Isolde. They were two of the most compatible monkeys at the zoo, and they were as cooperative as they were companionable. They were always tested together; they liked it that way.

Tristan and Isolde each carefully watched the reward being concealed under an object. They then, simultaneously, turned away and ambled off to a far corner of the cage, away from the test setting. They became very affectionate. At a respectable interval, they together returned to the experimental scene. They each made the correct choice. There was no doubt that the pair could solve delayed reaction tests without maintaining specific orientation in any one direction.

A NEW-OLD LABORATORY

It is difficult to place an exact date on Harlow's acquisition of the first scientific laboratory. Since research had been conducted at the Vilas Park Zoo and the rhesus had replaced rodents as the experimental subjects, the size requirements for the lab had increased more than threefold. The search had extended to new fields.

In 1932 the University officials discovered that the forest products department had outgrown two buildings. One was a spacious red brick building with modern improvements and facilities inside. This was not destined to be the primate laboratory.

The psychology department inherited the other forest products building, the one which had been called the Box Factory. It was a twenty-four foot square structure on the wrong side of the Milwaukee Railroad tracks. The building had one-and-one-half stories. This fact was evident only from the inside. There was no ceiling until just under the roof on one side of the building, whereas the other half boasted two complete stories. The entire building was filled with steel-reinforced concrete pillars of varied heights.

The first of Harlow's students to work at the zoo was Paul Settlage. The first of the students to work at the old but new lab was again Paul Settlage. You could not find a finer student to set the standard. The story of his recruitment is interesting. By the time Dr. Harlow had started at the zoo, we were quite well acquainted. One day I told him very seriously that one of my students in mental development was being wasted. Mental development was just about as close to child development as you could find in the curriculum of the thirties, but it was a long way off. I told

Harry Harlow that Paul was too good for educational psychology and that he should rescue him. I did not realize what a great team they would actually make. They thought on the same level. Paul could appreciate Harlow's dry and wry wit, and he was even more intelligent than he was serious.

Harlow and Settlage began attacking the pillars with sledge hammers. The sledge hammers did not break, but neither did the pillars—they didn't even budge. The next day Paul brought along with him his cousin Walter Grether. The next day both Paul and Walter brought along pneumatic hammers. This effective demolition squad conquered.

Walter Grether was so intrigued with the challenge of the lab that he joined the fast-growing group of psychology majors under Harlow's tutelage.

Equipment was the next priority. By late 1932 the Great Depression was in full force, and money was a verboten topic. There was no such entity as a government grant in existence. If any researcher received a little donation from an alumni fund, it was like manna from heaven.

There was, however, Miss Sage, the psychology department secretary, who found a balance of $300 in the account of the old laboratory which had been torn down. With this, beginning equipment was purchased. Harlow was encouraged; progress was being made. It was not very much later that Harry Harlow was informed that the $300 had been a deficit.

The subhuman primate population of the laboratory was at first a mixed population including one spider monkey, a number of South American cebus, and the balance all rhesus. It was obvious from the beginning that the twenty-four square-foot building was going to be crowded. As the animals began arriving, the facts were even more evident. The inside cages were rapidly being filled.

The first actual construction after the pillars had been removed was a high wire fence, which was being covered with honeysuckle. Harlow thought it improved the whole desolate surroundings.

As the cages began to fill, Harlow ordered some materials for the construction of outside summer observation cages, and the lab crew began building them—even Abe Maslow, who had recently joined the lab group. Abraham Maslow was Harry Harlow's first Ph.D. student. With his usual pleasant manner, Abe had suggested to Dr. Harlow that he did not think it necessary for him to do an experiment for his dissertation. In fact, he preferred not to. In an equally gracious and even firmer manner, Dr. Harlow stated that Abe Maslow would do an experiment, and he was sure that it would be a very good one. The experiment was on dominance, and it dominated the field on the subject for many years. Everyone liked Abe Maslow, and even though he knew as little as Dr. Harlow did about building cages, they both pitched in and did their part.

There were still quite a number of monkeys in the summer observation cages when the weather began turning cold. Since the inside cages were all occupied, it seemed like a very good idea to winterize the outdoor cages to protect the experimental animals. These cages had been accessible from the inside of the building for quite a time. While arranging for heat, the lab crew might just as well paint them to match the rest of the building. Harlow was rather relieved that the honeysuckle had completely covered the fence while they were working. It made it so nice and private.

The old laboratory tended to be quite informal. The students even called the professor "Doc" sometimes. Doc and the students worked well together. When vacations came the students all left, and then Doc worked well without them. One Christmas Eve, Harry Harlow was feeding the monkeys. They were always fed at six o'clock, leaving the rest of the day open for testing.

Harry was in a hurry to get home. It *was* Christmas Eve. He had only two cages left to do, both of which were outside cages. He picked up the food and went out and around to Cage 20. That finished, he opened the door to Cage 21, went in, and put the food on the floor near the two monkeys. He turned to go out and heard a click. It was the click of the latch on the outside door locking.

Although there was access to the outside cages from inside the laboratory, the reverse was not true. Harlow had heard the phrase: "Hoist with his own petar." However, he had not known its significance before. How could he have planned one-way traffic only? At least the cages were warm! The monkeys were acting quite suspicious of him. After all, it was more crowded than anyone had planned. The monkeys began to calm down, and Harlow began to think strange thoughts. He did like being innovative, but not so innovative as to be the first and only professor ever to be locked in a small cage with two monkeys on Christmas Eve.

There was a narrow tunnel connecting the cage with the building, and even though it had no door in, there was a small trapdoor on the roof. It lifted up, just enough for him to peer over. He heard caroling outside. It was far off, but he thought it was "O Come All Ye Faithful." He thought that "Away in a Manger" would be more appropriate. The caroling stopped, but Doc decided it was time to put the last shreds of pride away and call for help. He yelled. His eyes were barely above the opening, but he thought he saw some people on the closest street. They stopped. They seemed to be looking around. They heard the next yell and moved toward the noise. They proved to be three sailors and within earshot.

Harry explained briefly about how to reach him from the inside and where the door was to go in. He sat down on the floor to rest. Time passed. A horrible thought came to him: he had just finished the last cages. He had planned to leave at that time. He had locked the lab door. He reached in his pocket and felt his keys.

Harlow began to feel imprisoned again, but he underestimated the sailors. He never found out for what unusual crises the sailors had been trained. They certainly knew what to do in his crisis. They pulled out the door pins which the carpenters had put in from the outside, lifted off the door, and entered the lab. They opened up the door from the inside and let Harlow in.

And to think that the laboratory had purposely been built to be secure against invasion by any children, dogs, or sailors on leave.

COPING

Several years had passed since Dr. Terman had referred to a "timid" Harry Harlow destined for a junior college position, the same Harry Harlow who had termed himself a timid graduate student. It was customary for new members of the psychology department faculty to be assigned fairly small classes before they lectured to elementary psychology classes. Lecturing to the latter was sometimes described as being thrown to the wolves. The classes numbered into the hundreds. Harlow was still timid and still suffered his childhood difficulty of correctly pronouncing the letter "r."

During his freshman year at Reed College before going to Stanford, Harry enrolled in beginning French. At the very first meeting, his instructor announced, "I wish to make very clear the fact that in the French language, we have three distinct ways of pronouncing the letter 'r.'" Poor Harry. All he could think was that he could never catch up to numbers two and three.

Dr. Harlow lectured to his first class in elementary psychology the first fall after we were married. He faced about 100 students. He began to remember he was timid, and the "r's" took him over. The first masculine boos came as he mumbled over the first "r." They weren't very loud, but the next ones were.

At least Harry Harlow did not have to come home to a lonely, masculine abode. We began to think about methods of solving the escalating attack. How does one undo a "boo"? The first attempt was a diversionary approach. The *Reader's Digest* had just appeared on the newsstand. It offered some short, catchy anecdotes which from time to time could be fitted into a lecture. The students liked them, but unfortunately, the boos had become a habit too strong for them to dislodge. Harlow then tried something which only a desperate person would do—he started using puns. At first just a little pun would slide into a sentence. As the puns became more obnoxious, the boos commenced. Harlow became more daring. As the booing became louder, there were also fewer directed toward the "r's." Harlow had been concentrating so hard on the puns that he forgot to stumble over the "r's."

People stopped thinking of Harry Harlow as timid. There was certainly nothing timid about his research. The only trouble was that he never did stop punning!

THE CORTICAL RESEARCH PROGRAM

"First things first" was the motto at the new-old lab, and on that basis an operating room was constructed before there was even the semblance of an inside or outside rest room. With the operating room and well-planned background of testing at the zoo, Harlow could begin his long-delayed research on the cortex.

Paul Settlage later added a complete M.D. to his Ph.D., but he started at this point. Under the direction of a neurosurgeon from the medical school, the advice of an instructor in physiology, and some voluminous reading of his own, Settlage conducted pioneer studies from which a long series of brain researches stemmed.

John Bromer soon joined the graduate students at the laboratory and added oddity tests to the delayed reaction and discrimination learning tests in use. Bromer, by himself, accustomed the rhesus to this next step in complexity and trained them to solve the oddity problems.

Even during the very early days of cortical investigation, Harlow felt that the cortical areas designated for sensory and motor centers had sufficient excess space to be used as association or "thinking" areas. A note scribbled on Harlow's paper added, "It was only the scientists who had not enough room left over for thought."

Harlow's ventures into unraveling the secrets of the cortex reinforced his belief in the complexity of primate behavior. His strongest criticism of the Lashley theory of equipotentiality was the inclusion of all learning behavior in the sweeping hypothesis. From the beginning, learning tests showed evidence of certain localization of behavior and that a large variety of tests would be required, tests differing not only in the kind of behavior, but also in its degree of difficulty.

When a variety of investigators had demonstrated that the cortex had a number of layers, the amount of room available suddenly increased significantly. There was even room for a great diversity of functions to be located and furthermore, to be located specifically and differentially. In most of the animals studied, sensory behaviors were found to be in layer 4 and motor functions in layer 5. The subdivisions of the layers also had their significance.

Three different association areas could be recognized: one in the frontal area of the brain, one in the temporal lobe, and one in the posterior or occipital portion. Damage to any of these three areas produced various amount and degrees of intellectual loss in both man and monkeys. Memory impairment resulted from damage to the frontal or adjacent areas. Learning, and particularly complex learning, loss resulted from damage to the temporal lobe, and impairment of complex visual functions followed damage to the posterior associative cortex.

Teaching and training received a bonus from Harlow's definitive studies. After brain damage, a previously trained monkey regained learning skills faster than a naive monkey learned them.

Once Harry Harlow had embarked on researching a particular field, he never completely discontinued his experiments in that area. This was true of his interest in the cortex. Because of the variety and extent of his accomplishments, details and coverage must be selective. Should the reader wish for additional material on the cortex, there are three articles listed in the complete bibliography contained in this volume: No. 18 (Harlow, 1938), No. 34 (Spaet and Harlow, 1943), and No. 80 (Harlow, Davis, Settlage, and Meyer, 1952). These three concentrate on the occipital, the frontal, and the posterior association areas.

LEARNING SETS

Harlow was very interested in the cortical research, but his deep involvement with learning for his cortical research had turned his interests more toward behavioral than psychological studies. There was so much to be learned about learning! During the forties the complexity of the various tests was increased: there were many factors to be explored including the characteristics of objects used, the effect of multiple signs in solution of the tests, the position of objects, pattern discrimination, and the effect of shifting variables. How far could the monkey go?

Harry Harlow's most innovative research in the field of learning was on the formation of learning sets, to be discussed in detail in Chapter 4. Harlow threw down the gauntlet. Many people for many years had held the belief that subhuman animals could not generalize or comprehend the abstract. In the new series of learning problems, Harlow reversed the customary relationship of the subjects solving the problems and the problems themselves. Instead of a large number of subjects being tested on one problem, a very few subjects were tested on a large number of problems. Each of the problems was based on the same general principle while the characteristics of the objects used in the problem could vary.

For a number of years Harlow had suspected that the number of subjects in experiments was not a consistently vital factor in obtaining significant results. If the research was of enough importance, as few as four subjects should be sufficient. As Harlow would frequently add, if the research were truly important, one subject might be enough.

While he was proving his hypothesis and creating a new and valuable learning method for future teachers, Harlow was, ironically, saving research money at the same time. Rhesus monkeys were expensive, imported from India, but they made it up in the satisfactory results. They even suggested new experiments by their behavior. For instance, there was the rhesus monkey who looked at his own image in a mirror and then ran around to the back of the mirror to find the other monkey. Can you imagine rats doing that?

Harlow had been administering learning tests ever since he started at the zoo. During this entire period, he had, sometimes unconsciously, been observing and collecting items of information for his next major research. He had not found any theory of motivation which he could wholeheartedly support and was most critical of specific elements of behaviorism and motivation relying primarily on the internal, visceral drives.

When Watson dispensed with instincts, his behavioral theory was left with a great gap. To fill this gap, he enlisted a combination of habit and the emotions of fear, anger or rage, and love. These were, in name, the same as the "coarser" emotions of James, although they ignored James' favorite, the emotion of grief.

The theory gaining the most favor among psychologists was that of the internal drives, especially the reduction of the drives of hunger and thirst and the avoidance of pain. This theory was championed by Hull, who was soon followed by Spence.

In regard to hunger, the rhesus had their own theory and a habit which might have been borrowed from the chipmunk. Before and during testing, when a monkey had some food to its liking but too much to eat all at once, the balance would be tucked away in the pouches on both sides of the mouth to be eaten when desired. Many times the rhesus had their cheeks bulging before, during, and after successfully solving a problem. It was impossible to convince Harry Harlow that the monkeys' application and success resulted from a hunger which had not existed at any time during the experiment.

Not only did the monkeys do just as well when satisfied after eating—they did better. Harlow finally engineered an experiment which tested the learning ability of the subjects after escalation periods of food deprivation. The level of achievement dropped with each extension of the food deprivation period. The experimenters all decided that the law of parsimony indicated that the hungrier the monkeys became, the more they thought about food and the less they concentrated on solving the problem. Backing up common sense seemed like a waste of time to Harry Harlow, but if necessary he could back it up with scientific proof.

In addition to downplaying hunger as a motivational force, Harlow was acquiring another insight which further reduced the primacy of the visceral drives. One evening he had been working at the lab. When he was ready to leave, he remembered that the superintendent of buildings and grounds had noticed that the lab lights had been left on late several nights, and he urged Harry to remind the students to turn them off. Harlow did not want to be the culprit. He turned off the lights, went out, and turned the car around in the parking circle. As he drove past the front door, he saw the lights on again. He was an absentminded professor, but that was too much.

In he went, turned off the light, and stood still for a few moments. The light flashed on, and he was just able to catch sight of a tail sliding beneath the bars of the nearest cage. That was the cage of Granny, the spider monkey who had been at work, or play, with her prehensile tail.

Many observers might have just passed over the incident or said, "How smart of Granny" or muttered about having to come back in. Harlow, instead, was mentally outlining his first experiments on curiosity, a motive *not* one of the internal visceral drives. The next behavioral drive to be examined was the last of the major researches to take place at the new-old lab. This program centered on three related sources of motivation: curiosity, exploration, and manipulation. Simple and complex mechanical puzzles constituted the first step.

Harlow had often remarked that when he started on an experiment he knew the outcome in advance. In the first days of the lab, about fifteen years earlier, the lab crew watched their South American cebus monkeys solve tool-using problems, whereas the Old World rhesus monkeys were morons with any engineering projects. Harlow was convinced the difference must result from some unlearned difference in abilities. When they tested representative rhesus and cebus on large batteries of manual exploration situations, Harlow was almost chagrined to find that both cebus and rhesus were indefatigable explorers.

With the mechanical puzzles Harlow expected all the monkeys to work happily for the sheer joy of solving the puzzles, and so they did.

Dr. Robert Butler, a post-doctorate researcher at the lab, was testing monkeys on delayed response tests. Since the screen was down in front of him during the delay interval limiting his vision, he placed a properly angled mirror at the side. To his surprise the subjects then completely stopped doing the delayed response tests and spent all their time watching him in the mirror.

Since both curiosity and exploration may take visual as well as manual forms, Butler created the Butler Box to test the extent of curiosity through visual exploration. The box was large enough to contain an upright monkey. Inside there were two windows, one covered by a locked blue door and a second concealed by a yellow door which opened. They were each at a height just right for the monkey to look out if he tried the correct door.

The rhesus quickly discovered that the yellow door was the rewarding choice, and Butler discovered that the monkey would open this door repetitively for five hours at a time. In order to test the curiosity to its limit, Butler started another attempt after an evening gathering of the graduate group. He kept track for twenty-two hours and then fell asleep, but no one has ever been sure whether the monkey or the experimenter was the first to do so.

In 1949 Dr. Harlow went to Washington to serve for eighteen months as chief psychologist for the U.S. Army. With the welcome cooperation of Col. Jay Mowbry, he created the Human Resources Research Office, or Humro.

A NEW LAB AND VISTAS EXTENDED

When Harlow returned to Wisconsin, he was greeted by a real surprise. He had persuaded Dr. Norman Gutman to take his place in Wisconsin when he was gone, and Dr. Gutman, in his turn, had persuaded the University officials of the urgent need for a much larger laboratory and, as Harlow said, had hypnotized them into providing a building that actually resembled a laboratory.

The building was a deserted cheese factory, located at least one-half mile from any other university building. (Just where a monkey laboratory should be located, the dean of men would have thought.)

Mr. Gallistel, the superintendent of grounds who had been after Harlow each time he had managed to add little and not-so-little structures to the old lab, took Harry Harlow on a tour when remodeling of the cheese factory was well along. Suddenly they came upon a door which did not seem to lead anywhere, and Harlow asked why it was there. Mr. Gallistel said he though it more economical to have the door all ready for the time when Harlow planned to put on the next addition.

The new laboratory made it possible to expand, and Harlow initiated long-term research on the maturation of learning. Doing such a study correctly requires that the monkeys be tested from the first day of life onward. Of course a neonatal nursery was vital to insure the safe survival of the infants. Dr. Blomquist, one of Harlow's students, would manage it well. He was raised during the depression and had never hear of a forty-hour week. (His place was eventually taken by a staff of seven.)

The series of studies on the affectional systems of primates continued Harry Harlow's experiments on motivation and reflected his impatience with the persisting emphasis on internal, visceral motives. Before the researches on infant-mother love, there was agreement between the majority of child analysts, represented primarily by Anna Freud, and the behaviorists, especially Miller and Dollard (200), that the infant's attachment to the mother stemmed from internal drives which triggered activities connected with the libations of the maternal breast. This belief, according to Harlow, was the only one these two theoretical groups ever had in common.

In August of 1958, Harry Harlow's presidential address to the annual convention of the American Psychological Association had the title, "The Nature of Love." The "love" was the affection of the infant for the mother, based on mother's gifts to the infant. When the speech was concluded, the audience gave the new president a standing ovation in admiration, but the title alone was enough to startle the audience to attention.

The word "love" just did not exist in the scientific language. The word was not in any scientific dictionary nor was it used in casual professional jargon. Long ago I did find the word in the index of Woodworth's 1921 *Psychology*, but upon turning to the designated pages, the word was not once repeated. All I could find was a discussion of the specific sex motive. The same was true in the use of the word "love" in the lists of emotions by both James and Watson, although the actual definitions of each were not identical. The word "love" was in the bailiwick of the romantic troubadour, the medieval painters, and later poets, but not of the scientist.

This attitude toward love must have been quite widespread. For the first time even Harlow's enthusiastic, admiring students did not show their customary excitement at the first announcement of Dr. Harlow's plans for his next new experiments. It is possible that the students did not trust such a drastically innovative addition to scientific investigation to such equally unusual experimental participants as the cloth and wire surrogate mothers.

On August 22, 1984, there was a dedication ceremony at the University of Wisconsin at which the Psychology Primate Laboratory was renamed in honor of Harry Harlow, the Harlow Primate Laboratory. One of the Harlow Ph.D. students who requested the privilege of speaking at this occasion brought up the subject of the love experiment. There must have been a profound change in the attitude of the graduate students toward the surrogate study since Dr. Robert Zimmerman mentioned that there was an aura of pure magic at the laboratory as the experiments developed.

Both the academic and the wider world liked the results of the experiments on the affectional systems. *The Competent Infant* (Stone, Smith, & Murphy, 1971) emphatically emphasizes throughout the book the part played by the contributions of Dr. Harlow to the burst of experimental studies in the sixties, research which altered the concept of infant competence. Harlow, as might be expected, accepted all the attention with his customary aplomb, even the inclusion of his findings in books on baby care for expectant mothers.

At least ten years ago in an article on psychoanalysis, I read that the theory and beliefs of some of the more extreme of the followers of Freud had persisted stronger and longer in the United States than in Europe. I began to believe this when Harry came home from a meeting for a grant site visit. The chairman, a psychiatrist, had become livid when Harlow used the word "love." Harry immediately changed to his customary substitute "affection," but the visitor continued to pursue a coronary. Harry was not quite sure how to refer to the Baby Grant which funded the research on the affectional systems without referring to either love or affection, but he finally settled on the term "proximity." He thought this word might pass scrutiny because it could be measured: ten feet from proximity, five feet from proximity, six inches from proximity, and proximity.

DEVIOUS ROADS TO DISCOVERY

During the years at the first laboratory, Harlow and his students had no intention of studying depression or any other pathological state. They were on the trail of love. However, to adequately ascertain the strength of bonds between baby and mother, as well as the amount of dependency of the infant upon the mother, they proceeded, briefly, to break the bonds through separation and along with separation came depression. Harlow also did not have any suspicion of the deleterious effects which would be caused by asocial rearing of the monkeys in individual cages. It was just as far from his thought as depression was from love.

The individual cages were planned to prevent another ill fate. For many years, too many years, the lab had suffered from a tuberculosis problem, either active T.B. of the rhesus monkeys imported from the Orient or latent T.B., which could be transferred by carriers to healthy monkeys. The new laboratory had room for a breeding colony along with the neonatal nursery. To avoid any contact with carriers in the existing population, the breeders-to-be would be raised in separate cages.

The monkeys in separate cages grew strong and healthy. They were well-built animals. When the time was right and the monkeys were at an age to be sexually mature, a male rhesus was moved into the cage of a mother-to-be, and it was not until then that the disastrous effects of the asocial rearing began to emerge. The two monkeys sat staring out from the cage as if still all alone. Neither showed any interest in the other nor in anything else. They might just as well have been solid sphinx. The experimenters had started a brooding, not a breeding, colony.

This experience brings to our attention the changes which had been taking place in Harlow's research. Unexpected developments indicated diverse research needs. One could no longer say that one major area of research was inexorably leading to the next. Instead, as one behavioral field after another was included in the programs of the primate laboratory, the interrelationships of the different behaviors became even more apparent. Again, Harlow's concept of the complexity of behavior was being substantiated.

When Harlow's surrogate research was first launched, the relative effectiveness of contact comfort and the reduction of hunger was all-important as a form of motivation. After contact comfort won top laurels, it became clear that the infant's caretaker, mother or other, was capable of producing other sensations which also aided the development of a sense of security for the young monkeys. These were rocking motion, warmth, and the satisfaction of hunger as well. The mother became a symbol of security so that when fears began to be a part of the infant's reactions, the presence of the mother could lessen the impact. The infant was terrified by large, open spaces unless the surrogate was present and of strange objects under the same conditions.

Social rearing and the timing of early experiences gained in importance. Play had its own puckish part to add. If the young primates had guided, early opportunities to be with peers, play appeared early of its own accord. When the caretaker and baby were separated, play slowed and even disappeared, but the presence of peers eased the depression.

HARLOW IN SUMMARY

These are but a few of the interrelationships, but the time has come to review the second purpose of this introduction, and we return to the dedication ceremony. In arranging the entire program in honor of Harry Harlow, Mrs. Helen Lauersdorf LeRoy, Dr. Harlow's executive secretary and coauthor of Chapter 13, alerted former Harlow students, colleagues, and friends from all corners of the United States and other countries. She also enticed Dr. Stephen Suomi from his new position near Washington, D.C., to be master of ceremonies. Twenty persons of the many to assemble requested the privilege of speaking of their personal reminiscences of Harry Harlow.

From these memories came some interesting thoughts as to what made Harlow Harlow. Dr. Delos Wickens, recently retired from Ohio

State University and a colleague and friend of Harry Harlow since the early forties, was the first speaker. "What Harry wanted, Harry usually got, and one reason why he was so successful was that he did not let insurmountable obstacles stop him." Lack of money? If there wasn't a lot of money, he did not need a lot. When he needed new, three-dimensional objects for his learning set experiments, he and Wickens went down to Woolworth's and had a fine time picking them out. As Wickens commented, "Harry not only turned dross into gold, but he made true the song, 'I found a million dollar baby in the five-and-ten-cent store.'" When he didn't have a lab for his rats, he went to the zoo and changed from the animal subjects to which he was accustomed, two moves which might have been readily rejected by other academicians.

Both Wickens and Dr. Roger Davis of Washington State University psychology department were among a number who mentioned serendipity in connection with Harlow, serendipity in his recognition of chances and in his follow-through until he had made the most of the opportunity. Davis added, "Harlow could see consequences of projected experimental research, whereas lesser investigators could not even recognize them in their own findings." Davis was also highly impressed by the heavy work loads Harlow handled successfully. As an example he quoted one year during which Dr. Harlow was chairman of the psychology department, editor of the *Journal of Comparative and Physiological Psychology* (JCPP), taught five classes weekly, directed the lab, and published his customary ten or more outstanding journal articles.

Robert Dodsworth, the excellent photographer for the primate laboratory, first complimented Harry Harlow for his recognition of the importance of illustrations in his articles, speeches, and books. As Harry's most productive characteristic, however, he chose his sense of timing—the timing of his dry wit, the timing for his order of succession of research in relation to the theoretical atmosphere, and the timing of his brief chidings to keep order in the lab. Harlow would casually amble in on an overly long coffee break and remark "Making progress?" turn around, and amble out. Robert Zimmerman added his own contribution in the dry wit category, stating: "Harlow needed to buy a still to make necessary distilled water and was chided by the purchasing department for his extravagance. Harlow's answer was, 'Still water runs steep.'"

At one point when the graduate students were vainly attempting to divert Dr. Harlow from his surrogate research, they kept as many monkeys as possible engaged in their own experiments. To discourage Harlow, Zimmerman told him one day, "You need some rhesus for controls." Harlow stared at him. Said he, as he worked on the experiments to back his speech at APA, "I cannot write speeches about control animals."

Robert Leary described himself as "the oldest, longest lived student at the primate laboratory." His experiences extended from the learning-set period to the experiments on the age factor as it affects learning. He emphasized two facts about Harlow research which have not received due recognition over the years. One is that Harry Harlow could often take the common activities of human everyday life, behaviors of which we all are aware, see theoretical importance, and establish it through experiments. The second was that after Harry had established his facts and made his point, he did not fall in love with the subject and pursue it so long that people did not care whether or not it was correct.

Arthur Riopelle said that although he had not officially been a student of Dr. Harlow, he must have been at the lab enough that they all thought he had. He told a fine story to illustrate Harry's sense of humor. Among Harlow's early publications was one on fear, published by the University of Wisconsin Typing Service. On the front page there was just the title, "Fear," with an asterisk after it. At the bottom of the page after the asterisk was the phrase: "one of the most common fears is the fear of footnotes."

John Gluck, a professor at the University of New Mexico and a coauthor of Chapter 5, described the feeling among the students at the primate laboratory as a fever—a fever to act, to accomplish, to look, and to be curious.

Melinda Novak was Dr. Harry Harlow's last Ph.D. student and a coauthor of the last chapter of this book. She remarked that at one period Harlow was especially concerned about the question of generalization. He concluded his discussion saying, "The generalizations of behavioral data from species to species are relatively simple. One may not wish to generalize, but one must. If the competent do not generalize, the incompetent will take over the field."

Rosenblum, not of a common mold himself, recognized the unique in Harlow. When he arrived for graduate study, there was at that time in psychology strong interest in creating models to use in experiments. Rosenblum had plans for a fear-inducing model of a beast. He spent hours on a gruesome head which would thrust forward toward the subject. When it was finished, he rushed to Harlow's office and took him to see it. He stationed Harry before the beast, turned two switches, and the head thrust forward. Then, suddenly, there was a mass of flying sparks and all the lights went out. Said Harlow, "Very impressive." Rosenblum never got over the fact that Harlow held no hard feelings.

Even before Gene Sackett had received his Ph.D., he corresponded with Harry Harlow about a job. Harlow answered that when Sackett had his degree he should come for a talk. If he wanted to work he probably could, for a year if he were willing to work time-and-a-half for half pay. Sackett accepted and appeared at the proper time. Harlow was out of town but had left money for a student to take Gene to dinner. The student hadn't seen $12 for a long time and saw red—red steaks. He took them home and cooked the dinner. Sackett became the "man who came to dinner." He left the lab seven years and many, many published articles later.

Two psychologists who asked to speak had been neither students of Harlow nor at the University of Wisconsin. One of them had never met Harlow but became fascinated by his articles. There were no monkeys at his college, but J. Dee Higley majored in primatology and carried the banner of Harlow. Both he and Seymour Levine, the other non-student of Harlow, felt that his work was being carried on throughout the entire field of psychology, often by way of Harlow's students. Higley was also very proud of Harlow's revolutionizing the care of subhuman primates throughout the nation, showing the need for social rearing and the knowledge of the complexity of subhuman animals.

Since Harry Harlow began this introduction, I think it highly proper for him to have the last word in his own inimitable way. I also find it appropriate that it be concluded with excerpts from his final editorial upon retiring from the JCPP (161):

> Almost all scientific papers include an introduction even though large parts of it are frequently buried in the sections labeled Methods and Results. However, the total omission of an introduction constitutes a glaring error, and anyway, it is fun to write introductions—one is not constrained by facts.
>
> One way to write an introduction is to state what the experiment is all about and make predictions about the outcome.... However, prediction is one of the great booby traps into which young and inexperienced psychologists often fall. All their predictions are confirmed; older men know that this never happens. The proper technique is to select the prediction of minimum import, or throw in a completely extraneous one, and have this prediction fail. Honesty is the best policy.
>
> Although some psychologists write simple, straightforward introductions, this is commonly considered to be declassé. In the sophisticated or 'strip-tease' technique, you keep the problem a secret from the reader until the very last paragraph. Indeed, some very sophisticated authors keep the problem a secret forever. Since I am interested in readers as well as authors, I advise that readers always approach introduction sections using the Chinese technique—begin at the end and read backward.

From Learning to Love

PART ONE
LEARNING

1

The Effect of Application of Anesthetic Agents on Circumscribed Motor and Sensory Areas of the Cortex

H.F. Harlow and P.H. Settlage

INTRODUCTION

The purpose of the following investigation was to test the feasibility of using anesthetic agents to effect temporary inactivation of localized cortical areas. That such a method might be effective was suggested by the work of Dusser de Barenne (1,2) who used strychnine and novocaine to produce excitation and inhibition respectively of cortical functions in cats and monkeys.

EFFECT OF DRUGS ON THE MOTOR CORTEX

Although our ultimate aim was to effect temporary inactivation of sensory and association centers, preliminary tests were carried out to determine the effect of drugs on the motor area. This was done because the method of electrical stimulation of motor points is possible in animals which are in a

Harlow, H.F., and Settlage, P. The effect of application of anesthetic agents on circumscribed motor and sensory areas of the cortex. *J. Psychol.*, 1936, 2, 193–200. Copyright 1936 by the American Psychological Association. Reprinted by permission of the publisher and author.

state of general anesthesia, and thus offers a ready method of determining quantitatively the effect of a given drug in depressing cortical areas.

In this preliminary work two drugs, nupercaine and novocaine, in concentrations varying from 1–10 per cent, were used; and two methods of application were employed. These methods were (a) injection with a hypodermic needle and (b) application with a small piece of filter paper which has been soaked in the anesthetic agent—the latter was the method used by Dusser de Barenne. The several techniques were used on seven *Macacus rhesus*, each animal being subject in a number of investigations. The data indicated (a) that the motor areas could be depressed, (b) that novocaine gave more satisfactory results than nupercaine, (c) that Dusser de Barenne's filter-paper technique was the more satisfactory, and (d) that concentrations of novocaine up to 10 per cent could be applied without any residue of functional or morphological injury to nerve tissues. This 10 per cent concentration is considerably greater than the solutions used by Dusser de Barenne, 1–4 per cent. Its failure to produce permanent damage in our investigations was probably due to the fact that a small degree of absorption took place.

With 4 per cent novocaine, decreased excitability (as measured by the threshold for stimulation of motor points) usually began in 10–15 minutes; with 10 per cent novocaine, the decrease in excitability became evident more rapidly, the time of onset being 3–5 minutes after application. The effect of the novocaine lasted about 30–50 minutes, findings which also agree with Dusser de Barenne's.

The effect of the drug on the poisoned area varied considerably. Often motor points which had been previously determined were completely blocked out; at other times depression of excitability was only partial, and increased current strengths would cause sufficient excitation to bring about movement. In order to control for changes in excitability which may have been produced by other factors than the independent variable— factors such as lighter general anesthesia, changes in the temperature of the cortex, circulatory changes, etc.,—the excitability of the locally poisoned area was equated with non-poisoned regions.

This method of equating normal and poisoned areas was found to be reasonably satisfactory in spite of the fact that variations in the tests for excitability occasionally gave discordant results.

The increase in threshold due to local application of the anesthetic agents was clearly shown by the differential effect on the excitability of motor points lying inside and outside of the poisoned area. Points within the area invariably suffered loss or extinction of excitability. Points outside of it showed no such loss, excitability remaining quite constant throughout the experiment.

The area affected by the anaesthetic agents was sharply defined, all points within the area being frequently rendered non-excitable, when points only 1 *mm* from the outer border showed no demonstrable loss. (Toluidine blue, mixed with the given anesthetic agent, served to enable ready discrimination of the poisoned area. This techinique was also devised by Dusser de Barenne.)

Having demonstrated that drugs may be used successfully to inactivate circumscribed portions of the motor cortex, we employed the principle in attempting to inactivate sensory areas. This attempt was first carried out on an animal which had been conditioned to a stimulus of light touch. The monkey tested in this experiment was trained to sit quietly in a chair device, the essential features of which are shown in the accompanying plate. He was then conditioned to turn the head sharply to the right to obtain food, the substitute stimulus being light touch to the plantar surface of the left foot. The stimulating instrument was a piece of paper 3/16's of an inch wide and an inch long, glued to a toothpick. Although this is a crude stimulus, in comparison to those used in obtaining measurements on human beings, we believed the touch to be light enough to be epicritic rather than protopathic in nature (see Head, 5). (This animal's eyes were bandaged to exclude visual cues and his hands were restrained....)

After the conditioned response had been firmly established, a craniotomy was performed over the somesthetic area for the right foot, and the scalp closed with temporary sutures. The following day the monkey was tested and the integrity of the response demonstrated. Immediately thereupon he was subjected to light ether anesthesia, a dural flap was made, novocaine and epinephrine were injected subcutaneously in the entire region surrounding the scalp incision, sterile bandages were placed on the head, and the animal was allowed to recover from the effects of the ether. An area somewhat larger than the somesthetic area for the foot was treated with 10 per cent novocaine by the filter paper technique, and the monkey was again tested.

No impairment resulted from this application, the conditioned head turning responses to light-touch stimulation of the plantar surface occurring as usual.

Then two successive operations were carried out to determine whether this retention of the conditioned responses may have resulted from failure of the novocaine to inactivate the somesthetic area, or whether it may have been because the essential centers for this response were more extensive than the poisoned areas. The first operation consisted of an excision of an area somewhat larger than the somesthetic area for the foot. Upon recovery, the animal was retested and the conditioned response proved itself to have been retained. Thus the operation showed that there had been no real test of the effect of novocaine on the somesthetic area, since the area which had been treated was not essential for the existence of the conditioned response in question.

In the second operation the entire somesthetic area for the foot, as outlined by Dusser de Barenne's strychnine experiments (1), was excised. The boundaries of the excised portion extended laterally to include a portion of the hand area, anteriorly as far as the inferior limb of the inferior precentral sulcus[1] and posteriorly as far as the parieto-occipital sulcus. Subsequent to this operation it was found that the conditioned response was still retained, suggesting that the essential sensory centers for this response were subcortical or that there was bilateral cortical representation.

EFFECT OF DRUGS ON THE VISUAL AREA

Since the above experiments suggested that the somesthetic area did not present a favorable field for testing the effect of anesthetic agents on sensory functions, tests were made on the visual area. The monkey tested was trained to respond positively to red, and negatively to yellow, blue, and green.... Although the colors were far from pure spectral colors, such as have been produced by the monochromators devised in our laboratory (see Grether, 4), there can be no doubt that the monkey was forced to make a discrimination on the basis of hue rather than brightness. Special care was taken to rule out the possibility of response to secondary cues.

After the habit had been thoroughly established, the lateral surface of the left occipital lobe was exposed by a two-stage operation such as that described in the earlier part of this report. (The entire right occipital lobe had been resected previous to training to avoid the difficulty which would otherwise be occasioned by the necessity of working on both lobes at the same time.) The entire lateral surface of the left occipital lobe was treated with 10 per cent novocaine by the filter-paper technique, but resulted in no decrement in the animal's ability to make the chromatic discriminations. Succeeding this attempt, there was an application of 4 per cent butyn (which is reported to be comparable to cocaine in strength and in absorptive properties). No loss of visual capacity resulted from this. During the course of these two tests, the monkey made 125 discriminations without a single error, though rigorous controls for secondary cues were maintained throughout.

Following this the entire lateral surface of the occipital lobe was treated with ethyl chloride. The first attempt to inactivate with this agent gave no result in spite of the fact that freezing had been continued until the surface of the lobe was frosted. A second treatment, in which the time of application was considerably prolonged, did bring about inactivation.

Upon release, the animal appeared to be completely blind, since he did not respond to threatening gestures, movements of the experimenter's hand in front of the eyes, or to offers of food. In about one minute of time the animal showed signs of responding to these stimuli. There appeared to be a gradual, progressive recovery, since the first signs of visual perception indicated an imperfect orientation to distance and a failure to discriminate forms accurately. As soon as ability to react to visual stimuli was recovered, tests for color discrimination were initiated. For a brief period the animal made no responses to the color vision apparatus; a short time later he did give responses, but several errors occurred in the first 10 trials, in spite of the fact that the monkey appeared to be highly motivated and well orientated to the general situation; following this, recovery was complete and the animal executed a series of 20 trials without error.

The entire procedure of inactivation by cold was repeated on the same animal two more times, and the same results were obtained.

DISCUSSION OF EXPERIMENTS ON VISION

The results are strikingly reminiscent of observations on soldiers suffering from occipital injuries. Various investigators such as Piéron (9), Monbrun (7), and Morax (8) have pointed out that recovery tends to follow a definite sequence in which responses to light, form, and color return in the order given. The findings herein described parallel this phenomenon, save for the fact that recovery from cold application took place in a few minutes whereas it was much delayed in the cases of the soldiers suffering from severe traumatic injury.

The fact that *total* blindness transiently resulted from application of ethyl chloride to only the *lateral* surface of the occipital lobes is of some theoretical importance, since anatomical studies (see Poliak, 10) show that the visual gateway... (primary projection area, Brodman's area, 17) in the monkey extends over the occipital pole and onto the medial surface. Furthermore, according to the studies, parts of both the peripheral and macular portions of the retina are represented in these areas. Freezing of only the lateral surface would therefore be expected to produce large scotomatous regions, but to leave part of the visual field intact. These facts are of interest also since Marquis (6) was able to obtain conditioned responses to visual stimuli from monkeys following bilateral extirpation of the occipital lobes.[2] It is necessary to keep in mind, when considering this problem, that the tests of blindness which we used were necessarily crude. The rapid recovery of function did not allow much opportunity to make a careful study, but it cannot be doubted that marked amblyopia existed. It is possible that the inactivation of a part of the visual area temporarily inactivated the remainder as the result of a "diaschisis" effect, though there is no direct proof of this.

CONCLUSIONS

1. Application of 10 per cent novocaine to circumscribed areas within the motor cortex of the rhesus monkey produced marked decrease in excitability to electrical stimulation.

2. Applications of 10 per cent novocaine and 4 per cent butyn to the lateral surface of the occipital lobe were ineffective in abolishing any visual functions.

3. The visual cortex was temporarily inactivated by freezing. The period of inactivation was longest for the "highest" functions (color, form discrimination) and shortest for the simpler functions.

REFERENCES

1. Dusser de Barenne, J.G. Some aspects of the problem of "corticalization" of function and of functional localization in the cerebral cortex. *Proc. Asso. Res. Nerv. Ment. Dis.*, 1934, *13*, 85-106.
2. ———.On a release-phenomenon in electrical stimulation of the "motor" cerebral cortex. *Science*, 1931, *73*, 213-214.
3. Geist, F. The brain of the rhesus monkey. *J. Comp. Neur.*, 1930, *50*, 333-375.
4. Grether, W. A new spectral color apparatus for studies of primate color vision. *J. Gen. Psychol.*, 1935, *12*, 450-455.
5. Head, H., & Others. Studies in neurology. (2 vols.) London: Frowde & Hodder, 1920. Pp. 338; 537.
6. Marquis, D. Phylogenetic interpretation of the functions of the visual cortex. *Arch. Neur. & Psychiat.*, 1935, *33*, 807-815.
7. Monbrun, A. Le centre cortical de la vision. *Arch. Ophth.*, 1919, *36*, 11.
8. Morax, V. L'hemianopsie par contusion du crane. *Ann. d'ocul.*, 1918, *158*, 112-121.
9. Piéron, H. Thought and the brain. (Trans. by C.K. Ogden.) New York: Harcourt, Brace, 1927. Pp. xvi+262.
10. Poliak, S. Projection of the retina upon the cerebral cortex, based upon experiments with monkeys. *Proc. Asso. Res. Nerv. Ment. Dis.*, 1934, *13*, 535-557.

NOTES

The authors wish to thank Drs. Geist and Seevers for valuable emendations. The work was financed in part by a grant from the University of Wisconsin research fund for 1934–35.

[1] Terminology is that given by Geist.

[2] In a private communication, Dr. M.H. Seevers, of the University of Wisconsin pharmacology department, has made the following suggestions. The failure of novocaine and butyn to inactivate the sensory fields of the cortex was probably due to failure of the agents to come into contact with the strata of cell bodies which subserve the given sensory functions. Also, he suggests that the effectiveness of prolonged treatment with ethyl chloride may have been due to vascular disturbances, which resulted in a condition of ischemia. The latter hypothesis is useful in attempting to explain the fact that freezing brought about no permanent damage to the nervous tissues, and it may also help to account for the complete blindness which resulted from application to a limited part of the visual area.

2

The Effects of Large Cortical Lesions on the Solution of Oddity Problems by Monkeys

H.F. Harlow, D. Meyer, and P.H. Settlage

Earlier studies of the behavior of rhesus monkeys with severe unilateral brain damage (3,5) have demonstrated impairments in a wide variety of performances. These losses are typically quantitative and subject to reduction by appropriate training. Indeed, no task has yet been devised that will permanently differentiate normal monkeys from animals with lesions in one hemisphere which spare little except motor and somatic areas. The present experiment adds to the battery of tests a problem of greater complexity, and evaluates the effects of additional lesions in the contralateral frontal and posterior association areas. The task is known as the oddity problem. On a given trial in the training procedure for this problem, three small objects are presented to the monkey for choice. Of these, two are physically identical. The third is dissimilar—or odd—and its selection is rewarded by food. A particular object is odd on half and paired on the other half of a series of such trials, but it is correct only when it is odd.

The use of this task in the analysis of cerebral function in monkeys has been limited to a study by Bromer (1), but variants have been used as indicators of the "abstraction" factor in Halstead's (2) theory of "biological intelligence." Although the oddity principle is consistently reinforced,

Harlow, H.F., Meyer, D.R., and Settlage, P.H. The effects of large cortical lesions on the solution of oddity problems by monkeys. *J. comp. physiol. Psychol.*, 1951, 44, 320–326. Copyright 1951 by the American Psychological Association. Reprinted by permission of the publisher and author.

the reward values of the objects and positions involved in the presentation of this pattern are frequently reversed. Perseverational responses to position or to object provide inadequate solutions. Such tendencies are, of course, inimical to the acquisition of the patterning response, which is well within the capacity of the normal monkey.

METHOD

Subjects

Sixteen rhesus monkeys, all with extensive laboratory experience, participated in this experiment. Four of the animals (Nos. 127, 128, 129, and 130) were a control *Normal Group*. Four others (Nos. 120, 131, 114, and 126), the *Frontal Group*, had undergone extensive unilateral decortication two years before the experiment began, and had more recently (5) been subjected to extirpation of the lateral surface of the contralateral prefrontal region. The extensive unilateral lesion included blunt dissection of the frontal pole anterior to a plane passing through the rostral extremities of the arcuate sulcus, blunt dissection of the occipital pole posterior to a plane 3 to 5 mm. rostral to the lunate sulcus, blunt dissection of the temporal lobe inferior to a plane parallel to and 4 to 5 mm. below the lateral fissure, aspiration of the remaining temporal cortex with the exception of a small amount at the extreme tip, aspiration of the parietal cortex with the exception of a 2 to 3 mm. strip caudal to the central fissure, and aspiration of the remaining frontal cortex anterior to the arcuate sulcus.

The third group of animals (Nos. 125, 122, 123, and 117) were reoperated after oddity learning and before oddity relearning. In the initial learning phase of the present experiment, this group of monkeys had extensive unilateral ablations of the type just described. Before the second series of problems was presented, decortications were performed in the contralateral posterior region. The lesion began near the midline at the junction of the lunate sulcus and the vein representing continuation of the intraparietal and superior temporal sulci. The lesion followed laterally along the lunate sulcus and caudal to this vein, broadening into and completely destroying the temporal lobe. These animals are designated first as the *Unilateral Group* and subsequently as the *Posterior Group*.

A fourth group of animals with unilateral occipital lobectomies (Nos. 119, 134, 135, and 132) were trained on the initial learning series of problems, but not on the second, since one of the monkeys died in the interim period. The test experience of these animals was never strictly comparable to that of the other subjects. Anatomical verification of lesions in all but one of the operated animals is currently forestalled by continued experimentation.

Apparatus and Procedure

The Wisconsin General Test Apparatus (3, Fig. 120) was used throughout. On each trial three objects on a movable tray were presented to the monkey for choice. Selection of the odd object was rewarded with a small piece of food placed in an underlying foodwell. The animal reached through the bars of a restraining cage to make his selection, which was defined as displacement of any object far enough to uncover any portion of the foodwell. Correction of errors was not permitted. During the choice period the animal was observed through a one-way vision screen.

Double pairs of objects, e.g., tobacco tins and match boxes, were used for arranging the six possible oddity combinations. Each kind of object was odd (correct) an equal number of times and appeared in each position an equal number of times. These arrangements were presented in a balanced order. During the setting of a trial an opaque screen was lowered just in front of the restraining cage.

The initial acquisition of the oddity learning set was studied for 60 test days. A given double-pair of stimulus objects was used in a single daily experimental session of 24 trials. The 60 sets of objects employed in the course of this series of problems were an unbiased choice from the laboratory's large and randomly ordered collection.

The data for the matched groups of Normal, Unilateral, and Frontal monkeys were collected by four experimenters, and one monkey of each group was assigned to each experimenter. The Occipital Group was tested at a later time and by other experimenters.

In the interim between the learning and relearning series the Unilateral Group was converted into the Posterior Group. Additional laboratory experience for the animals during this four-month period included two studies of delayed response performance, a transfer problem patterned after one originally described by Spence, a multiple-reversal problem, six-trial object-quality discrimination training, and six-trial pattern discrimination training.

The relearning phase of the experiment lasted for 15 days. Each day 24 trials were presented, but a given set of objects was used for only six trials. Four sets of objects were employed each day, and a total of 60 problems were completed. Again, the objects were chosen from the randomized laboratory collection.

RESULTS

Learning Series

Group curves which represent per cent error performances for each of five successive blocks of 12 problems are shown in Figure 2-1. The Normal

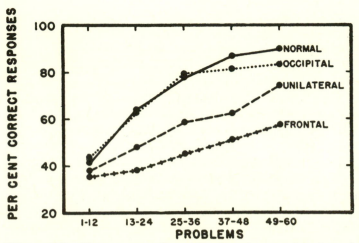

Figure 2-1   Group curves for oddity learning as a function of the number of problems presented.

Group trend is almost indistinguishable from that of the Occipital Group, but mean scores of the other two groups of monkeys are uniformly inferior. The over-all performance of the Normal Group is significantly (by *t* test) superior to that of the Frontal Group (0.1 per cent level), but not to that of the Unilateral Group (10 per cent level). On the final block

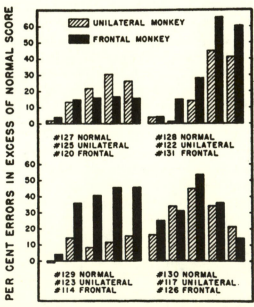

Figure 2-2   Individual comparisons of the performances of matched normal and brain-damaged monkeys.

of problems, however, the performance of the Normal animals is significantly superior to that of both the Unilateral and the Frontal monkeys at the 1 and the 2 per cent levels of confidence, respectively.

The substantial differences in the group mean performances of the Unilateral and Frontal groups are not statistically demonstrable and the degree of overlap is illustrated in Figure 2-2. Here four separate bar charts have been drawn, each based on data for three matched animals. In these diagrams the baselines are the performances of the respective control monkeys, and the scores of the matched brain-damaged animals appear as per cent deviations. Each pair of bars represents performance on one of the five blocks of 12 oddity problems. In each of the 20 instances the performance of the normal animal is superior to that of the matched frontal monkey, and the differences are large. In 19 or 20 instances the performance of the normal monkey is superior to that of the matched unilateral subject, and the single reversal is of negligible magnitude. In 15 instances the frontal monkeys are inferior to the unilateral animals, but large reversals are present in the other five comparisons.

Individual performances for the final block of 12 problems, in terms of per cent correct responses, range from 83 to 93 in the Normal Group, from 79 to 85 in the Occipital Group, from 54 to 77 in the Unilateral Group, and from 47 to 69 in the Frontal Group. These scores show that some animals in each of the experimental groups are at this time solving oddity problems with efficiency.

The performances of the least efficient animals in the Frontal and Unilateral groups, which approximate 50 per cent correct responses, suggested that these monkeys attempted to solve the problems as object discriminations. This hypothesis was examined by comparing the number of errors made with ABB, BAB, and BBA arrangements (where A and B represent dissimilar objects) to those made with BAA, ABA, and AAB arrangements. The distribution of errors between the two kinds of objects indicated the operation of object preferences in all groups, but the distributions were too similar to permit quantitative differentiations. Variations in object preference errors as a function of practice are extremely complex.

Trends of performance within problems are presented in Figure 2-3. These curves summarize data from all of the 60 problems in the series, since probable systematic changes with practice are too small to be detected. Improvements from trial to trial are small. Over-all performance for the Normal Group on the first trial alone was also tabulated and found to be in very close agreement with the pooled data for the first six trials.

Relearning Series

Interproblem relearning functions for the series of six-trial oddity problems are shown in Figure 2-4. The trends for the two operated groups which

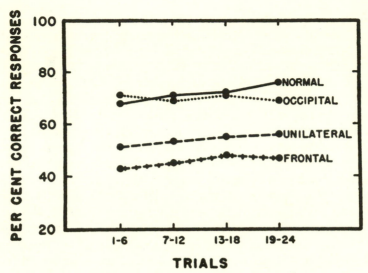

Figure 2-3   Trends of performance as a function of trials within oddity learning problems.

were tested in this phase of the experiment, the Posterior (formerly Unilateral) and the Frontal, are much closer than during the initial acquisition series, but it should be emphasized that the earlier differences were not statistically significant. Over-all performances of the individuals of

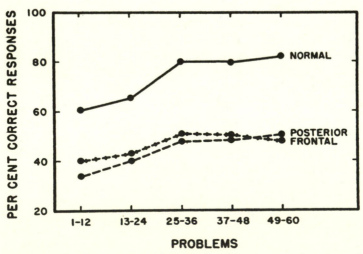

Figure 2-4   Group curves for oddity relearning as a function of the number of problems presented.

the Frontal Group remain essentially the same, but three of the animals of the Posterior Group have scores which suggest deterioration. The performance of the Normal Group, both for over-all and last-block scores, are significantly superior to those of the Posterior and Frontal groups at the 1 and the 5 per cent levels, respectively.

A comparison of the Normal Group trends in Figures 2-1 and 2-4 shows that the rate of interproblem improvement is markedly reduced in the later series, for the initial superiority of the relearning curve is not maintained as problem practice proceeds. If, however, learning and relearning are plotted as a function of trials, and not as a function of problems, the two curves are quite similar. This has been done in Figure 2-5.

The relearning function is based upon relatively few trials, and the irregularities do not permit a precise evaluation of slope. Nevertheless, these data suggest that the relearning rate per trial is slightly greater than the learning rate.

If we assume that transfer of training changes the intercept of the relearning function, this finding is a new clue to the optimal length of problem for maximally efficient oddity learning. In another experiment (4) it was shown that over-all performance on a series of 96 trials with a given set of objects was no better than over-all performance on the initial 24 trials with this set of objects. From the available evidence, then, the optimal problem is certainly less than 96 trials long, probably less than 24 trials long, and possibly less than 6 trials long. Extrapolation of this relationship strongly suggests that acquisition of the oddity learning set

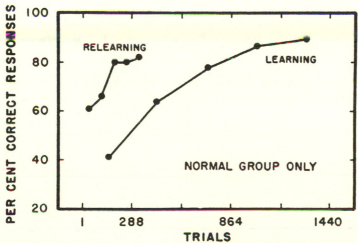

Figure 2-5   Oddity learning and relearning as a function of the total number of trials.

would be maximally rapid if objects were used for a single trial, but this must remain for the present a matter of conjecture.

DISCUSSION AND SUMMARY

The data of the present experiment show that acquisition, by monkeys, of the general solution to oddity problems is markedly retarded by extensive cortical lesions restricted to a single hemisphere. The deficit cannot be attributed to the loss of a visual field, for the effect is not produced by resection of one occipital lobe.

Invasion of the contralateral hemisphere yields a trend toward additional impairment that is not specific to damage in the frontal or the posterior association areas.

Contrasting results are obtained when other tests are used. The animals with the additional frontal lesion show conspicuous delayed response impairment. Subjects with additional posterior ablation are retarded in discrimination learning.

REFERENCES

1. Bromer, J.A. A genetic and physiological investigation of concept behavior in primates. Unpublished Doctor's dissertation, Univ. Wisconsin, 1940.
2. Halstead, W.C. *Brain and intelligence.* Chicago: University of Chicago Press, 1947.
3. Harlow, H.F., and Settlage, P.H. The effect of extirpation of frontal areas upon learning performance of monkeys. In J.F. Fulton, C.D. Aring, and S.B. Wortis (Eds.), *The frontal lobes. Res. Publ. Ass. nerv. ment. Dis.*, Vol. 27. Baltimore: Williams & Wilkins, 1948. Pp. 446–459.
4. Meyer, D.R., and Harlow, H.F. The development of transfer of response to patterning by monkeys. *J. comp. physiol. Psychol.*, 1949, *42*, 454–462.
5. Meyer, D.R., Harlow, H.F., and Settlage, P.H. A survey of delayed response performance by normal and brain-damaged monkeys. *J. comp. physiol. Psychol.*, 1951, *44*, 17–25.

3

The Development of Learning in the Rhesus Monkey

Harry F. Harlow

During the last five years we have conducted an integrated series of researches tracing and analyzing the learning capabilities of rhesus monkeys from birth to intellectual maturity. Control over the monkey's environment has been achieved by separating the infants from their mothers at birth and raising them independently, using techniques and methods adapted from those described by van Wagenen (12).

There are many characteristics that commend the rhesus monkey as a subject for investigation of the development of learning. At birth, or a few days later, this animal attains adequate control over its head, trunk, arm, and leg movements, permitting objective recording of precise responses on tests of learning. The rhesus monkey has broad learning abilities, and even the neonatal monkey rapidly learns problems appropriate to its maturational status. As it grows older, this monkey can master a relatively unlimited range of problems suitable for measuring intellectual maturation. Although the rhesus monkey matures more rapidly than the human being, the time allotted for assessing its developing learning capabilities is measured in terms of years—not days, weeks, or months, as is true with most subprimate forms. During this time a high degree of control can be maintained over all experimental variables, particularly those relating to

Harlow, H.F. The development of learning in the rhesus monkey. *American Scientist*, 1959, 47, 459–479.

the animal's learning experiences. Thus, we can assess for all learning problems the relative importance of nativistic and experiential variables, determine the age at which problems of any level of difficulty can first be solved, and measure the effects of introducing such learning problems to animals before or after this critical period appears. Furthermore, the monkey may be used with impunity as a subject for discovering the effects of cerebral damage or insult, whether produced by mechanical intervention or by biochemical lesions.

The only other creature whose intellectual maturation has been studied with any degree of adequacy is the human child, and the data from this species attest to the fact that learning capability increases with age, particularly in the range and difficulty of learned tasks which can be mastered. Beyond this fact, the human child has provided us with astonishingly little basic information on the nature or development of learning. Obviously, there are good and sufficient reasons for any and all such deficiencies. There are limits beyond which it is impossible or unjustifiable to use the child as an experimental subject. The education of groups of children cannot be hampered or delayed for purposes of experimental control over either environment or antecedent learning history. Unusual motivational conditions involving either deprivation or overstimulation are undesirable. Neurophysiological or biochemical studies involving or threatening physical injury are unthinkable.

Even aside from these cultural limitations, the human child has certain characteristics that render him a relatively limited subject for the experimental analysis of the maturation of learning capability. At birth, his neuromuscular systems are so undeveloped that he is incapable of effecting the precise head, arm, hand, trunk, leg, and foot movements essential for objective measurement. By the time these motor functions have adequately matured, many psychological developmental-processes, including those involving learning, have appeared and been elaborated, but their history and nature have been obscured or lost in a maze of confounded variables.

By the time the normal child has matured physically, he is engaging each day in such a fantastic wealth of multiple learning activities that precise, independent control over any single learning process presents a task beyond objective realism. The multiple, interactive transfer processes going on overwhelm description, and their independent experimental evaluation cannot be achieved. Even if it were proper to cage human children willfully, which it assuredly is not, this very act would in all probability render the children abnormal and untestable and again leave us with an insuperable problem.

It might appear that all these difficulties could be overcome best by studying the development of learning abilities in infraprimate organisms rather than monkeys. Unfortunately, the few researches which have been completed indicate that this is not true. Animals below the primate order are intellectually limited compared with monkeys, so that they learn the same problems more slowly and are incapable of solving many problems that are relatively easily mastered by monkeys. Horses and rats, and even cats and dogs, can solve only a limited repertoire of learning tasks, and they learn so slowly on all but the simplest of these that they pass from infancy to maturity before their intellectual measurement can be completed. Even so, we possess scattered information within this area. We know that cats perform more adequately on the Hamilton perseverance test than do kittens and that the same relationship holds for dogs compared with puppies (2, 3). It has been demonstrated that mature and aged rats are no more proficient on a multiple-T maze than young rats (11), and that conditioned responses cannot be established in dogs before 18–21 days of age (1); but such data will never give us insight into the fundamental laws of learning or maturation of learning.

NEONATAL AND EARLY INFANTILE LEARNING: THE FIRST SIXTY DAYS

Because learning and the development of learning are continuous, orderly processes, classifying learning into temporal intervals is an arbitrary procedure. However, a criterion that may be taken for separating early learning from later learning is the underlying motive or incentive. Solid foods are precluded as incentives for monkey learning prior to 40–60 days of age, forcing the experimenter to depend upon such rewards as liquid nutrients, shock avoidance, exploration, and home cage conditions. It is recognized that these same rewards may be used to motivate older primates on learning tasks, but for them the convenient incentive of solid food becomes available. Another arbitrary criterion that may be taken for choosing this temporal period lies in the fact that fear of strange, new situations—including test situations—only appears toward the end of this period.

Conditioned Responses

The earliest unequivocal learned responses which we obtained from the rhesus monkey were conditioned responses in a situation in which an auditory stimulus was paired with electric shock. The standard procedure was to adapt the neonatal monkeys during the first two days of life by placing them for ten minutes a day in the apparatus, which consisted of a cubic Plexiglas stabilimeter with a grid floor, enclosed in a sound-deadened cabinet with a one-way-vision screen on the front (see Figure 3-1).

Figure 3-1 Neonatal monkey in stabilimeter.

Conditioning trials were initiated on the third day, the tone and shock
intervals being mechanically fixed at two seconds and one second, respectively, and administered either separately or paired. The animals were
divided into three groups and were given daily trials as follows: five
experimental subjects (T-S group) were given eight paired tone-shock
trials and two tests trials; four pseudoconditioning controls (P-C group)
were given eight shock trials and two test trials in which tone only was
presented; and four stimulus-sensitization controls (T-O group) received
ten tone trials but never received shock from the grid floor. Conditioned
and unconditioned responses were measured in terms of both the continuous, objective activity records taken from an Esterline-Angus recorder
and the check-list records made by two independent human observers.

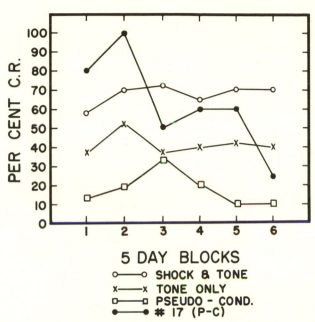

Figure 3-2 Conditioning in 5 day blocks.

The learning data presented in Figure 3-2 show early and progressive learning. The differences between the frequency of conditioned responses by the five experimental subjects and the four subjects in each of the control groups were significant, even though clear-cut evidence of pseudoconditioning was found in one of the P-C animals. It will be noted that the observers recorded a higher frequency of conditioned responses than could be identified from the stabilimeter record. The observational data indicate that these tone-shock conditioned responses were learned by three subjects on the second test day and that unequivocal conditioning took place in four of the five subjects. The observational data also show that the form of the conditioned response changes with training, starting as a diffuse response and gradually becoming more precise. As training progressed, most subjects responded to the conditioned stimulus by standing erect, sometimes on one foot.

Limited tests failed to demonstrate any generalization of the conditioned response to the experimenter or to auditory stimuli presented outside the test situation. Retention tests made fifteen days after the completion of the original training revealed very considerable learning loss, ranging among individual subjects from no definite indication of retention, to conditioned responses on about half the test trials.

Straight-Runway Performance

An apparently simple learned response, which has been frequently used by psychologists in studying rat learning, is the straight runway. We produced such an apparatus by simply using the monkey's living cage as the runway and introducing a nursing booth at one end prior to each feeding period. At the time of testing, the subject was taken to the far end of the home cage, faced toward the nursing booth, released, and allowed thirty seconds to enter the booth. The number of daily trials was determined by number of feeding sessions, twelve a day during the first two weeks, and ten a day subsequently.

The subjects were divided into three groups: For the light-conditioned animals (L-C group) the nursing booth was suffused with flashing green light during each of the training trials; for the no-light monkeys (N-L group) there were no conditioning cues other than those afforded by the test situation and the act of orientation; for the light-extinguished subjects (L-I group) the nursing booth was suffused with green light, but this light was immediately extinguished when the monkey entered the booth and simultaneously there began a five-minute delay period before feeding.

The data...offer evidence of rapid and progressive improvement in performance. Many of the failures during the first ten days resulted from locomotor limitations or from the disturbing effects of reorientation and restraint by the experimenter. It is clear, however, that learning occurred early in life and that the cue of green light added little or nothing to the cues provided by the presence of the experimenter and postural orientation. The L-I group, which did not receive food upon approach to the nursing booth, was significantly inferior to the other two groups, and it is possible that the green light became a cue for absence or delay of feeding.

Spatial Discrimination

Two groups of ten monkeys each were tested on a spatial discrimination problem requiring choice of the right or left alley of the Y-maze illustrated in Figure 3-3. One group of subjects began training at fifteen days of age (group 15), after four days of adaptation, and the other group started maze learning at forty-five days of age (group 45). Two trials were given each day, a correct trial being rewarded by entrance into the home cage, a highly effective incentive for the infant monkey, whereas an incorrect response, defined as entrance into the incorrect antechamber, was punished by a one-minute delay before rerunning. A rerun technique was used throughout this test, i.e., whenever the monkey made an error, it was returned to the starting position and run again until it made the correct choice and reached the home cage. Spatial discrimination learning was

Figure 3-3   Infant monkey Y-maze.

continued for twenty-five days; on the twenty-sixth day the position of the correct goal box was reversed and the same training schedule of two trials per day continued.

The percentage of correct initial responses made by group 15 on days 1, 2, 5, 10, and 15 are 45, 60, 75, 75, and 95, respectively. Comparable percentages for group 45 are 80, 55, 65, 85, and 100. Despite the high percentage of correct responses made by group 45 on day 1, the two learning curves...are very similar. Excluding a single member in each group that failed to adapt to the test situation and never met the criterion of 18 correct responses in 20 consecutive trials, the mean number of trials to this criterion, excluding the criterional trials, was 8.5 for group 15 and 6.2 for group 45.

The percentage of correct responses dropped below chance for both groups of monkeys during the first five reversal trials, and trial 1 was especially characterized by multiple, persistent, erroneous choices. During all these trials the animals made many violent emotional responses as indicated by balking, vocalization, and autonomic responses, including blushing, urination and defecation. Even so, all but one subject in group

15 attained the criterion of 18 correct responses in 20 consecutive trials, and the mean number of trials to learn, not including the criterional trials, was 19.2 for group 15 and 11.9 for group 45.

Although the performance of the older group was superior to that of the younger, particularly on the reversal problem, the differences were not statistically significant. Certainly the 15-day-old macaques solved this spatial learning task with facility, and their performance leaves little to be gained through additional maturation.

Object Discrimination

Two groups of four newborn monkeys were trained on a black-white discrimination, i.e., a nonspatial or object discrimination, by teaching them to select and climb up a black or white ramp for the reward of a full meal delivered through a nursing bottle. An incorrect choice was punished by a three-minute delay in feeding... Not only the ramp, but the entire half of the test situation was black or white, as the case might be, and the positions of these half-cages were reversed on fifty per cent of the trials. The number of test trials was stabilized at nine per day after the first few days of life.

Learning by the neonatal macaques in this test situation proved to be almost unbelievably rapid, even allowing for the fact that a maximally efficient stimulus display was provided by the totally black and totally white halves of the test chamber.... The group of infants trained from birth on the object-discrimination problem attained the criterion of ninety per cent correct responses on two consecutive days beginning at nine days of age. This was a total of less than 100 trials, many of which were failed through physical inability to climb the ramp. A second group, run as a maturational control, was rewarded for climbing up either of two gray ramps for the first ten days. On day 11 the black and white ramps were substituted, and these monkeys solved the black-white discrimination problem, the first formal learning problem they had ever faced, by the second test day, averaging less than thirteen trials to achieve the criterion.

After the black-white discrimination problem was solved, the infants were tested on discrimination reversal, i.e., the color of ramp previously correct was now made incorrect, and the color of the ramp previously incorrect became correct. The results were very similar to those obtained in the spatial discrimination problem. The infants made a great many errors when the problem was first reversed and showed very severe emotional disturbances. This was particularly true when the reversal went from white correct to black, since infant monkeys strongly prefer white to black.

We have also a considerable body of data showing that the infant monkey can solve form discriminations and color discriminations as well as the black-white brightness-discrimination problem. It is not possible in these other situations, particularly in the case of form discrimination, to attain the maximally efficient stimulus display previously described. For this reason—and a control study suggests that it is for this reason alone—the number of trials required to learn increases and the age at which learning can be demonstrated also advances. Even so, it has been possible to obtain discrimination between a triangle and a circle by the 20-to-30-day-old monkey after less than 200 training trials.

INFANT LEARNING: THE FIRST YEAR

The most surprising finding relating to neonatal learning was the very early age at which simple learning tasks could be mastered. Indeed, learning of both the simple conditioned response and the straight runway appeared as early as the animal was capable of expressing it through the maturation of adequate skeletal motor responses. Thus, we can in no way exclude the possibility that the monkey at normal term, or even before normal term, is capable of forming simple associations.

Equally surprising is the fact that performance may reach or approach maximal facility within a brief period of time. The five-day-old monkey forms conditioned reflexes between tone and shock as rapidly as the year-old or the adult monkey. The baby macaque solves the simple straight-alley problem as soon as it can walk, and there is neither reason nor leeway for the adult to do appreciably better. Although we do not know the minimal age for solution of the Y-maze, it is obviously under fifteen days. Such data as we have on this problem indicate that the span between age of initial solution and the age of maximally efficient solution is brief. One object discrimination, the differentiation between the total-black and total-white field, shows characteristics similar to the learning already described. The developmental period for solution lies between six and ten days of age, and a near maximal learning capability evolves rapidly. However, it would be a serious mistake to assume that any sharply defined critical periods characterize the development of more complex forms of learning or problem solving.

Object Discrimination Learning

Although the 11-day-old monkey can solve a total-black *versus* total-white discrimination problem in less than thirteen trials, the 20- to 30-day-old

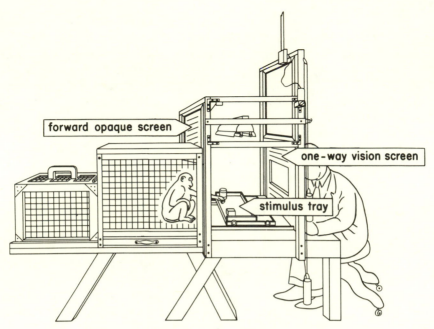

Figure 3-4 Wisconsin General Test Apparatus.

monkey may require from 150 to 200 trials to solve a triangle-circle discrimination problem when the stimuli are relatively small and placed some distance apart. It is a fact that, even though the capability of solving this more conventional type of object-discrimination problem exists at twenty days, object-discrimination learning capability has by no means attained full maturity at this time.

The development of complete object-discrimination capacity was measured by testing five different age groups of naive rhesus monkeys on a single discrimination problem. Discrimination training was begun when the animals were 60, 90, 120, 150, or 366 days of age, and, in all cases, training was preceded by at least fifteen days of adaptation to the apparatus and to the eating of solid food. There were eight subjects in group 366 (as defined by age), ten in group 60, and fifteen in each of the other groups. A Wisconsin General Test Apparatus, illustrated in Figure 3-4, was used throughout the test sessions. A single pair of three-dimensional stimuli differing in multiple attributes such as color, form, size, and material was presented on a two-foodwell test tray of the Klüver type. The animals were given twenty-five trials a day, five days a week, for four weeks, a total of 500 trials. A noncorrection method was always used.

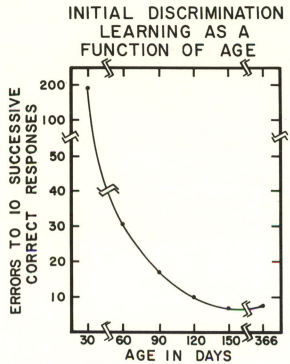

Figure 3-5 Initial discrimination learning as a function of age.

Figure 3-5 presents the number of trials taken by the five different groups of monkeys, and performance by a 30-day-old group on a triangle-circle discrimination is plotted on the far left. Whether or not one includes this group, it is apparent that the ability of infant monkeys to solve the object-discrimination problem increases with age as a negatively accelerated function and approaches or attains an asymptote at 120 to 150 days.

Detailed analyses have given us considerable insight into the processes involved in the maturation of this learning function. Regardless of age, the monkeys' initial responsiveness to the problem is not random or haphazard. Instead, almost all the subjects approached the problem in some systematic manner. About twenty per cent of the monkeys chose the correct object from the beginning and stayed with their choice, making no errors! Another twenty per cent showed a strong preference for the incorrect stimulus and made many errors. Initial preference for the left side and for the right side was about equally frequent, and consistent alternation-patterns also appeared. The older, and presumably brighter, monkeys rapidly learned to abandon any incorrect response tendency. The younger, and presumably less intelligent, monkeys persisted longer with the inadequate response tendencies, and very frequently shifted from one incorrect response tendency to another before finally solving the problem. Systematic responsiveness of this type was first described by Krechevsky (8) for rats and was given the name of "hypothesis." Although this term has unfortunate connotations, it was the rule and not the exception that our monkey subjects went from one "hypothesis" to another until solution, with either no random trials or occasionally a few random trials intervening. The total number of incorrect, systematic, response tendencies before problem solution was negatively correlated with age.

These data on the maturation of discrimination learning capability clearly demonstrate that there is no single day of age nor narrow age-band at which object-discrimination learning abruptly matures. If the "critical period" hypothesis is to be entertained, one must think of two different critical periods, a period at approximately twenty days of age, when such problems can be solved if a relatively unlimited amount of training is provided, and a period at approximately 150 days of age, when a full adult level of ability has developed.

Delayed Response

The delayed-response problem has challenged and intrigued psychologists ever since it was initially presented by Hunter (6). In this problem the animal is first shown a food reward, which is then concealed within, or under, one of two identical containers during the delay period. The problem was originally believed to measure some high-level ideational ability or "representative factor"—a capacity that presumably transcended simple trial-and error learning. Additional interest in the problem arose from the discovery by Jacobsen (7) that the ability to solve delayed-response problems was abolished or drastically impaired by bilateral frontal lobectomy in monkeys.

Scores of researches have been conducted on delayed-response problems. Almost all known laboratory species have been tested and all conceivable parameters investigated. In so far as the delayed response is difficult, it appears to be less a function of period of delay or duration of memory than an intrinsic difficulty in responding attentively to an implicit or demonstrated reward. However, in spite of the importance of the problem and the vast literature which has accumulated, there has been no previous major attempt to trace its ontogenetic development in subhuman animals.

Ten subjects in each of four groups, a 60-, 90-, 120-, and 150-day group, were tested on so-called zero-second and five-second delayed

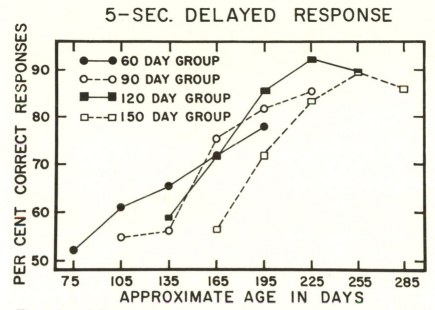

5–SEC. DELAYED RESPONSE

- ● ● 60 DAY GROUP
- ○---○ 90 DAY GROUP
- ■ ■ I20 DAY GROUP
- □---□ I50 DAY GROUP

Figure 3-6   5-Second delayed response performance of different maturational groups with age held constant.

responses (the actual delay period is approximately two seconds longer) at the same time they began their discrimination learning. A block of ten trials at each delay interval was presented five days a week for eighteen weeks, a total of ninety test days. These 900 trials at each delay interval constituted the test program for Series I, which was followed by Series II during which time delay intervals of 5, 10, 20, and 40 seconds were introduced in counterbalanced order for twelve test weeks of five days each at the rate of eight trials a day for each condition.

The results for the four infant groups on the five-second delayed responses were compared with the performance of a group of adults with extensive previous test experience on many different problems. The four infant groups showed increasing ability to solve delayed responses both as a function of experience and as a function of age. The performance of all infant groups was inferior to the adult group, but differences in past learning experiences preclude any direct comparison.

The performance of the four infant groups of monkeys on the five-second delayed responses for trials 1–100, 201–300, 401–500, 601–700, and 801–900 is plotted in Figure 3-6. Because performance during trials 1–100 is poor regardless of group, it is apparent that a certain minimum experience is required to master the delayed-response task. At the same time, the increasingly steep slopes of the learning curves make it apparent that efficiency of delayed-response learning and performance is in large part a function of age. The group data suggest that, after extensive training as provided in this study, seventy per cent correct responses may be attained by 150 days of age, eighty per cent by 200 days, and ninety per cent by 250 days.....

Very marked individual differences were disclosed during delayed-response testing, a finding which typifies this task regardless of species or age. Some monkeys, as well as some other animals, fail to adapt to the requirements of the test. Inspection of individual records reveals that the capability of solving this problem first appears at about 125 to 135 days of age and that essentially faultless performance may appear by 200 to 250 days in perhaps half the infant monkey subjects. Thus, some monkeys at this age may possess an adult capability, and these data are in keeping with the results obtained in the Series II tests. Recently, we have completed a study on a 30-month-old group of five monkeys on zero- and five-second delayed responses, and their learning rates and terminal performance are at adult levels. Thus, it appears that we have definitive data on the maturation and acquisition of delayed-response performance by rhesus monkeys.

It is obvious that the capability of solving the delayed-response problem matures at a later date than the capacity of solving the object-discrimination problem. This is true regardless of the criterion taken, whether it is the age at which the task can be solved after a relatively unlimited number of trials or the age at which a full adult level of mastery is attained. At the same time, it should be emphasized that this capacity does develop when the monkey is still an infant, long before many complex problems can be efficiently attacked and mastered. Thus, there is no reason to believe that the delayed response is a special measure of intelligence or of any particular or unusual intellectual function.

Object Discrimination Learning Set

The present writer, in 1949, demonstrated that adolescent or adult monkeys trained on a long series of six-trial discrimination problems showed progressive improvement from problem to problem. As successive blocks of problems were run, the form of the learning curve changed from positively accelerated, to linear, to negatively accelerated; finally, there appeared to be two separate curves or functions, i.e., performance changed from chance on trial 1 to perfection or near perfection on and after trial 2. From trial 1 to 2 the curve is precipitate and from trial 2 onward it is flat. This phenomenon, called "learning set formation" or "interproblem learning," has proved to be a useful tool in comparative, physiological, and theoretical psychology. To obtain evidence concerning the maturational factors involved, the performance of various age groups of monkeys was measured on this task.

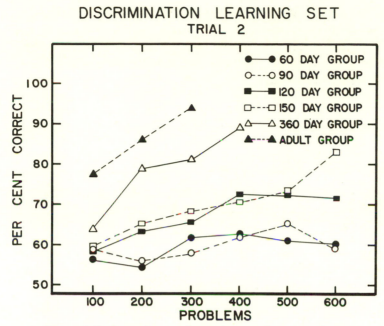

DISCRIMINATION LEARNING SET
TRIAL 2

Legend:
● — ● 60 DAY GROUP
○ - - - ○ 90 DAY GROUP
■ — ■ 120 DAY GROUP
□ - - - □ 150 DAY GROUP
△ — △ 360 DAY GROUP
▲ - - - ▲ ADULT GROUP

Y-axis: PER CENT CORRECT (50, 60, 70, 80, 90, 100)
X-axis: PROBLEMS (100, 200, 300, 400, 500, 600)

Figure 3-7   Learning set formation as a function of age.

The same five infant groups previously tested on a single object-discrimination problem served as subjects for learning-set training. Upon completion of the original discrimination problem they were tested on four discrimination problems a day five days a week, each problem six trials in length. Group 366 was trained on 400 problems and the other monkeys on 600 problems. The individual test-trial procedures were identical to those employed in regular object-discrimination learning, but a new pair of stimuli was introduced for each new problem.

The trial 2 performance of the five groups of infant monkeys is plotted in Figure 3-7, and data from mature monkeys tested in previous experiments are also given. The two younger groups fail to respond consistently above a sixty per cent level even though they were approximately ten and eleven months of age at the conclusion of training. The two older groups show progressive, even though extremely slow, improvement in their trial 2 performances, with groups 120 and 150 finally attaining a seventy and eighty per cent level of correct responding. These data are in general accord with those obtained from an earlier, preliminary experiment and indicate that the year-old monkey is capable of forming discrimination learning sets even though it has by no means attained an adult level of proficiency.

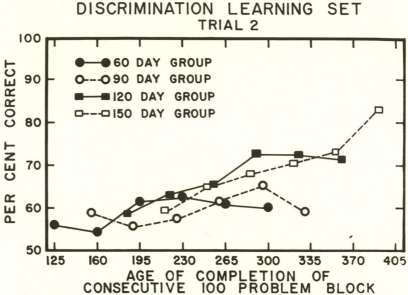

Figure 3-8 Learning set plotted for age of completion of consecutive 100 problem blocks.

In Figure 3-8 the trial 2 learning-set performance for the various groups is plotted in terms of age of completion of consecutive 100-problem blocks, and these data suggest that the capacity of the two younger groups to form discrimination learning sets may have been impaired by their early, intensive learning-set training, initiated before they possessed any effective learning-set capability. Certainly, their performance from 260 days onward is inferior to that of the earlier groups with less experience but matched for age. The problem which these data illustrate has received little attention among experimental psychologists. There is a tendency to think of learning or training as intrinsically good and necessarily valuable to the organism. It is entirely possible, however, that training can either be helpful or harmful, depending upon the nature of the training and the organism's stage of development.

Because of the fundamental similarities existing between the learning of an individual problem and the learning of series of problems of the same kind, it is a striking discovery that a great maturational gulf exists between efficient individual-problem learning and efficient learning-set formation. Information bearing on this problem has been obtained through detailed analyses by the author. The author's error-factor analysis technique (5) reveals that, with decreasing age, there is an increasing tendency to make stimulus-perseveration errors, i.e., if the initially chosen object is incorrect, the monkey has great difficulty in shifting to the correct object. Further-

Figure 3-9 Infant monkey responding incorrectly to crossed-string problem.

more, with decreasing age there is an increasing tendency to make differential-cue errors, i.e., difficulty in inhibiting, on any particular trial, the ambiguous reinforcement of the position of the stimulus which is concurrent with the reinforcement of the object *per se*.

In all probability, individual-problem learning involves elimination of the same error factors or the utilization of the same hypotheses or strategies as does learning-set formation. However, as we have already seen, the young rhesus monkey's ability to suppress these error factors in individual-problem learning does not guarantee in any way whatsoever a capacity to transfer this information to the interproblem learning-set task. The learning of the infant is specific and fails to generalize from problem to problem, or, in Goldstein's terms, the infant possesses only the capacity for concrete thinking. Failure by the infant monkey to master learning-set problems is not surprising inasmuch as infraprimate animals, such as the rat and the cat, possess the most circumscribed capabilities for these interproblem learnings, and it is doubtful if the pigeon possesses any such ability at all. Indeed, discrimination learning-set formation taxes the prowess of the human imbecile and apparently exceeds the capacity of the human idiot.

Most of the findings which we have reported for the maturation of learning in the rhesus monkey had been predicted, but this was not true in the case of the string tests. One of the two theoretically simple patterns, the parallel strings and the two crossed strings, is pictured in Figure 3-9.

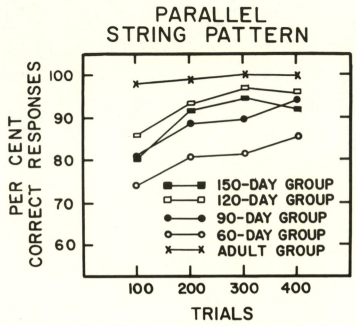

Figure 3-10   Parallel string pattern performance as a function of age.

We had assumed that the infant monkey would solve the parallel pattern with few or no errors, but, as can be seen in Figure 3-10, this assumption did not accord with fact. The infant monkeys made many errors, learned slowly, and in many cases failed to reach a level of perfect responsiveness after prolonged training. The data on the relatively simple two crossed-strings pattern (Figure 3-11) show that the six-month-old rhesus monkey is just beginning to reach the age at which this problem can be mastered. Unfortunately, our data on patterned-strings learning are incomplete, but it is obvious that this capacity is a function which is maturing during the second half of the first year of life and probably for a considerable period of time henceforward. In retrospect, we realized that the relatively late maturation of string-test learning was in keeping with known facts. The crossed-strings pattern has never been solved by any infraprimate animal, and this task cannot be resolved by the human infant (9, 10) until the second or third year of life.

THE DEVELOPMENT OF TERMINAL LEARNING ABILITY

At the present time we have completed a series of experiments which clearly demonstrate that the capability of solving problems of increasing

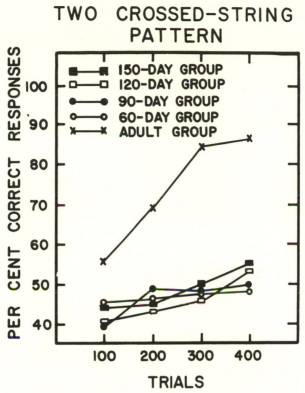

Figure 3-11 Two crossed-string pattern performance as a function of age.

complexity develops in rhesus monkeys in a progressive and orderly manner throughout the first year of life. Furthermore, when we compare the performances of the year-old monkey and the adult monkey, it becomes obvious that maturation is far from complete at the end of the first year. Although our data on early development are more complete than our data on terminal learning capacities, we have already obtained a considerable body of information on middle and late learning growth.

Hamilton Perseverance Test

Just as we were surprised by the delayed appearance of the capability of mastering the patterned-strings tests, so were we surprised by the delay before performance on the Hamilton perseverance test attains maximal efficiency.

Three groups of monkeys were initially tested at 12, 30, and 50 months of age, respectively. The groups comprised six, five, and seven

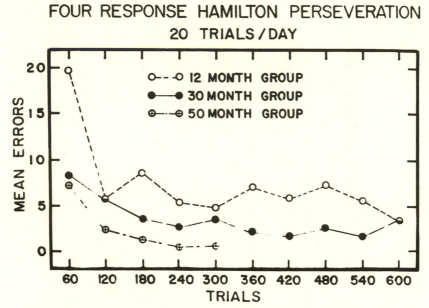

Figure 3-12 Mean number of errors per 60-trial block on Hamilton Perseverance Test.

monkeys, and all were tested twenty trials a day for thirty days. On the perseverance problem the animal is faced with a series of four boxes having spring-loaded lids which close as soon as they are released. Only one box contains food, and the rewarded box is changed in a random manner from trial to trial with the provision that the same box is never rewarded twice in succession. In the present experiment the subjects were allowed only four responses per trial, whether or not the reward was obtained, and an error was defined as any additional response to an unrewarded box after the initial lifting of the lid during a trial. Infraprimate animals make many errors of this kind, but as can be seen in Figure 3-12, the mature monkey makes few such errors and learns rather rapidly to eliminate these. We were surprised by the inefficient performance of the year-old monkey and unprepared to discover that maximally efficient performance was not attained by the 30-month-old monkeys.

The mature monkey finds a simple plan for attacking the perseverance problem. Typically, it chooses the extreme left or right box and works systematically toward the other end. If it adopts some more complex strategy, as responding by some such order as box 4–2–3–1, it will repeat this same order on successive trials.

Since the animal's procedural approach to the perseveration problem appeared to be an important variable, measures were taken of changes in

Figure 3-13   Infant monkey making correct response to oddity problem.

the animal's order of responding from trial to trial, and these were defined as response-sequence changes. The data...show that the 50-month-old monkeys adopt the invariant type of behavior described above but that this is not true for either the 12- or 30-month-old groups. If a subject adopts an invariant response pattern, the problem is by definition simple; failure to adopt such a pattern can greatly complicate the task. In view of this fact it is not surprising that the 30-month-old subjects made so many errors; rather, it is surprising that they made so few—their error scores represent a triumph of memory over inadequate planning.

Relatively little research on the Hamilton perseverance method has been conducted by psychologists in spite of the fact that the original studies resulted in an effective ordering of Hamilton's wide range of subjects in terms of their position within the phyletic series. Furthermore, the limited ontogenetic material gave proper ordering of animal perform-ance: kittens, puppies, and children were inferior to cats, dogs, and human adults. Above and beyond these facts, the perseverance data give support to the proposition that the rhesus monkey does not attain full intellectual status until the fourth or fifth year of life.

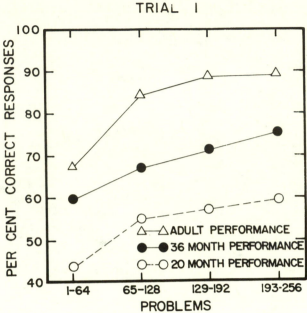

PERFORMANCE ON ODDITY PROBLEMS AS A FUNCTION OF AGE

TRIAL I

Figure 3-14   Performance on oddity problems as a function of age.

Oddity Test

Probably the most efficient tests that have been developed for measuring the maximal intellectual capability of the subhuman primates are the multiple-sign tests, whose solution is dependent upon appropriate responses to multiple, simultaneously presented cues. One of the simplest of these tests is that of oddity. Each oddity problem utilizes two identical pairs of stimuli, the "A" and the "B" stimuli. On any trial, three of the stimuli are presented simultaneously, as is shown in Figure 3-13, and the odd or different stimulus is correct and rewarded.

We have now completed a series of experiments using the two-position oddity problem, in which the correct stimulus is either in the right or left position, never in the center. In Figure 3-14 are presented data from a group of ten monkeys tested on 256 problems at 20 months of age and again at 36 months of age. Comparable data for a group of six adult rhesus monkeys are also graphed. These data indicate increasingly efficient performance as a function of age. The performance differences at each of the three age levels are statistically significant, and there is every reason to believe that intellectual maturation as measured by this test is incomplete at three years...

A group of ten monkeys was trained on oddity, first at 12 months of age and subsequently at 36 months of age. At 30 months of age, however, this group was divided into two groups of five monkeys each, one group being trained on a series of 480 six-trial discrimination problems and the other, 2400 delayed-response trials. The differences between the two groups on the oddity problems are statistically significant, with every indication of negative transfer from the learning-set to the oddity training. This is consistent with the fact that a single stimulus is uniformly correct on every discrimination problem but reverses frequently during the trials of each oddity problem. The transfer from delayed response to oddity may have been positive, since performance of the 36-month-old group with delayed-response training is superior to the comparable 36-month-old group whose performance is included in Figure 3-14. But, in neither case does a 36-month-old group attain an adult performance level.

For the neonatal and infant rhesus monkey each learning task is specific unto itself, and the animal's intellectual repertoire is composed of multiple, separate, and isolated learned experiences. With increasing age, problem isolation changes to problem generalization, and this fundamental reorganization of the monkey's intellectual world apparently begins in its second year of life. From here on, we can no longer specify the monkey's learning ability for any problem merely in terms of maturational age and individual differences. The variable of kind and amount of prior experience must now be given proper value. This is the characteristic of monkey learning, and, in fact, learning by all higher primates as they come of intellectual age.

Monkeys do not attain full oddity performance at three years of age, and oddity learning is by no means the most complicated learning task that the adult rhesus monkey can solve. Oddity-nonoddity learning, in which the subject is required to choose either the odd or the nonodd stimulus, depending upon the color of the test tray presented on a particular trial, can be solved relatively routinely by the adult monkey. Considerably more complex learning problems have been mastered by highly trained rhesus subjects. We are in no position to determine the monkey's age of intellectual maturity, but four or five years of age is a reasonable estimate.

SUMMARY AND INTERPRETATION

Half a decade is entirely too brief a period to establish a definitive program on the maturation of learning ability in the rhesus monkey, particularly in the later age ranges. However, within this period of time we have developed the techniques and conducted tests which demonstrate that such a program is entirely feasible. The monkey is capable of solving simple learning problems during the first few days of life and its capability of solving ever increasingly complex problems matures progressively, probably for four to five years.

Early in life, new learning abilities appear rather suddenly within the space of a few days, but, from late infancy onward, the appearance of new learning powers is characterized by developmental stages during which particular performances progressively improve. There is a time at which increasingly difficult problems can first be solved, and a considerably delayed period before they can be solved with full adult efficiency.

The monkey possesses learning capacities far in excess of those of any other infrahuman primate, abilities probably comparable to those of low-level human imbeciles. The monkey's learning capabilities can give us little or no information concerning human language, and only incomplete information relating to thinking. These are the generalizable limits of learning research on rhesus monkeys, but they still leave us with an animal having vast research potentialities. There is a wealth of learning problems which the monkey can master, and at present the field is incompletely explored. The maturation of any learning function can be traced and the nature and mechanisms underlying interproblem and intertask transfer can be assessed. There exist great research potentialities in analyzing the fundamental similarities and differences among simple and complex learnings within a single species. The monkey is the subject ideally suited for studies involving neurological, biochemical, and pharmacological correlates of behavior. To date, such studies have been limited to adult monkeys, or monkeys of unspecified age, but such limited researches are no longer a necessity. We now know that rhesus monkeys can be raised under completely controlled conditions throughout a large part, and probably all, of their life span, and we may expect that the research of the future will correlate the neurophysiological variables, not with the behavior of the static monkey, but with the behavior of the monkey in terms of ontogenetic development.

REFERENCES

1. Fuller, J.F., Easler, C.A., and Banks, E.M. Formation of conditioned avoidance responses in young puppies. *Am. J. Physiol.*, *160*, 462–466 (1950).
2. Hamilton, G.V. A study in trial and error reactions in animals. *J. Anim. Behavior*, *1*, 33–66 (1911).
3. Hamilton, G.V. A study of perseverance reactions in primates and rodents. *Behav. Monogr.*, *3*, No. 2, 1–63 (1916).

4. Harlow, H.F. The formation of learning sets. *Psychol. Rev.*, *56*, 51–65 (1949).
5. Harlow, H.F. Analysis of discrimination learning by monkeys. *J. Exp. Psychol.*, *40*, 26–39 (1950).
6. Hunter, W.F. The delayed reaction in animals and children. *Behav. Monogr.*, *2*, 21–30 (1913).
7. Jacobsen, C.F. An experimental analysis of the frontal association areas in primates. *Arch. Nerv. Ment.Dis.*, *82*, 1–14 (1935).
8 Krechevsky, I. "Hypothesis" vs. "chance" in the pre-solution period in sensory discrimination learning. *Unv. Calif. Publ. Psychol.*, *6*, 27–44 (1932).
9. Matheson, E. A study of problem solving behavior in pre-school children. *Child Develpm.*, *2*, No. 4, 242–262 (1931).
10. Richardson, H.M. The growth of adaptive behaviour in infants. *Gent. Psychol. Monogr.*, *12*, 195–357 (1932).
11. Stone, C.P. The age factor in animal learning: II. Rats on a multiple light discrimination box and a difficult image. *Genet. Psychol. Monogr.*, *6*, No. 2, 125–202 (1929).
12. van Wagenen, G. The monkey. In *The care and breeding of laboratory animals*, E.J. Farris (Ed.), pp. 1–42, New York: Wiley, 1950.

NOTE

A Sigma Xi-RESA National Lecture, 1958–1959.

4

The Formation of Learning Sets

Harry F. Harlow

In most psychological ivory towers there will be found an animal laboratory. The scientists who live there think of themselves as theoretical
psychologists, since they obviously have no other rationalization to explain
their extravagantly paid and idyllic sinecures. These theoretical psychologists have one great advantage over those psychological citizens who
study men and women. The theoreticians can subject their subhuman
animals, be they rats, dogs, or monkeys, to more rigorous controls than
can ordinarily be exerted over human beings. The obligation of the
theoretical psychologist is to discover general laws of behavior applicable
to mice, monkeys, and men. In this obligation the theoretical psychologist
has often failed. His deductions frequently have had no generality beyond
the species which he has studied, and his laws have been so limited that
attempts to apply them to man have resulted in confusion rather than
clarification.

One limitation of many experiments on subhuman animals is the brief
period of time the subjects have been studied. In the typical problem, 48
rats are arranged in groups to test the effect of three different intensities of
stimulation operating in conjunction with two different motivational
conditions upon the formation of *an isolated* conditioned response. A
brilliant Blitzkrieg research is effected—the controls are perfect, the results
are important, and the rats are dead.

If this *do and die* technique were applied widely in investigations with
human subjects, the results would be appalling. But of equal concern to the

Harlow, H.F. The formation of learning sets. *Psychol. Rev., 1949, 56,* 51–65. Copyright 1949 by the
American Psychological Association. Reprinted by permission of the publisher and author.

psychologist should be the fact that the derived general laws would be extremely limited in their application. There are experiments in which the use of naive subjects is justified, but the psychological compulsion to follow this design indicates that frequently the naive animals are to be found on both sides of the one-way vision screen.

The variety of learning situations that play an important role in determining our basic personality characteristics and in changing some of us into thinking animals are repeated many times in similar form. The behavior of the human being is not to be understood in terms of the results of single learning situations but rather in terms of the changes which are affected through multiple, though comparable, learning problems. Our emotional, personal, and intellectual characteristics are not the mere algebraic summation of a near infinity of stimulus-response bonds. The learning of primary importance to the primates, at least, is the formation of learning sets; it is the *learning how to learn efficiently* in the situations the animal frequently encounters. This learning to learn transforms the organism from a creature that adapts to a changing environment by trial and error to one that adapts by seeming hypothesis and insight.

The rat psychologists have largely ignored this fundamental aspect of learning and, as a result, this theoretical domain remains a *terra incognita.* If learning sets are the mechanisms which, in part, transform the organism from a conditioned response robot to a reasonably rational creature, it may be thought that the mechanisms are too intangible for proper quantification. Any such presupposition is false. It is the purpose of this paper to demonstrate the extremely orderly and quantifiable nature of the development of certain learning sets and, more broadly, to indicate the importance of learning sets to the development of intellectual organization and personality structure.

The apparatus used throughout the studies subsequently referred to is illustrated in Figure 3-4. The monkey responds by displacing one of two stimulus-objects covering the food-wells in the tray before him. An opaque screen is interposed between the monkey and the stimulus situation between trials and a one-way vision screen separates monkey and man during trials.

The first problem chosen for the investigation of learning sets was the object-quality discrimination learning problem. The monkey was required to choose the rewarded one of two objects differing in multiple characteristics and shifting in the left-right positions in a predetermined balanced order. A series of 344 such problems using 344 different pairs of stimuli was run on a group of eight monkeys. Each of the first 32 problems was run for 50 trials; the next 200 problems for six trials; and the last 112 problems for an average of nine trials.

In Figure 4-1 are presented learning curves which show the per cent of correct responses on the first six trials of these discriminations. The data

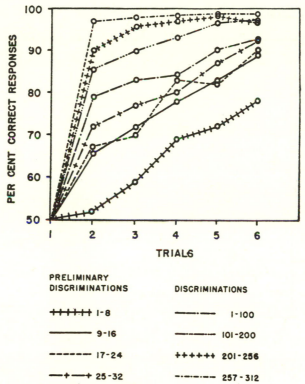

Figure 4-1 Discrimination learning curves on successive blocks of problems.

for the first 32 discriminations are grouped for blocks of eight problems, and the remaining discriminations are arranged in blocks of 100, 100, 56, and 56 problems. The data indicate that the subjects progressively improve in their ability to learn object-quality discrimination problems. The monkeys *learn how to learn* individual problems with a minimum of errors. It is this *learning how to learn a kind of problem* that we designate by the term *learning set.*

The very form of the learning curve changes as learning sets become more efficient. The form of the learning curve for the first eight discrimination problems appears S-shaped; it could be described as a curve of "trial-and-error" learning. The curve for the last 56 problems approaches linearity after Trial 2. Curves of similar form have been described as indicators of "insightful" learning.

We wish to emphasize that this *learning to learn*, this *transfer from problem to problem* which we call the formation of a learning set, is a highly *predictable, orderly* process which can be demonstrated as long as controls are maintained over the subjects' experience and the difficulty of the problems. Our subjects, when they started these researches, had no previous

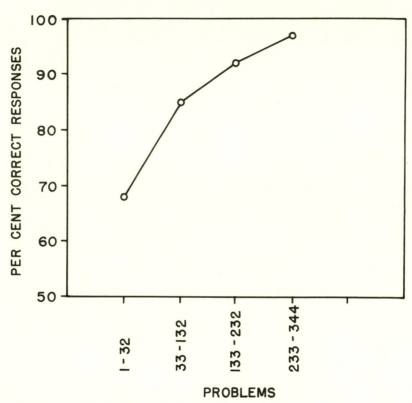

Figure 4-2 Discrimination learning set curve based on Trial 2-6 responses.

laboratory learning experience. Their entire discrimination learning set history was obtained in this study. The stimulus pairs employed had been arranged and their serial order determined from tables of random numbers. Like nonsense syllables, the stimulus pairs were equated for difficulty. It is unlikely that any group of problems differed significantly in intrinsic difficulty from any other group.

In a conventional learning curve we plot change of performance over a series of *trials;* in a learning set curve we plot change in performance over a series of *problems.* It is important to remember that *we measure learning set in terms of problems* just as *we measure habit in terms of trials.*

Figure 4-2 presents a discrimination learning set curve showing progressive increase in the per cent of correct responses on Trials 2–6 on successive blocks of problems. This curve appears to be negatively accelerated or possibly linear.

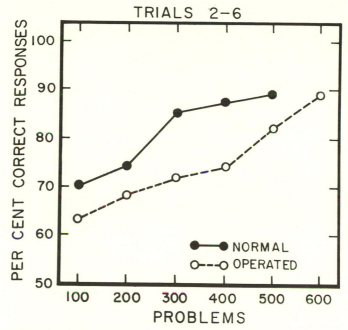

Figure 4-3 Discrimination learning set curves based on Trial 2-6 responses: normal and operated monkeys.

Discrimination learning set curves obtained on four additional naive normal monkeys and eight naive monkeys with extensive unilateral cortical lesions, are shown in Figure 4-3. Brain-injured as well as normal monkeys are seen to form effective discrimination learning sets, although the partial hemidecorticate monkeys are less efficient than the normal subjects. Improvement for both groups is progressive and the fluctuations that occur may be attributed to the small number of subjects and the relatively small number of problems, 14, included in each of the problem blocks presented on the abscissa.

Through the courtesy of Dr. Margaret Kuenne we have discrimination learning set data on another primate species. These animals were also run on a series of six-trial discrimination problems but under slightly different conditions. Macaroni beads and toys were substituted for food rewards, and the subjects were tested sans iron-barred cages.... In spite of the small number of cases and the behavioral vagaries that are known to characterize this primate species, the learning set curves are orderly and lawful and show progressive increase in per cent of correct responses.

Learning set curves, like learning curves, can be plotted in terms of correct responses or errors, in terms of responses on any trial or total trials.

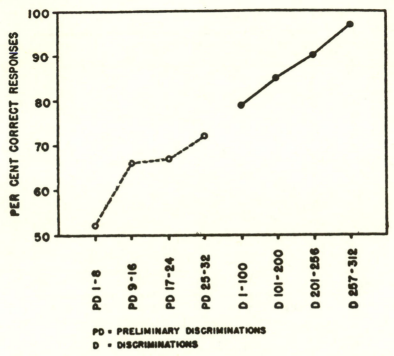

Figure 4-4   Discrimination learning set curve based on Trial 2 responses.

A measure which we have frequently used is per cent of correct Trial 2 responses—the behavioral measure of the amount learned on Trial 1.

Figure 4-4 shows learning set curves measured in terms of the per cent correct Trial 2 responses for the 344-problem series. The data from the first 32 preliminary discriminations and the 312 subsequent discriminations have been plotted separately. As one might expect, these learning set curves are similar to those that have been previously presented. What the curves show with especial clarity is the almost unbelievable change which has taken place in the *effectiveness of the first training trial.* In the initial eight discriminations, this single paired stimulus presentation brings the Trial 2 performance of the monkeys to a level less than three per cent above chance; in the last 56 discriminations, this first training trial brings the performance of the monkeys to a level *less than three per cent* short of perfection. Before the formation of a discrimination learning set, a single training trial produces negligible gain; after the formation of a discrimination learning set, *a single training trial constitutes problem solution.* These data clearly show that *animals can gradually learn insight.*

In the final phase of our discrimination series with monkeys there were subjects that solved from 20 to 30 consecutive problems with no errors whatsoever following the first blind trial, and many of the children, after the first day or two of training, did as well or better.

These data indicate the function of learning set in converting a problem which is initially difficult for a subject into a problem which is so simple as to be immediately solvable. The learning set is the mechanism that changes the problem from an intellectual tribulation into an intellectual triviality and leaves the organism free to attack problems of another hierarchy of difficulty.

For the analysis of learning sets in monkeys on a problem that is ostensibly at a more complex level than the discrimination problem, we chose the discrimination reversal problem. The procedure was to run the monkeys on a discrimination problem for 7, 9, or 11 trials and then to reverse the reward value of the stimuli for eight trials; that is to say, the stimulus previously correct was made incorrect and the stimulus previously incorrect became correct.

The eight monkeys previously trained on discrimination learning were tested on a series of 112 discrimination reversal problems.... Reversal Trial 2 is the first trial following the 'informing' trial, *i.e.*, the initial trial reversing the reward value of the stimuli. Reversal Trial 2 is the measure of the effectiveness with which the single informing trial leads the subject to abandon a reaction pattern which has proved correct for 7 to 11 trials, and to initiate a new reaction pattern to the stimulus pair. On the last 42 discrimination reversal problems the monkeys were responding as efficiently on Reversal Trial 2 as they were on complementary Discrimination Trial 2, *i.e.*, they were making over 97 per cent correct responses on both aspects of the problems. The eight monkeys made from 12 to 57 successive correct second trial reversal responses. Thus it becomes perfectly obvious that at the end of this problem the monkeys possessed sets both to learn and to reverse a reaction tendency, and that this behavior could be consistently and immediately elicited with hypothesis-like efficiency.

This terminal performance level is likely to focus undue attention on the one-trial learning at the expense of the earlier, less efficient performance levels. It should be kept in mind that this one-trial learning appeared only as the end result of an orderly and progressive learning process; insofar as these subjects are concerned, the insights are only to be understood in an historical perspective.

Although the discrimination reversal problems might be expected to be more difficult for the monkeys than discrimination problems, the data of Figure 4-5 indicate that the discrimination reversal learning set was formed more rapidly than the previously acquired discrimination learning set. The explanation probably lies in the nature of the transfer of training from the discrimination learning to the discrimination reversal problems. A detailed analysis of the discrimination learning data indicates the opera-

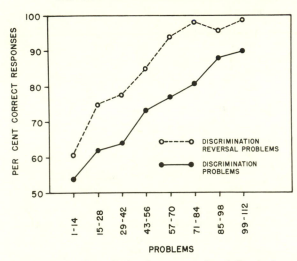

COMPARISON OF DISCRIMINATION REVERSAL
AND DISCRIMINATION LEARNING SET CURVES

Figure 4-5 Discrimination reversal and discrimination learning set curves based on Trial 2 responses.

tion throughout the learning series of certain error-producing factors, but
with each successive block of problems the frequencies of errors attributable
to these factors are progressively decreased, although at different rates and
to different degrees. The process might be conceived of as a learning of
response tendencies that counteract the error-producing factors. A description of the reduction of the error-producing factors is beyond the
scope of this paper, even though we are of the opinion that this type of
analysis is basic to an adequate theory of discrimination learning.

Suffice it to say that there is reason to believe that there is a large
degree of transfer from the discrimination series to the reversal series, of
the learned response tendencies counteracting the operation of two of the
three primary error-producing factors thus far identified.

The combined discrimination and discrimination reversal data show
clearly how the learning set delivers the animal from Thorndikian bondage.
By the time the monkey has run 232 discriminations and followed these
by 112 discriminations and reversals, he does not possess 344 or 456
specific habits, bonds, connections or associations. We doubt if our monkeys at this time could respond with much more than chance efficiency on
the first trial of any series of the previously learned problems. But the
monkey does have a generalized ability to learn *any* discrimination problem
or *any* discrimination reversal problem with the greatest of ease. Training
on several hundred specific problems has not turned the monkey into an

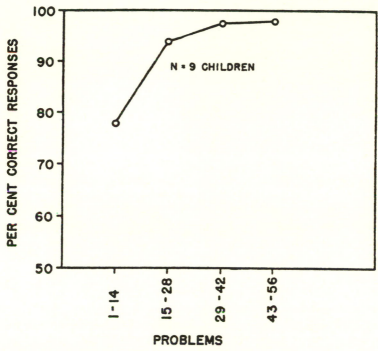

Figure 4-6 Discrimination reversal learning set curve based on Trial 2 responses: children.

automaton exhibiting forced, stereotyped, reflex responses to specific stimuli. These several hundred habits have, instead, made the monkey an adjustable creature with an *increased capacity* to adapt to the ever-changing demands of a psychology laboratory environment.

We believe that other learning sets acquired in and appropriate to the monkey's natural environment would enable him to adapt better to the changing conditions there. We are certain, moreover, that learning sets acquired by man in and appropriate to his environment have accounted for his ability to adapt and survive.

Before leaving the problem of discrimination reversal learning we submit one additional set of data that we feel merits attention. Nine of the children previously referred to were also subjected to a series of discrimination reversal problems. The outcome is partially indicated in Figure 4-6 which shows the per cent of correct Reversal Trial 2 responses made on successive blocks of 14 problems. It can be seen that these three- to five-year-old children clearly bested the monkeys in performance on this series of problems. Trial 2 responses approach perfection in the second block of 14 discrimination reversal problems. Actually, over half of the total Trial 2 errors were made by one child.

These discrimination reversal data on the children are the perfect illustration of set formation and transfer producing adaptable abilities rather than specific bonds. Without benefit of the monkey's discrimination reversal set learning curves we might be tempted to assume that the children's data indicate a gulf between human and subhuman learning. But the *extremely rapid* learning on the part of the children is not unlike the *rapid* learning on the part of the monkeys, and analysis of the error-producing factors shows that the same basic mechanisms are operating in both species.

Following the discrimination reversal problem the eight monkeys were presented a new series of 56 problems designed to elicit alternation of unequivocally antagonistic response patterns. The first 7, 9, or 11 trials of each problem were simple object-quality discrimination trials. These were followed immediately by ten right-position discrimination trials with the same stimuli continuing to shift in the right-left positions in predetermined orders. In the first 7 to 11 trials, a particular object was correct regardless of its position. In the subsequent 10 trials, a particular position—the experimenter's right position—was correct, regardless of the object placed there. Thus to solve the problem the animal had to respond to object-quality cues and disregard position cues in the first 7 to 11 trials and, following the failure of reward of the previously rewarded object, he had to disregard object-quality cues and respond to position cues.... It is to be noted that the object-quality curve, which is based on Trials 1 to 7, begins at a very high level of accuracy, whereas the position curve, plotted for Trials 1 to 10, begins at a level little above chance. This no doubt reflects the operation of the previously well-established object-quality discrimination learning set. As the series continues, the object-quality curve shows a drop until the last block of problems, while the position curve rises progressively. In the evaluation of these data, it should be noted that chance performance is 50 per cent correct responses for the object-quality discriminations and 45 per cent for the position discriminations, since each sequence of 10 position trials includes an error "informing" trial. It would appear that the learning of the right-position discriminations interferes with the learning of the object-quality discriminations to some extent. In spite of this decrement in object-quality discrimination performance for a time, the subjects were functioning at levels far beyond chance on the antagonistic parts of the problems during the last half of the series. We believe that this behavior reflects the formation of a right-position learning set which operates at a high degree of independence of the previously established object-quality discrimination learning set.

The precision of the independent operation of these learning sets throughout the last 14 problems is indicated in Figure 4-7. Since the right-position part of the problem was almost invariably initiated by an

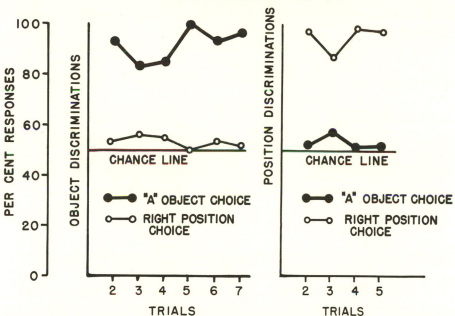

Figure 4-7 Object and position choices following initial errors on both phases of object-position shift series, based on problems 42–56.

error trial, these data are limited to those problems on which the first trial object-quality discrimination response was incorrect. The per cent of correct Trial 7 responses to the 'A' object, the correct stimulus for the object-quality discriminations, is 98. The initiating error trial which occurs when the problem shifts without warning to a right-position problem, drops this per cent response to the 'A' object to 52—a level barely above chance. The per cent of Trial 7 responses to the right position during the object-quality discriminations is 52. The single error trial initiating the shift of the problem to a right-position discrimination is followed by 97 per cent right-position responses on the next trial. In other words, *it is as though* the outcome of a single *push of an object* is adequate to switch off the 'A'-object choice reaction tendency and to switch on the right-position choice reaction tendency.

The cue afforded by a single trial produces at this point almost complete discontinuity of the learning process. The only question now left unsettled in the controversy over hypotheses in subhuman animals is whether or not to use this term to describe the behavior of a species incapable of verbalization.

Again, it should be remembered that both the object-quality discrimination learning set and the right-position discrimination learning set developed in a gradual and orderly manner. Only after the learning sets are formed do these phenomena of discontinuity in learned behavior appear.

Further evidence for the integrity of learning sets is presented in an additional experiment. Six monkeys with object-quality discrimination learning experience, but without training on reversal problems or position discriminations, were given seven blocks of 14 problems each, starting with a block of 25-trial object-quality discriminations, followed by a block of 14 25-trial positional discriminations composed of right-position and left-position problems presented alternately. The remaining five blocks of problems continued the alternate presentation of 14 object-quality discrimination problems and 14 right-left positional discrimination problems.... The complex positional discrimination learning set curve shows progressive improvement throughout the series, whereas the object-quality discrimination curve begins at a high level of accuracy, shows decrement on the second block, and subsequently recovers. By the end of the experiment the two basically antagonistic learning sets had "learned" to live together with a minimum of conflict. These data are the more striking if it is recalled that between each two blocks of object-quality discriminations there were 350 trials in which no object was differentially rewarded, and between each two blocks of 14 positional discriminations there were 350 trials in which no position was differentially rewarded....

Although our objective data are limited to the formation of learning sets which operate to give efficient performance on intellectual problems, we have observational data of a qualitative nature on social-emotional changes in our animals. When the monkeys come to us they are wild and intractable but within a few years they have acquired, from the experimenter's point of view, good personalities. Actually we believe that one of the very important factors in the development of the good personalities of our monkeys is the formation of social-emotional learning sets organized in a manner comparable with the intellectual learning sets we have previously described. Each contact the monkey has with a human being represents a single specific learning trial. Each person represents a separate problem. Learning to react favorably to one person is followed by learning favorable reactions more rapidly to the next person to whom the monkey is socially introduced. Experience with additional individuals enables the monkey to learn further how to behave with human beings, and eventually the monkey's favorable reactions to new people are acquired so rapidly as to appear almost instantaneous.

The formation of social-emotional learning sets is not to be confused with mere stimulus generalization, a construct applied in this field with undue freedom. Actually a learning set once formed determines in large part the nature and direction of stimulus generalization. In the classic study in which Watson conditioned fear in Albert, the child developed a fear of the rat and generalized this fear, but failed to develop or generalize fear to Watson, even though Watson must have been the more conspicuous stimulus. Apparently Albert had already formed an affectional social-emotional learning set to people, which inhibited both learning and simple Pavlovian generalization.

Our observations on the formation of social-emotional learning sets have been entirely qualitative and informal, but there would appear to be no reason why they could not be studied experimentally.

The emphasis throughout this paper has been on the role of the historical or experience variable in learning behavior—the forgotten variable in current learning theory and research. Hull's Neo-behaviorists have constantly emphasized the necessity for an historical approach to learning, yet they have not exploited it fully. Their experimental manipulation of the experience variable has been largely limited to the development of isolated habits and their generalization. Their failure to find the phenomenon of discontinuity in learning may stem from their study of individual as opposed to repetitive learning situations.

The field theorists, unlike the Neo-behaviorists, have stressed insight and hypothesis in their description of learning. The impression these theorists give is that these phenomena are properties of the innate organization of the individual. If such phenomena appear independently of a gradual learning history, we have not found them in the primate order.

Psychologists working with human subjects have long believed in the phenomenon of learning sets and have even used sets as explanatory principles to account for perceptual selection and incidental learning. These psychologists have not, however, investigated the nature of these learning sets which their subjects bring to the experimental situation. The determining experiential variables of these learning sets lie buried in the subjects' pasts, but the development of such sets can be studied in the laboratory as long as the human race continues to reproduce its kind. Actually, detailed knowledge of the nature of the formation of learning sets could be of such importance to educational theory and practice as to justify prolonged and systematic investigation.

In the animal laboratory where the experiential factor can be easily controlled, we have carried out studies that outline the development and operation of specific learning sets. We believe that the construct of learning sets is of importance in the understanding of adaptive behavior. Since this is our faith, it is our hope that our limited data will be extended by those brave souls who study *real* men and *real* women.

NOTES

This paper was presented as the presidential address of the Midwestern Psychological Association meetings in St. Paul, May 7, 1948.

The researches described in this paper were supported in part by grants from the Special Research Fund of the University of Wisconsin for 1944–48.

PART TWO
DISCUSSION

5

Generalization of Behavioral Data Between Nonhuman and Human Animals

Harry F. Harlow, John P. Gluck,
and Stephen J. Suomi

The justification for generalizing nonhuman behavioral data to similar data obtained on human beings has long been questioned. It is pointless to attempt to provide a definitive answer since no definitive answer has ever existed and never will. This sounds like a thesis of ghastly gloom, but it can be said that from the depths and through the darkness that have always pervaded the problem of interspecies generalization, there have been researchers who have provided illumination and light, the reflections sometimes being scintillating and sometimes coruscant.

Most biologically trained scientists are of the opinion that generalization from nonhuman behavioral data to man is justifiable, and they differ only in the degree to which they believe this to be true. Some biological scientists are convinced that there are behavioral areas beyond the pale, whereas other scientists pale at any suggestion relative to interspecies generality. There is only one way to test the limits of interspecies generalization and that is by experimentation. Positive results could prove the existence of generality. Negative results may prove nothing other than the limitations of the method or mind of the experimenter. The sanguine position is to believe that the maximal degree of generalization has not yet

Harlow, H.F., Gluck, J.P., & Suomi, S.J. Generalization of behavioral data between nonhuman and human animals. *American Psychologist*, 1972, 27, 709–716. Copyright 1972 by the American Psychological Association. Reprinted by permission of the publisher.

been discovered. It is safe to maintain the assumption that a world of wealth related to nonhuman-human homologues is yet to be disclosed. Men and methods will presumably advance rather than regress. This is, of course, an expression of faith.

Although we believe that the degree to which nonhuman animal behavior generalizes to man should be tirelessly tested, we do not believe that positive results will always be disclosed no matter how elegant the research and apparently pervasive the findings may be. At the risk of offending all and pleasing none, we take the example of Lorenz's (1952) imprinting, which we believe does not generalize to man and does not totally generalize to the greylag goose. If the maternal imprinting response of greylag goslings were really irreversible and forever persistent, no greylag goose could have ever broken away from maternal bondage, and the greylag goose as a species would have become extinct long ago.

Imprintinglike phenomena obviously exist in many species of birds and may exist in some species of mammals (Klopfer, 1971). The data are certainly not definitive. We would gladly nominate as imprinting mammals some of the ungulates—deer, elk, moose, and wild horses—whose infants must move with the mother almost from birth onward in order to survive. Imprintinglike phenomena are more apt to be found in precocial than in altricial animals. We do not believe that the imprinting phenomenon aids in the analysis of infant-mother ties in monkeys and men. It does, however, lend support to the position that infant-mother ties in an enormous range of mammals and presumably other classes are formed by a host of variables other than lactational libations.

Although the question of behavioral generalization from nonhuman to human animals has led to redundant ruminations and has been discussed for decades, the converse question has seldom appeared in print. If nonhuman animal data do not generalize to data derived from human beings, can human data be used to predict within reason the supposedly homologous behavior of nonhuman animals? Of even more practical importance, can human data and human experimental designs be used to create and achieve meaningful and important animal experiments? Most biological scientists are probably sympathetic to the possibility of this proposition and can cite countless cases where generalization from man to lower forms has been pursued successfully in the biomedical sciences. Actually, generalization from human to nonhuman animal data should be as probable and pervasive as generalization from nonhuman animals to man. However, most people feel more interest and empathy for human-oriented researches than for researches stemming from the behavioral capabilities of hoot owls and hummingbirds.

Probably because Harlow spent his effective scientific life studying monkeys, most of our researches are designed to test the maximal generality of various behaviors from man to monkeys. Occasionally when we believed that the human facts were foolish or the human theories were false, we designed experiments that would clarify cant or expiate error. In any and all cases we wanted to determine the replicability or relative replicability of human data by using rhesus monkeys as subjects. In addition, this research approach gave rise to satisfactory data and deductions demonstrating reasoned and rational relationships between man and lower animals. Actually, some of our researches have disclosed truths either unknown or previously unacceptable to a respectable body of human beings.

No one will question that monkeys can learn many things, some of which are intellectually complex. Whether or not monkeys can think is a problem we leave to the individual reader. Being an avowed monkey man, Harlow has struggled to demonstrate the maximal intellectual generality from man to the rhesus macaque, just as others have struggled to deny it.

INTELLECTUAL GENERALIZATION
BETWEEN MONKEY AND MAN

By the late 1930s, Harlow had begun measuring the capability of monkeys to solve complex learning problems. In 1940, he spent a year at Columbia University, where he attended a seminar given by the eminent neurologist, Kurt Goldstein, who took a strong position concerning intellectual generalization from animals to men. Harlow was informed by a young, but long-time Goldstein admirer, that in order to understand Goldsteinian animal learning theory one would have to be aware of the fact that Goldstein did not believe in evolution. Goldstein believed that there were *men* and there were *animals,* not *men* and *other* animals. Men alone were capable of abstract thinking, and animals were capable only of concrete thinking (Goldstein, 1939). Without attempting to present details, Goldstein's abstract thinking had connotations similar to Köhler's insight learning, and concrete thinking had connotations like those of Thorndike's trial-and-error learning. This class of theory restricts generalization between animals and men to limited kinds of learning and denies all species, other than man, even access to abstract learning.

One particular problem which Goldstein believed could be solved only by abstract thinking was a problem designed by Weigl, a student of Goldstein's late-departed colleague, Gelb. It might be added that there were cynical and suspicious people who believed that Gelb had created almost all of Goldstein's ideas, including the concepts of concrete and abstract thinking. Some authorities even held that after Gelb's death, Goldsteinian theory suffered, drifting from the Gelb abstract level to the Goldstein concrete level. These may have been jealous people. At any rate, Goldstein had absolute faith that solution of the Weigl problem required abstract intelligence.

In the Weigl test, a human subject, child or adult, was presented with three different stimuli, one of which differed from the other two in form alone and a second that differed only in color. Thus, there might be a blue triangle, a red cross, and a red triangle. Responding to an appropriate cue, the human subject chose the object odd in color; and to a different cue, the subject chose the object odd in relation to form. Goldstein was convinced that the Weigl test was a measure of abstract thinking since it could not be solved by young children or by German soldiers who had suffered severe brain damage, particularly damage to the frontal lobes. Goldstein had great faith in the human frontal lobes, and he commonly talked with pride about the frontal lobe syndrome he had described.

Since we believed in evolution and knew that chimpanzees and monkeys had solved similar but simpler problems, we regarded Goldstein's abstract thinking pronouncements as a challenge. We cheerfully concede that the Weigl problem strained the "abstract thinking" ability of our rhesus monkeys and that the Weigl was more abstract than the simpler oddity and matching-from-sample problems which chimpanzees and monkeys had already solved. However, by providing our monkeys with distinctive differential signs on cues for differential color and form choice and by devising and utilizing a slow, stepwise training procedure, we trained the monkeys to master the Weigl problem (Young & Harlow, 1943). By Goldsteinian criteria, the monkeys had then achieved the capability of abstract thought.

We do not believe that this macaque monkey tour de force endowed the rhesus with human intelligence. It merely demonstrated that a greater degree of intellectual generality existed between man and monkey than Goldstein could concede. These data seemed so interesting to us that we were shocked and surprised to discover how many psychologists did not care. At least Goldstein cared!

Having conducted research on the degree of cortical localization of function, we are intrigued by the generalization of malfunction after damage to one cortical area to malfunction extant after damage to a different area. This statement of generalization is buttressed by a literature more lengthy than lucid. The British diagram makers of the nineteenth century believed that each and every intellectual function was localized in a specific cortical area and that there was no generalization of effect from one area to another. Subsequent neurologists, particularly Jackson (1932), Pick (1922), and Head (1920), questioned this pinpoint precision. Finally, Lashley (1929) presented his theory of equipotentiality of all cortical areas, a classic puddle-of-mud theory. Taken at face value, this theory held that all cortical areas contributed equally to all intellectual functions.

Most monkey researchers have disclosed the fact that lesions in the frontal cortex and lesions in the posterior cortex are associated with different types of intellectual impairment (Blum, Chow, & Pribram, 1950; Warren & Harlow, 1952). Frontal lesions produce severe delayed memory response loss and little or no discrimination or learning set loss. Posterior lesions produce severe discrimination and learning set loss but little or no delayed response loss. Apparently intellectual loss in the frontal and posterior lobes does not generalize, as Lashley doubtless believed.

Occasional authorities have agreed with Lashley, even in the case of human lesions, as illustrated by the previously mentioned position taken by Kurt Goldstein. Although Goldstein did not believe in a generalization of significant learning from nonhuman to human animals he had vast faith in the generalization in performance produced by massive cortical lesions in diverse lobes of the brain, or so he inadvertently disclosed. For half a year Harlow listened to Goldstein, who was an inspiring teacher, talk about the behavior of the brain-injured German soldier whose exploits formed the basis for Goldstein's frontal lobe syndrome.

After convivial postseminar sessions of some months duration, Harlow questioned the master.

> Dr. Goldstein, you know that the soldier whose performances you cited to illustrate your frontal lobe syndrome was shown on autopsy to have massive lesions in the thalamic and pulvinar nuclei and the striate (visual) areas of the cortex and in no other areas. How can this case with only occipital lesions be the basis for providing the data for your frontal lobe lesions syndrome?

Without hesitation, Goldstein rose with conviction and enthusiasm to reply, "Completely simple, completely simple; in man vision is so important to abstract thinking that lesions in the visual cortex give you the frontal lobe syndrome." Perhaps Goldstein was right. Generalization may be largely a matter of faith.

A fascinating field example of attempted generalization from human to nonhuman beings is found in the many attempts of humans to teach chimpanzees to speak or to otherwise master human language (Furness, 1916; Kellogg & Kellogg, 1933; and eventually Hayes, 1951). Their attempts represented a series of unmitigated, painful, perilous, and prolonged tragedies. Anyone familiar with the data would conclude that human language abilities do not generalize to anthropoid apes. Nevertheless, a parcel of orangs and chimpanzees learned to speak, providing the confused and unclear vocalization of three or possibly four sounds, none of which closely mirrored any human word, can be considered speech. The Hayeses, probably in a transient triumphant tribute to surrogate parental love, produced a sound movie proving that their chimpanzee,

Vicki, could speak. Any nonparent who listened to the sound effects could come to only one conclusion. Chimpanzees cannot speak, and no chimpanzee ever will speak, regardless of the training technique. Every time Vicki learned a new word she suffered severe loss in the efficient use of the previous word or words. The Hayeses were the victims of either vicarious love or Vickarious love; it makes little difference. We have already uttered the pronouncement that multiple failures to achieve interspecies generalization do not prove that it cannot exist. Perhaps in the depths of some jungle there exists one chimpanzee, one orangutan, or one gorilla capable of mastering human speech.

Do human language data generalize to chimpanzees? No, if one is concerned with vocal language. As for sign language, that may be another matter. A very important question relevant to the failure of human language development to generalize from man to chimpanzee concerns the channel of speech selected. There are now data showing that the mouth and throat structure of simians is such that they cannot conceivably effectively evoke human language sounds. A fundamental principle in the formulation of a conditioned response is the preexistence of an appropriate unconditioned response in both species, human and subhuman. Failure to obtain generalization from men to lower animals or vice versa is often due to the lack of an appropriate unconditioned response in one or the other. This has nothing to do with the question of generalization of learning.

We would be the first to agree that human vocal language capabilities show little generalization to the chimpanzee, and we are glad that they do not. The chimpanzees probably feel the same way. However, a new twist to this problem of generalization of language from man to ape is the gestural approach recently achieved by the Gardners (1967). Instead of attempting to teach Washoe, their chimpanzee subject, an inappropriate vocal language, the Gardners trained Washoe in the use of sign language. Chimpanzees do not speak spontaneously, but chimpanzees gesture spontaneously. The Gardners' gifted infant chimpanzee, wondrous Washoe, rapidly mastered—with pleasure to him and profit to the Gardners—gestural language. One can almost hear Washoe say by gestures, "Look, mother, see me talk."

After living for three years in a world in which all human beings with whom he came into contact spoke and spoke only the American Sign Language, Washoe possessed a vocabulary of about 100 words (in 1971). He usually differentiated precisely between words, spoke spontaneously, and even combined the signs in proper serial order to form simple sentences. As far as we know, Washoe has not taught other chimpanzees the American Sign Language, but anything can happen.

Another nonverbal approach to the generalization of language in apes was Premack's (1970) work with Sarah, a six-year-old African-born female chimpanzee. Premack used small plastic metal-backed object "words" as the physical basis of his language, requiring his subject to place the objects in designated orders on a magnetic board. He formulated a schedule of tasks progressively increasing in difficulty, beginning with the association of specific object "words" with different types of fruits. Sarah rapidly learned to both name and request fruit. She subsequently was taught to place more than one "word" on the magnetic board to form simple "sentences"; for example, "Mary [the tester] give apple Sarah." Eventually, Sarah was able to express relationships among stimuli (e.g., same versus different) by placing the appropriate relationship-designating words on the magnetic board following the presentation of the stimulus objects.

Premack further demonstrated that his subject ascribed properties of a given stimulus to the actual word designated for that stimulus. To do so he employed an independent features analysis. On each trial of this analysis, Sarah was presented with an apple and a pair of response alternatives, one of which was related to some dimension of the apple. Alternatives included red versus green, round versus square, square with stemlike protuberances versus plain square, and plain round versus square with protuberances. After compiling Sarah's feature analysis with the actual apple present, a similar analysis was performed with the plastic word apple present instead of the apple. Premack found that Sarah ascribed the same properties to the plastic word as she did to the actual apple. He concluded that Sarah's analysis of the word was based on the object that the word represented.

The generalization of data from man to monkey or from monkey to man is doubtless well substantiated when we deal with simple learning, but there are limitations and reservations when we consider thinking and language in the erudite human form. The neocortices of monkeys, apes, and men differ, and although man may think about monkeys, monkeys probably never will think seriously about men. If, instead of problems of learning, we concern ourselves with problems of motivation, we find much more widespread generalization.

MOTIVATIONAL TRANSFER BETWEEN MONKEY AND MAN

Motivational behavior studies not only may produce more evidence of generalization from human beings to animals but also may throw new light on the theories of human behavior per se. The question of determination of the degree of transfer between complex behaviors in man and lower animals is pursued by many, either because of intellectual curiosity or some theoretical or philosophical position. No nonhuman animal can think like man, speak like man, or mold his behavior in terms of complex human cultural variables. However, many important human behaviors, particularly neonatal and infantile behaviors, occur without the intervention of thinking, recondite language, or formidable cultural variables.

Freudian theorists and behavioral theorists had long speculated about the variables binding the neonatal infant to the mother, and the leaders of both of these diverse, dichotomous camps came by different speculative routes to the same conclusion. The infant loved the mother because of repetitive association of the mother's breasts with the alleviation of the pangs of hunger. Mother love was conceived of as a learned or derived motive, conditioned upon the internal, homeostatic drive of hunger. Human data, human replication, and human need give rise to no other conclusion.

Harlow had no objection to homeostatic drives as human motives, nor secondary reinforcement as a motivational mechanism, but he had such respect for mother love that he felt it should be based at least in part on complex unlearned motives, more picturesque and less pragmatic than lactational loneliness. Furthermore, in a flash of insight it dawned on him how the real mechanics of mother love might be tested experimentally using nonhuman animals. The problem involved the degree of generalization of theories of infant love from human beings to monkeys and properly assumed that generalization existed and that it would be found by those who kept abreast with their research. Harlow believed that basic bodily contact was probably an unlearned, nativistic force that caused the child to love the mother. We tested this thesis by creating two artificial mother surrogates, one cloth covered, the other comprised of a wire-mesh body, which in final design equated all other variables (Harlow & Zimmermann, 1958). In half of the cases, the good cloth surrogate nursed from a tiny bottle on its thoracic midline and the wire did not. In the other cases, the wire mother nursed and the cloth surrogate did not. A direct test could be made of the relative importance of bodily contact in contradistinction to activities associated specifically with the breast. The infant monkeys continually clasped and clung to the cloth mother, and thus the original research showed that body texture, the skin we love to touch, was a variable of completely overwhelming importance over all activities associated with the breast, including the ingestion of milk.

These were informational studies on generalization. The data of the human theorists did not generalize to monkeys because the human theory was false. Monkey theories basically generalized to human infants because the monkey facts were true.

Having closed the doors on Anna Freud's cupboard theory of love, where infant love is associated with maternal mien and bubbling breast, we subsequently designed a family of studies (e.g., Harlow & Suomi,

1970; Harlow & Zimmermann, 1958) showing the relative importance of many variables in the formation of maternal love. All important behaviors are mediated by many variables. Body contact remained the variable of primary importance if it were skin, terrycloth, or spun nylon. Infant-mother love did not develop from satin, which is for show (Furchner & Harlow, 1969), and sandpaper and welded wire connoted not skin but sin to the neonatal animal.

In these experiments, we were able to demonstrate that activities associated with the breast, including nursing, were variables of importance secondary to good, soft bodily contact, and we believe that human breasts were put there by God for more than aesthetic purposes. Furthermore, rocking motion was a positive variable of value, and temperature was a variable with impact. Hot, or at least warm, mothers were cheerfully chosen over others, and cold mothers were adversive. An infant upon contacting an ice-cold mother designed by Suomi fled screaming in horror and never returned to the mother over a 30-day period.

In many ways these were classical experiments demonstrating that generalization from animals, even inanimate animals, to man can be better in limited ways for specific limited purposes and in limited circumstances than the generalization from men to lower animals. The researches on inanimate mothers probably generalized better to idealized real mothers than the previous research conducted on fleshy, fulsome human females themselves. Sometimes when monkey data fail to generalize to human data the answer lies in the superiority of the monkey data and the need to revise those data that are human.

GENERALIZATION OF PSYCHOPATHOLOGY FROM MAN TO NONHUMAN ANIMALS

At the present time we are engaged in an epic effort to produce simulated human psychopathic states. We are plagued by the question, Do the monkey data generalize to man or not? Some authorities believe our monkey data generalize to man. Some authorities believe they do not. This might lead one to the assumption that one group of external arbitrators is right and one group is wrong. This conclusion is in error. Probably both groups are right and both groups are wrong. Cross-species generalization is seldom, if ever, complete, and the evaluation of cross-species generalization may be more an art than a science.

Some years ago we produced a syndrome of childhood depression in infant monkeys that is so much like child anaclitic depression that no thinking man has, and no thinking man ever will, question an enormous, near total generality from monkey to man. Oddly enough, the experiments were conducted in the opposite order. Human anaclitic depression was achieved by retrospective clinical data, and taking the clinical models of Spitz (1946) and Bowlby (1960), we fashioned the monkey anaclitic depression studies. The near perfect generalization which was found has since been confirmed by others on two other species of macaque monkeys and also on patas monkeys.

The etiology of the anaclitic depression was basically the same for both genera, man and macaque: maternal separation or at least the loss of a loved one. The behavioral syndrome was clearly parallel for both genera. Finally, the techniques of successful rehabilitation were for all practical purposes identical. The primary procedure was that of reinstatement of the loved object.

The simplicity in achieving de facto generalization between men and monkeys along the dimensions of anaclitic depression might suggest that behavioral generalization of any and all psychopathological patterns among primates would be simple, safe, and universally acceptable. Nothing could be further from the truth. Even adolescent reactive depression (McKinney, Suomi, & Harlow, 1972) offers uncertain generality between men and monkeys at the present time. Beyond depression, interspecies psychopathological generality is a proposition based more on faith than fact.

DEGREES OF GENERALIZATION

Leaving psychopathology and returning to love, we find areas where a high level of interspecific generality is obvious and others where behavioral generality is humble or hidden. Maternal love and infant love of the mother are behaviors in which the obtained data have enormous interspecies generality in most primates. Probably there is higher interspecies behavioral generality among infants than adults since maturational differentiation progressively separates different species along all dimensions. Thus, mother love and infant love for the mother are related to neonatal responses with high interspecies generality; agemate or peer love that is based on play and matures later shows less interspecific generality; father or paternal love that matures even later in life, since there are no neonatal fathers, is controlled by variables known only to God and shows low interspecies generality (Mitchell, 1969).

A criterion for making a best guess as to the degree that human data generalize to animals, and that animal data generalize to human beings, is that of anatomical similarity. Furthermore, all homologous or analogous anatomy and structures have not and should not be given equal consideration. The primary interspecies anatomical correlates for complex behaviors are those relating to the structures of the central nervous system. Thus, if we know the differential complexity of the central nervous system of two closely related or divergent species of animals and know the level of learning ability of one, we can make a reasonable prediction about the learning ability of the other, be it more complex or less complex. Frequently the degree of likelihood of behavioral generalization from one species to another can be predicted by anatomical similarities and dissimilarities. In predicting behavioral generalization, we are properly prone to seeking similarities and dissimilarities in brain structures and particularly cortical structures.

Total brain weight is a measure that has been used to predict similarities in behavioral capabilities between different species, but total brain weight is a controllable measure that is both perilous and ponderous. The elephant may never forget, but its vast cerebral mass finds problems requiring any abstract thinking to be unsolvable. Its inability to forget may stem from an absence of retroactive inhibition. The porpoise, in spite of the many kind words written by porpoise friends, with its large mass of cerebral tissue is limited in its behavior to tasks that are porpoiseful but not purposeful. The porpoise's most learned lover was Lilly (1961), and it is pointless to try to gild this kind of love.

A slightly more recondite anatomical measure is wealth of fissuration rather than mass, but even this anatomical measure is correlated poorly with complex problem solution. In all probability it is more highly correlated with brain weight than with behavioral wisdom.

A highly sophisticated anatomical criterion for complex behavioral capability is that of the cytoarchitectonic structure of the neocortex, not the mass of the brain but the delicacy of organization of the cells in or near the cortical outer fringe. This criterion works very well in seriating men, apes, monkeys, carnivores such as dogs and cats, and ungulates including the horse and possibly the pig.

Unfortunately, the criterion of neocortical complexity and intellectual eminence comes apart at the seams when we include birds, at least certain representative birds like the pigeon. Birds have little or no cortex, and they are multiple millions of years away from a trace of any neocortex. Birds have extremely complex and differentiated striated structures, but how these came to operate in behavioral regulation as if they were neocortical neurons will remain a mystery within our life and for a longer period within the lifetimes of Aves. Yet, some of the bird-brained beasts successfully solve oddity-principle and matching-from-sample problems at a performance level equal to or beyond representative carnivores and at a level approaching that of performance of the higher primates. No one has yet tested pigeons on Weigl problems.

These data indicate that there is no single or simple anatomical measure to account for the generalization or lack of generalization between animals in relatively disparate orders. Instead of bringing order out of chaos, we have brought chaos out of orders, beaten and battered by a bird-brained beast. When correlating behavioral capabilities and cortical complexity, one need not abandon the effort to search for criteria underlying behavioral generalization.

Having agonized about the generalization or lack of generalization of behavioral performances between monkey and man and also between man and monkey, let us meditate upon a hypothetical discovery of the worst of all contingencies. Suppose we discovered that there was no generalization between behavioral performances within selected members of the primate order or within the class of mammals. Under these circumstances, would we of necessity abandon the field of comparative psychology and comparative study and devote all of our time to brooding about human uniqueness?

No, we would not. Even if behavioral data had no generalization between members of different species, similar or divergent, there might still be merit in conducting research on subhuman forms. If facts fail to generalize, one facet of facts—the research ideas behind the facts—would still generalize. Significant results obtained on lower forms have suggested, even to some individuals not enormously intellectually endowed, experiments that should be conducted on man. Many human experiments of meaning and merit would never have been created through an act described as insight, if the acts of insight had not previously been generated by observations of some proper and pious behavior of some nonhuman animal.

From the point of view of cold facts—and most facts are—it is commonly believed that some animal data generalize to man and some data do not. The only problem then is that of selecting between or among the data that generalize and those that do not. This is never an easy task since there is no completely logical or absolutely objective way to make the separation.

Perhaps the best way to struggle with the problem of behavioral generalization between different animal species is to think of it as a game, even if a dangerous game, which one pursues at his own peril. There will always be company in such endeavors. The very fact that a problem cannot be solved with certainty and is pursued with peril may come to carry a source of pleasure in its own right.

Some people wrestle with alligators as a pastime even though there is not total generality in behavior from one alligator to another. Some people play Russian roulette, trusting in total generality from one barrel to the next, particularly if the first one fails to fire. However, the behavioral acts in Russian roulette are so stereotypical that they offer little cheer or charm to the creative mind. A better illustration of the game of interspecies behavioral generalization is that of the few people who jump across the Grand Canyon for pleasure. The behavioral generality is within a single organism and not between two different organisms, but generality from leap to leap is assumed. Testing one's own generality can be an exciting and educational game even though you do not expect to always get to the other side in a single jump. But have faith, for after all there is no worthwhile activity in which there is total safety and security from a drastic letdown.

Basically the problems of generalization of behavioral data between species are simple—one cannot generalize, but one must. If the competent do not wish to generalize, the incompetent will fill the field.

REFERENCES

Blum, J. C., Chow, K. L., & Pribram, K. H. A behavioral analysis of the organization of the parieto-temporo-preoccipital cortex. *Journal of Comparative Neurology,* 1950, 93, 53–100.

Bowlby, J. Grief and mourning in infancy and early childhood. *Psychoanalytic Study of the Child,* 1960, 15, 9–52.

Furchner, C. S., & Harlow, H. F. Preference for various surrogate surfaces among infant rhesus monkeys. *Psychonomic Science,* 1969, 17, 279–280.

Furness, W. H. Observations on the mentality of chimpanzees and orang-utans. *Proceedings of the American Philosophical Society,* 1916, 55, 281–290.

Gardner, B. T., & Gardner, R. A. Teaching sign language to a chimpanzee: Methodology and preliminary results. *Psychonomic Bulletin,* 1967, 1, 36.

Gardner, B. T., & Gardner, R. A. Two-way communication with an infant chimpanzee. In A. M. Schrier & F. Stollnitz (Eds.), *Behavior of nonhuman primates. Vol. 4.* New York: Academic Press, 1971.

Goldstein, K. *The organism.* New York: American Book Company, 1939.

Harlow, H. F., & Suomi, S. J. The nature of love—simplified. *American Psychologist,* 1970, 25, 161–168.

Harlow, H. F., & Zimmermann, R. R. The development of affectional responses in infant monkeys. *Proceedings of the American Philosophical Society,* 1958, 102, 501–509.

Hayes, C. *The ape in our house.* New York: Harper, 1951.

Head, H. Discussion on aphasia. *Brain,* 1920, 43, 412–450.

Jackson, J. H. *Selected writings of J. Hughlings Jackson. Vol. 2* (Ed. by J. Taylor). London: Hodder & Stoughton, 1932.

Kellogg, W. N., & Kellogg, L. A. *The ape and the child.* New York: McGraw-Hill, 1933.

Klopfer, P. H. Mother love: What turns it on? *American Scientist,* 1971, 59, 404–407.

Lashley, K. S. *Brain mechanisms and intelligence.* Chicago: University of Chicago Press, 1929.

Lilly, J. C. *Man and dolphin.* Garden City, N.Y.: Doubleday, 1961.

Lorenz, K. *King Solomon's ring.* London: Metheun, 1952.

McKinney, W. T., Suomi, S. J., & Harlow, H. F. Repetitive peer separations of juvenile age rhesus monkeys. *Archives of General Psychiatry,* 1972, 27, 200–204.

Mitchell, G. D. Paternalistic behavior in primates. *Psychological Bulletin,* 1969, 71, 399–417.

Pick, A. Schwere Denkstörung infolge einer kombination perseveratorischer, amnestifch-aphasischer und kontaminatorischer Störungen. *Zetschrist fuer Die Gesamte Neurologie und Psychiatrie,* 1922, 75, 309–322.

Premack, D. A functional analysis of language. *Journal of the Experimental Analysis of Behavior,* 1970, 14, 107–125.

Spitz, R. A. Anaclitic depression. *Psychoanalytic Study of the Child,* 1946, 2, 313–342.

Warren, J. M., & Harlow, H. F. Discrimination learning by normal and brain operated monkeys. *Journal of Genetic Psychology,* 1952, 81, 45–52.

Young, M. L., & Harlow, H. F. Generalization by rhesus monkeys of a problem involving the Weigl principle using the oddity method. *Journal of Comparative Psychology,* 1943, 36, 201–216.

NOTE

Supported in part by United States Public Health Service Grant MH-11894 from the National Institute of Mental Health to the University of Wisconsin Primate Laboratory.

PART THREE
MOTIVATION

6

Learning Motivated by a Manipulation Drive

Harry F. Harlow, Margaret Kuenne Harlow, and Donald R. Meyer

A preliminary study of puzzle solution in four rhesus monkeys suggested that a manipulation drive might operate in these animals and with sufficient strength to provide adequate motivation for learning. Psychologists have traditionally utilized the homeostatic drives in learning studies with subhuman animals, and have neglected, if not actually been blind to, the importance of externally elicited drives in learning.

The primary purpose of this study is to investigate the performance of monkeys on mechanical puzzles whose manipulation is accompanied by no extrinsic reward. A secondary purpose is to investigate the effect of the subsequent introduction of a food reward.

The study is comparable to the Blodgett (1) and the Tolman and Honzik (8) latent learning experiments, and the repetition of the Blodgett experiment by Reynolds (6), in that the initial training was conducted without special incentives, and later in training food incentives were introduced. The study differs from the earlier studies, however, in that the design of the present investigation places emphasis on the performance during the non-reward period, whereas the design of the other investigations places emphasis on the performance after the introduction of reward.

Harlow, H. F., Harlow, M. K., and Meyer, D. R. Learning motivated by a manipulation drive. *J. Exp. Psychol.*, 1950, *40*, 228–234. Copyright 1950 by the American Psychological Association. Reprinted by permission of the publisher and author.

SUBJECTS

Subjects in this investigation were eight rhesus monkeys with previous laboratory experience confined to discrimination, delayed reaction, and multiple discrimination reversal learning problems. The animals were matched in pairs and assigned to two groups on the basis of emotionality as judged by one person familiar with all the subjects under both living cage and experimental conditions. Group A, the experimental animals, contained Monkeys 138, 143, 150 and 151. Group B, the matched control subjects, included Monkeys 140, 146, 142 and 147.

APPARATUS

The essential experimental apparatus, illustrated in Figure 6-1, consisted of a metal-edged unpainted wooden base to which was attached, flush, a hasp restrained by a hook which was, in turn, restrained by a pin. The pin and hook are referred to as Restraining Devices 1 and 2, respectively, and had to be opened in serial order before the hasp, referred to as Device 3, could be raised. The apparatus was screwed to a wooden perch 24 in. long and 6 in. wide fastened to one side of an inside living cage 6 ft. long, 2½ ft. wide, and 6 ft. high. The animals at all times had access, through a runway, to an outside living cage 4 by 2½ by 6 ft.

For tests conducted in the experimental room, a puzzle identical with

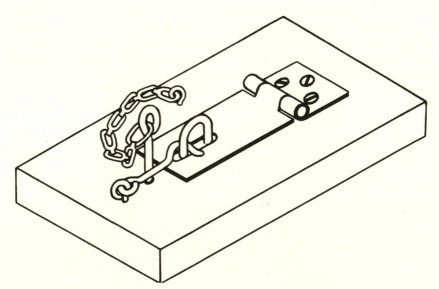

Figure 6-1 Multiple device mechanical puzzle.

the one described except for a food-well one in. in diameter cut in the board and covered by the hasp, was screwed onto a 24 by 10 in. test tray placed on the floor of a 24 by 24 by 24 in. cage. A restraining cage 27 by 26 by 16½ in. adjoined the test cage.

PROCEDURE

Throughout the experiment each subject was housed in individual quarters consisting of an inside and outside cage, and fed daily, as is the customary procedure for the colony, between 5:30 and 6:00 P.M..

Tests without food reward.—During the first 10 days of the investigation, Group A subjects had the assembled puzzle attached to their perches and Group B subjects had the puzzle attached with the restraining devices unassembled and the hasp raised. At convenient times, an experimenter checked the puzzles in all the cages and recorded any successful manipulations that had occurred. Approximately 50 checks were made on each animal in the 10-day period. Any devices released by Group A subjects were reset at the time of the check. It was planned to unfasten any devices found assembled at the checking time for Group B subjects, but no instance of assembling behavior occurred. On both the 11th and 12th days, 10 checks were made on each subject at hourly intervals.

On both Days 13 and 14 five five-min. observations one hour apart were made on each subject. For the observation, the experimenter assembled the puzzle, left the cage, started the stop watch and observed from outside the cage without staring directly at the animal. A record was made in sec. of the time the subject initially touched the puzzle, released the restraining devices, and lifted the hasp. The order in which the parts were touched or manipulated was also recorded. At the conclusion of each of the observations except the last one on Day 14, the apparatus was reset if any devices had been released. Upon the experimenter's return an hour later or the following day for the next observation, a record was made of the successful manipulations accomplished in the interval.

Tests with and subsequent to food reward.—Approximately one hour before the daily feeding on Days 4 to 13 of the experiment, the animals in both groups were brought into the laboratory for adaptation to a special test situation to be administered on Day 14. The procedure on each adaptation day was to release the animal from the transport cage into the restraining cage, give him a few raisins, and then raise the cage door to permit entrance into the adjoining test cage. On the floor against the far side of the test cage rested a standard test tray 24 in. by 10 in., containing two one-in. food wells 12 in. apart, center to center. On the first five days, the subject obtained raisins from both food wells, took additional raisins introduced through the cage bars, then returned to the restraining cage.

On each of the next five days, 20 delayed reaction trials were run. The monkey was kept in the restraining cage until the experimenter baited one food well and covered both wells with identical objects. The restraining cage door was then opened and the monkey allowed to displace the object and take the raisin. He then returned to the restraining cage and awaited the next trial. These tests were run merely to accustom the Group A animals to obtaining hidden raisins in the experimental cage situation. Group B animals were given identical training so that general adaptation would be constant for both groups.

The special puzzle test with food reward was conducted on Day 14, approximately two hours after the last living cage observation. Each Group A monkey was released into the restraining cage as on previous days. The tray in the test cage, however, now had the puzzle apparatus attached to it. While the animal watched, the food-well was baited with a raisin, the hasp lowered, and the restraining devices set. The restraining cage door was opened and the animal allowed to enter the test cage. A record was made of behavior for a five-min. period using the procedure described for Days 13 and 14 on the non-reward tests. The monkey was then returned to the living cage and immediately given a trial on his own puzzle apparatus which was baited in his presence with a raisin crushed beneath the hasp. A five-min. observation was made from outside the cage. The apparatus was reassembled immediately (this time without food) while the animal watched, and behavior was once more observed for five min.

RESULTS

Tests without food reward. —The data of Table 6.1 present for each subject the total number of Day 13 and 14 solutions in 10 tests. A solution is defined as release of both restraining devices. The table also shows the number of solutions accomplished within 60 sec. of initial contact with the apparatus.

The Group A monkeys made a total of 31 solutions and the Group B monkeys a total of 4 solutions in 40 trials. The difference is significant at the one percent confidence level as determined by a *t*-test for related measures. There was no overlapping in the scores made by the individual animals of the two groups. None of the Group B monkeys ever solved the problem within 60 sec. of initial contact, whereas all the Group A monkeys solved the problem three or more times within this time limit. Over 50 percent of all solutions by the Group A monkeys were made in 20 sec. or less, and over 35 percent were made in 10 sec. or less. Monkey 151 twice failed to touch the puzzle in the five-min. test period but solved the

TABLE 6.1   Puzzle Solutions on Days 13 and 14

Total Solutions				Solutions Attained Within 60 Sec.			
Group A		Group B		Group A		Group B	
Subject	Solutions	Solutions	Subject	Subject	Solutions	Solutions	Subject
138	8	1	140	138	5	0	140
143	6	1	146	143	3	0	146
150	9	2	142	150	7	0	142
151	8	0	147	151	7	0	147
Total	31	4			22	0	

problem without error in less than five sec. when the experimenter passed to the next cage.

The number of errors made before initial solution on Days 13 and/or 14 are given in Table 6.2. An error is defined as contact with or manipulation of any device out of sequence, or any incorrect manipulation of the restraining devices. Three of the four Group A animals made the initial solution in the first observation period and without error. All Group B monkeys made errors before the initial solution and one monkey failed to solve the problem during the 10 five-min. tests. The difference between the two groups, as determined by a *t*-test of related measures, is significant at the one percent confidence level.

A comparison of the total number of correct and erroneous responses of the Group A and Group B monkeys is presented in Table 6.3. All Group A monkeys made more than twice as many correct as incorrect responses, whereas all Group B monkeys made more than twice as many incorrect as correct responses. The differences are again significant at the one percent confidence level as measured by a X^2 test of independence.

A further indication of the difference in proficiency of the two groups lies in the finding that the Group A monkeys made *no errors* in 21 of the 38

TABLE 6.2   Number of Errors Before Initial Solution on Days 13 and/or 14

Group A		Group B	
Subject	Errors	Subject	Errors
138	0	140	11
143	6	146	16
150	0	142	7
151	0	147	15*

*Total errors. No solution attained.

TABLE 6.3 Total Correct and Incorrect Responses on Days 13 and 14

| | Group A | | | | Group B | | |
| | Correct | Error | Correct R | | Correct | Error | Correct R |
Subject	Responses	Responses	Incorrect R	Subject	Responses	Responses	Incorrect R
138	25	9	2.8	140	7	16	0.4
143	20	7	2.9	146	4	24	0.2
150	20	1	20.0	142	7	19	0.4
151	24	11	2.2	147	2	15	0.1

times that puzzle manipulations were observed, while the Group B monkeys *always made errors* in the 25 times that puzzle manipulations were observed.

Solution of the problem, it will be recalled, was defined in terms of releasing both Restraining Devices 1 and 2. Responses to Device 3 in the five-min. observation periods were variable (a finding confirmed in a subsequent study), even though all Group A monkeys invariably displaced the hasp in the one hour period between observations. Subject 138 ignored the hasp in one of eight solutions, Monkey 143 in two of six solutions, Monkey 150 in eight of nine solutions, and Monkey 151 in none of eight solutions.

Tests with and subsequent to food reward.—The data of Table 6.4 show that in three of the four Group A subjects, the introduction of food rewards seriously disrupted the efficient puzzle solution which they had repeatedly demonstrated previously. In the experimental room test with food reward, Monkey 143 touched the apparatus and then retreated and refused to work, while Monkeys 138 and 150 worked on the problem, but failed after making 5 and 9 errors, respectively. On the food trial in the home cage, Subject 138 again failed, and the other three subjects made errors before their successful manipulations. It is to be noted that Monkey

TABLE 6.4 Errors on Tests With and Subsequent to Food Reward
F = failure; NR = no response

Subject	Test Room With Food	Home Cage With Food	Home Cage Without Food
138	5F	6F	3
143	NR	4	10
150	9F	1	1
151	0	2	1

143 performed very poorly in the subsequent home cage test without food.

The degree of disruption of the acquired puzzle responses in the case of Monkeys 138, 143, and 150 during and following the introduction of food is indicated by their total of 39 errors in these three five-min. tests, although they had made a total of only 17 errors in the previous 10 five-min. tests. The difference in the *kind of errors* is also very striking. In the initial 10 tests without food reward, the monkeys *never* approached the problem by touching the hasp first; in the subsequent tests, all three monkeys *always* erred by attacking (literally) the hasp first. In the initial 10 tests without food reward the three monkeys had made a total of 2, 2, and 0 hasp errors, respectively, in contrast to the 8, 8, and 7 hasp errors made by the same monkeys subsequently.

DISCUSSION

The behavior obtained in this investigation poses some interesting questions for motivation theory, since significant learning was attained and efficient performance maintained without resort to special or extrinsic incentives. It is obvious, of course, that a number of physiological drives might have operated to activate the animals. Hunger must certainly have been present, since 14 to 22 hours had elapsed between the last feeding and the puzzle performances. Thirst may have been present, at least part of the time, for water bottles occasionally run dry during the day. Data obtained in a subsequent study suggest that temperature drive played a role. Sex drive might also have operated. Granted that these physiological drives were present, the problem remains of explaining how such drives could operate to direct behavior on the puzzle problem. Solution did not lead to food, water, or sex gratification. The precise serial manipulations could not have provided greater temperature relief than random manipulation or locomotor behavior.

Whether one assumes a reinforcement or non-reinforcement theory of learning, the behavior of the monkeys is not explained by attributing their performance directly to the homeostatic drives. The reinforcement theorist is left to account for the drive or drives reduced by performance. The non-reinforcement theorist is faced with the problem of explaining the channeling of behavior.

The authors propose that an externally elicited drive operated to channel behavior on the mechanical puzzle, and that the performance of the task provided intrinsic reward. The idea of an externally-stimulated drive eliciting intrinsically-motivating behavior is not, of course, a new one. The exploratory-investigatory drive proposed by previous workers would fit in this category. The curiosity motive frequently attributed to human infants and children can also be characterized in this way. Tolman (7) has proposed play and aesthetic drives in apes and, presumably, human beings as primary drive conditions which might be externally elicited.

In spite of previous suggestions of such drives, little experimental work has been conducted relating to them, and the work that has been done appears to be limited to the exploratory drive. Nissen (5) obtained data on the behavior of rats in crossing a charged grid to a Dashiell checkerboard maze, and attributed the behavior to an exploratory drive. This same drive has been proposed by some to explain latent learning in the studies of Blodgett (1), Haney (3), Buxton (2), and others. In several of these experiments control over the possible escape incentive was obtained by housing the animals in the maze during the "latent" learning part of the investigation. In another study, Mote and Finger (4) found a marked drop in latency of the simple running response of naive rats after an initial trial without food reward on the Graham and Gagne elevated runway. Because of lack of food reinforcement, however, the investigators did not interpret this improvement as a learning phenomenon.

An exploratory drive might have operated, in the present experiment, to initiate behavior towards the puzzle but some motivation in addition to the exploratory drive must be adduced to account for the persistence of the puzzle solving behavior through the course of the experiment without suggestion of extinction.

A secondary reinforcement explanation seems inadequate for a number of reasons. The only extrinsic incentive previously provided these subjects was food, and so presumably any secondary reinforcement would be derived from hunger reduction. Introduction of food in the present experiment served to disrupt performance, a phenomenon not reported in the literature on secondary reinforcement. Furthermore, the animals' history raises serious doubts about a secondary reinforcement interpretation. The previous experimental experience of the animals includes no problems of manipulation beyond pushing an object on a tray, and no problems of any kind presented in the living quarters. Some monkeys have been noted to reach through their living cages and manipulate the latches on the doors, but such responses have never led to solution and escape, and would thus provide no opportunity in the present experiment for secondary reinforcement of manipulatory responses based on escape. Additional evidence against a secondary reinforcement interpretation lies in the relative indifference during the observation tests of three of the four monkeys to the hasp, the only device that in any way resembled discrimination or delayed reaction objects. Finally, no evidence of extinction appeared after numerous trials without food or other extrinsic incentives. It seems far-fetched to propose that secondary reinforcement derived from hunger reduction in discrimination learning and delayed reaction problems conducted in the test rooms generalized to the puzzle problem presented in the living quarters, and once generalized, was maintained for 80 trials without any primary reinforcement.

Persons unfamiliar with monkeys might suspect social reinforcement of the responses, and theoretically it is possible that the experimenter might serve as a secondary reinforcing agent or provide reinforcement for a derived or secondary motive. The animals' history provides opportunities for such motivation, for taming procedures utilize food, and the human being is also associated with the daily feeding and watering. During the previous experimental work, however, interaction between subject and experimenter was minimized through the use of screens in all but one group of delayed reaction problems. General observation of the subjects has not suggested any affectional attachment to the experimenters which might have motivated performance. In the puzzle study, the experimenter was not present during the trials on the first 12 days, and during the observations on Days 13 and 14, the presence of the experimenter produced negative rather than positive effects. Certainly for Animals 146 and 151, the departure of the experimenter was a stronger stimulus than his presence to puzzle attack and solution. Social motivation is a possible explanation, but it appears to be an unlikely one.

It is the opinion of the experimenters that a manipulation drive can best account for the behavior obtained in this investigation. The stimuli to the drive are external and, in conjunction with the animals' capacities, set the pattern of behavior. The manipulation is conceived of as having reinforcing properties that account for the precision and speed the subjects acquire in carrying out the solution, and the persistence they show in repeated performances. Observations of subhuman animals and human beings provide abundant illustrations of directed manipulatory behavior unassociated with homeostatic drive reduction or social approval, but to the authors' knowledge no previous investigations have utilized this drive experimentally.

In conclusion we would like to emphasize the strength and the persistence of the manipulatory drive as described in this paper. It would appear that this drive, and probably a broad category of drives to which manipulation belongs, may be as basic and as strong as the homeostatic drives. Furthermore, there is some reason to believe that these drives can be as efficient in facilitating learning as the homeostatic drives.

The homeostatic drives have been such convenient drives for the comparative-theoretical psychologist that the potentialities of other drives have been ignored and their role in behavior has been neglected or belittled. The unsatisfactory nature of modern drive theory may stem in large part from the biases of experimenters who have tended to cast all studies in a limited common mold.

SUMMARY AND CONCLUSIONS

1. Four rhesus monkeys were given 12 days' experience in manipulating a mechanical puzzle whose solution did not lead to any special incentive such as food or water. Four matched control subjects had the puzzles placed in their home cages the same period of time, but unassembled.

2. The performance of the two groups was then compared by observing their responses to the assembled puzzle during five five-min. periods on Days 13 and 14.

3. The experimental monkeys were more efficient than the control monkeys in puzzle solution as measured by total number of solutions, solutions attained in 60 sec., and ratio of correct to incorrect responses. The differences were significant at the one percent confidence level.

4. Subsequent introduction of food in the puzzle situation tended to disrupt, not facilitate, the learned performances of the experimental subjects.

5. A manipulation drive, strong and extremely persistent, is postulated to account for learning and maintenance of the puzzle performance. It is further postulated that drives of this class represent a form of motivation which may be as primary and as important as the homeostatic drives.

REFERENCES

1. Blodgett, H. C. The effect of the introduction of reward upon the maze performance of rats. *Univ. Calif. Publ. Psychol.,* 1929, *4,* 113–134.
2. Buxton, C. E. Latent learning and the goal gradient hypothesis. *Cont. to Psychol. Theory,* 1940, *2,* No. 2, 3–75.
3. Haney, G. W. The effect of familiarity on the maze performance of albino rats. *Univ. Calif. Publ. Psychol.,* 1931, *4,* 319–333.
4. Mote, F. A., & Finger, F. W. Exploratory drive and secondary reinforcement in the acquisition and extinction of a simple running response. *J. exp. Psychol.,* 1942, *31,* 57–68.
5. Nissen, H. W. A study of exploratory behavior in the white rat by means of the obstruction method. *J. genet. Psychol.,* 1930, *37,* 361–76.
6. Reynolds, B. A repetition of the Blodgett experiment on "Latent Learning." *J. exp. Psychol.,* 1945, *35,* 504–516.
7. Tolman, E. C. Motivation, learning and adjustment. *Proc. Amer. phil. Soc.,* 1941, *84,* 543–563.
8. Tolman, E. C., & Honzik, C. H. Introduction and removal of reward and maze performance in rats. *Univ. Calif. Publ. Psychol.,* 1930, *4,* 257–275.

NOTE

Supported in part by the Research Committee of the Graduate School from funds supplied by the Wisconsin Alumni Research Foundation.

7

Mice, Monkeys, Men, and Motives

Harry F. Harlow

Many of psychology's theoretical growing pains—or, in modern terminology, conditioned anxieties—stem from the behavioral revolution of Watson. The new psychology intuitively disposed of instincts and painlessly disposed of hedonism. But having completed this St. Bartholomew-type massacre, behavioristic motivation theory was left with an aching void, a nonhedonistic aching void, needless to say.

Before the advent of the Watsonian scourge the importance of external stimuli as motivating forces was well recognized. Psychologists will always remain indebted to Loeb's (21) brilliant formulation of tropistic theory, which emphasized, and probably overemphasized, the powerful role of external stimulation as the primary motivating agency in animal behavior. Unfortunately, Loeb's premature efforts to reduce all behavior to overly simple mathematical formulation, his continuous acceptance of new tropistic constructs in an effort to account for any aberrant behavior not easily integrated into his original system, and his abortive attempt to encompass all behavior into a miniature theoretical system doubtless led many investigators to underestimate the value of his experimental contributions.

Thorndike (30) was simultaneously giving proper emphasis to the role of external stimulation as a motivating force in learning and learned performances. Regrettably, these motivating processes were defined in terms of pain and pleasure, and it is probably best for us to dispense with such lax, ill-defined, subjective terms as pain, pleasure, anxiety, frustration, and hypotheses—particularly in descriptive and theoretical rodentology.

Instinct theory, for all its terminological limitations, put proper emphasis on the motivating power of external stimuli; for, as so brilliantly described by Watson (31) in 1914, the instinctive response was elicited by "serial stimulation," much of which was serial external stimulation.

The almost countless researches on tropisms and instincts might well have been expanded to form a solid and adequate motivational theory for psychology—a theory with a proper emphasis on the role of the external stimulus and an emphasis on the importance of incentives as opposed to internal drives per se.

It is somewhat difficult to understand how this vast and valuable literature was to become so completely obscured and how the importance of the external stimulus as a motivating agent was to become lost. Pain-pleasure theory was discarded because the terminology had subjective, philosophical implications. Instinct theory fell into disfavor because psychologists rejected the dichotomized heredity-environment controversy and, also, because the term "instinct" had more than one meaning. Why tropistic theory disappeared remains a mystery, particularly inasmuch as most of the researches were carried out on subprimate animal forms.

Modern motivation theory apparently evolved from an overpopularization of certain experimental and theoretical materials. Jennings' (14) demonstration that "physiological state" played a role in determining the behavior of the lower animal was given exaggerated importance and emphasis, thereby relegating the role of external stimulation to a secondary position as a force in motivation. The outstanding work in the area of motivation between 1920 and 1930 related to visceral drives and drive cycles and was popularized by Richter's idealized theoretical paper on "Animal Behavior and Internal Drives" (26) and Cannon's *The Wisdom of the Body* (3).

When the self-conscious behavior theorists of the early thirties looked for a motivation theory to integrate with their developing learning constructs, it was only natural that they should choose the available tissue-tension hypotheses. Enthusiastically and uncritically the S-R theorists swallowed these theses whole. For fifteen years they have tried to digest them, and it is now time that these theses be subjected to critical examination, analysis, and evaluation. We do not question that these theses have fertilized the field of learning, but we do question that the plants that have developed are those that will survive the test of time.

It is my belief that the theory which describes learning as dependent upon drive reduction is false, that internal drive as such is a variable of little importance to learning, and that this small importance steadily decreases as we ascend the phyletic scale and as we investigate learning problems of progressive complexity. Finally, it is my position that drive-reduction theory orients learning psychologists to attack problems of limited importance and to ignore the fields of research that might lead us in some foreseeable future time to evolve a theoretical psychology of learning that transcends any single species or order.

There can be no doubt that the single-celled organisms such as the amoeba and the paramecium are motivated to action both by external and internal stimuli. The motivation by external stimulation gives rise to heliotropisms, chemotropisms, and rheotropisms. The motivation by internal stimulation produces characteristic physiological states which have, in turn, been described as chemotropisms. From a phylogenetic point of view, moreover, neither type of motive appears to be more basic or more fundamental than the other. Both types are found in the simplest known animals and function in interactive, rather than in dominant-subordinate, roles.

Studies of fetal responses in animals from opossum to man give no evidence suggesting that the motivation of physiological states precedes that of external incentives. Tactual, thermal, and even auditory and visual stimuli elicit complex patterns of behavior in the fetal guinea pig, although this animal has a placental circulation which should guarantee against thirst or hunger (4). The newborn opossum climbs up the belly of the female and into the pouch, apparently in response to external cues; if visceral motives play any essential role, it is yet to be described (20). The human fetus responds to external tactual and nociceptive stimuli at a developmental period preceding demonstrated hunger or thirst motivation. Certainly, there is no experimental literature to indicate that internal drives are ontogenetically more basic than exteroceptive motivating agencies.

Tactual stimulation, particularly of the cheeks and lips, elicits mouth, head, and neck responses in the human neonate, and there are no data demonstrating that these responses are conditioned, or even dependent, upon physiological drive states. Hunger appears to lower the threshold for these responses to tactual stimuli. Indeed, the main role of the primary drive seems to be one of altering the threshold for precurrent responses. Differentiated sucking response patterns have been demonstrated to quantitatively varied thermal and chemical stimuli in the infant only hours of age (15), and there is, again, no reason to believe that the differentiation could have resulted from antecedent tissue-tension reduction states. Taste and temperature sensations induced by the temperature and chemical composition of the liquids seem adequate to account for the responses.

There is neither phylogenetic nor ontogenetic evidence that drive states elicit more fundamental and basic response patterns than do external stimuli; nor is there basis for the belief that precurrent responses are more dependent upon consummatory responses than are consummatory responses dependent upon precurrent responses. There is no evidence that the differentiation of the innate precurrent responses is more greatly influenced by tissue-tension reduction than are the temporal ordering and intensity of consummatory responses influenced by conditions of external stimulation.

There are logical reasons why a drive-reduction theory of learning, a theory which emphasizes the role of internal, physiological-state motivation, is entirely untenable as a motivational theory of learning. The internal drives are cyclical and operate, certainly at any effective level of intensity, for only a brief fraction of any organism's waking life. The classical hunger drive physiologically defined ceases almost as soon as food—or nonfood—is ingested. This, as far as we know, is the only case in which a single swallow portends anything of importance. The temporal brevity of operation of the internal drive states obviously offers a minimal opportunity for conditioning and a maximal opportunity for extinction. The human being, at least in the continental United States, may go for days or even years without ever experiencing true hunger or thirst. If his complex conditioned responses were dependent upon primary drive reduction, one would expect him to regress rapidly to a state of tuitional oblivion. There are, of course, certain recurrent physiological drive states that are maintained in the adult. But the studies of Kinsey (17) indicate that in the case of one of these there is an inverse correlation between presumed drive strength and scope and breadth of learning, and in spite of the alleged reading habits of the American public, it is hard to believe that the other is our major source of intellectual support. Any assumption that derived drives or motives can account for learning in the absence of primary drive reduction puts an undue emphasis on the strength and permanence of derived drives, at least in subhuman animals. Experimental studies to date indicate that most derived drives (24) and second-order conditioned responses (25) rapidly extinguish when the rewards which theoretically reduce the primary drives are withheld. The additional hypothesis of functional autonomy of motives, which could bridge the gap, is yet to be demonstrated experimentally.

The condition of strong drive is inimical to all but very limited aspects of learning—the learning of ways to reduce the internal tension. The hungry child screams, closes his eyes, and is apparently oblivious to most of his environment. During this state he eliminates response to those aspects of his environment around which all his important learned behaviors will be based. The hungry child is a most incurious child, but after he has eaten and become thoroughly sated, his curiosity and all the learned responses associated with his curiosity take place. If this learning is conditioned to an internal drive state, we must assume it is the resultant of backward conditioning. If we wish to hypothesize that backward conditioning is dominant over forward conditioning in the infant, it might be possible to reconcile fact with S-R theory. It would appear, however, that alternate theoretical possibilities should be explored before the infantile backward conditioning hypothesis is accepted.

Observations and experiments on monkeys convinced us that there was as much evidence to indicate that a strong drive state inhibits learning as to indicate that it facilitates learning. It was the speaker's feeling that monkeys learned most efficiently if they were given food before testing, and as a result, the speaker routinely fed his subjects before every training session. The rhesus monkey is equipped with enormous cheek pouches, and consequently many subjects would begin the educational process with a rich store of incentives crammed into the buccal cavity. When the monkey made a correct response, it would add a raisin to the buccal storehouse and swallow a little previously munched food. Following an incorrect response, the monkey would also swallow a little stored food. Thus, both correct and incorrect responses invariably resulted in S-R theory drive reduction. It is obvious that under these conditions the monkey cannot learn, but the present speaker developed an understandable skepticism of this hypothesis when the monkeys stubbornly persisted in learning, learning rapidly, and learning problems of great complexity. Because food was continuously available in the monkey's mouth, an explanation in terms of differential fractional anticipatory goal responses did not appear attractive. It would seem that the Lord was simply unaware of drive-reduction learning theory when he created, or permitted the gradual evolution of, the rhesus monkey.

The langurs are monkeys that belong to the only family of primates with sacculated stomachs. There would appear to be no mechanism better designed than the sacculated stomach to induce automatically prolonged delay of reinforcement defined in terms of homeostatic drive reduction. Langurs should, therefore, learn with great difficulty. But a team of Wisconsin students has discovered that the langurs in the San Diego Zoo learn at a high level of monkey efficiency. There is, of course, the alternative explanation that the inhibition of hunger contractions in multiple stomachs is more reinforcing than the inhibition of hunger contractions in one. Perhaps the quantification of the gastric variable will open up great new vistas of research.

Actually, the anatomical variable of diversity of alimentary mechanisms is essentially uncorrelated with learning to food incentives by monkeys and suggests that learning efficiency is far better related to tensions in the brain than in the belly.

Experimental test bears out the fact that learning performance by the monkey is unrelated to the theoretical intensity of the hunger drive.

Meyer (23) tested rhesus monkeys on discrimination-learning problems under conditions of maintenance-food deprivation of 1.5, 18.5, and 22.5 hours and found no significant differences in learning or performance. Subsequently, he tested the same monkeys on discrimination-reversal learning following 1, 23, and 47 hours of maintenance-food deprivation and, again, found no significant differences in learning or in performance as measured by activity, direction of activity, or rate of responding. There was some evidence, not statistically significant, that the most famished subjects were a bit overeager and that intense drive exerted a mildly inhibitory effect on learning efficiency.

Meyer's data are in complete accord with those presented by Birch (1), who tested six young chimpanzees after 2, 6, 12, 24, and 48 hr. of food deprivation and found no significant differences in proficiency of performance on six patterned string problems. Observational evidence led Birch to conclude that intense food deprivation adversely affected problem solution because it led the chimpanzee to concentrate on the goal to the relative exclusion of the other factors.

It may be stated unequivocally that, regardless of any relationship that may be found for other animals, there are no data indicating that intensity of drive state and the presumably correlated amount of drive reduction are positively related to learning efficiency in primates.

In point of fact there is no reason to believe that the rodentological data will prove to differ significantly from those of monkey, chimpanzee, and man. Strassburger (29) has recently demonstrated that differences in food deprivation from 5 hours to 47 hours do not differentially affect the habit strength of the bar-pressing response as measured by subsequent resistance to extinction. Recently, Sheffield and Roby (28) have demonstrated learning in rats in the absence of primary drive reduction. Hungry rats learned to choose a maze path leading to a saccharin solution, a non-nutritive substance, in preference to a path leading to water. No study could better illustrate the predominant role of the external incentive-type stimulus on the learning function. These data suggest that, following the example of the monkey, even the rats are abandoning the sinking ship of reinforcement theory.

The effect of intensity of drive state on learning doubtless varies as we ascend the phyletic scale and certainly varies, probably to the point of almost complete reversal, as we pass from simple to complex problems, a point emphasized some years ago in a theoretical article by Maslow (22). Intensity of nociceptive stimulation may be positively related to speed of formation of conditioned avoidance responses in the monkey, but the use of intense nociceptive stimulation prevents the monkey from solving any problem of moderate complexity. This fact is consistent with a principle that was formulated and demonstrated experimentally many years ago as the Yerkes-Dodson law (32). There is, of course, no reference to the Yerkes-Dodson law by any drive-reduction theorist.

We do not mean to imply that drive state and drive-state reduction are unrelated to learning; we wish merely to emphasize that they are relatively unimportant variables. Our primary quarrel with drive-reduction theory is that it tends to focus more and more attention on problems of less and less importance. A strong case can be made for the proposition that the importance of the psychological problems studied during the last fifteen years has decreased as a negatively accelerated function approaching an asymptote of complete indifference. Nothing better illustrates this point than the kinds of apparatus currently used in "learning" research. We have the single-unit T-maze, the straight runway, the double-compartment grill box, and the Skinner box. The single-unit T-maze is an ideal apparatus for studying the visual capacities of a nocturnal animal; the straight runway enables one to measure quantitatively the speed and rate of running from one dead end to another; the double-compartment grill box is without doubt the most efficient torture chamber which is still legal; and the Skinner box enables one to demonstrate discrimination learning in a greater number of trials than is required by any other method. But the apparatus, though inefficient, give rise to data which can be splendidly quantified. The kinds of learning problems which can be efficiently measured in these apparatus represent a challenge only to the decorticate animal. It is a constant source of bewilderment to me that the neobehaviorists who so frequently belittle physiological psychology should choose apparatus which, in effect, experimentally decorticate their subjects.

The Skinner box is a splendid apparatus for demonstrating that the rate of performance of a learned response is positively related to the period of food deprivation. We have confirmed this for the monkey by studying rate of response on a modified Skinner box following 1, 23, and 47 hr. of food deprivation. Increasing length of food deprivation is clearly and positively related to increased rate of response. This functional relationship between drive states and responses does not hold, as we have already seen, for the monkey's behavior in discrimination learning or in acquisition of any more complex problem. The data, however, like rat data, are in complete accord with Crozier's (6) finding that the acuteness of the radial angle of tropistic movements in the slug Limax is positively related to intensity of the photic stimulation. We believe there is generalization in this finding, and we believe the generalization to be that the results from the investigation of simple behavior may be very informative about even simpler behavior but very seldom are they informative about behavior of greater complexity. I do not want to discourage anyone from the pursuit of the psychological Holy Grail by the use of the Skinner box, but as far as I am concerned, there will be no moaning of farewell when we have passed the pressing of the bar.

In the course of human events many psychologists have children, and these children always behave in accord with the theoretical position of their parents. For purposes of scientific objectivity the boys are always referred to as "Johnny" and the girls as "Mary." For some eleven months I have been observing the behavior of Mary X. Perhaps the most striking characteristic of this particular primate has been the power and persistence of her curiosity-investigatory motives. At an early age Mary X demonstrated a positive valence to parental thygmotatic stimulation. My original interpretation of these tactual-thermal erotic responses as indicating parental affection was dissolved by the discovery that when Mary X was held in any position depriving her of visual exploration of the environment, she screamed; when held in a position favorable to visual exploration of the important environment, which did not include the parent, she responded positively. With the parent and position held constant and visual exploration denied by snapping off the electric light, the positive responses changed to negative, and they returned to positive when the light was again restored. This behavior was observed in Mary X, who, like any good Watson child, showed no "innate fear of the dark."

The frustrations of Mary X appeared to be in large part the results of physical inability to achieve curiosity-investigatory goals. In her second month, frustrations resulted from inability to hold up her head indefinitely while lying prone in her crib or on a mat and the consequent loss of visual curiosity goals. Each time she had to lower her head to rest, she cried lustily. At nine weeks attempts to explore (and destroy) objects anterior resulted in wriggling backward away from the lure and elicited violent negative responses. Once she negotiated forward locomotion, exploration set in, in earnest, and, much to her parents' frustration, shows no sign of diminishing.

Can anyone seriously believe that the insatiable curiosity-investigatory motivation of the child is a second-order or derived drive conditioned upon hunger or sex or any other internal drive? The S-R theorist and the Freudian psychoanalyst imply that such behaviors are based on primary drives. An informal survey of neobehaviorists who are also fathers (or mothers) reveals that all have observed the intensity and omnipresence of the curiosity-investigatory motive in their own children. None of them seriously believes that the behavior derives from a second-order drive. After describing their children's behavior, often with a surprising enthusiasm and frequently with the support of photographic records, they trudge off to their laboratories to study, under conditions of solitary confinement, the intellectual processes of rodents. Such attitudes, perfectly in keeping with drive-reduction theory, no doubt account for the fact that there are no experimental or even systematic observational studies of curiosity-investigatory-type external-incentive motives in children.

A key to the real learning theory of any animal species is knowledge of the nature and organization of the unlearned patterns of response. The differences in the intellectual capabilities of cockroach, rat, monkey, chimpanzee, and man are as much a function of the differences in the inherent patterns of response and the differences in the inherent motivational forces as they are a function of sheer learning power. The differences in these inherent patterns of response and in the motivational forces will, I am certain, prove to be differential responsiveness to external stimulus patterns. Furthermore, I am certain that the variables which are of true, as opposed to psychophilosophical, importance are not constant from learning problem to learning problem even for the same animal order, and they are vastly diverse as we pass from one animal order to another.

Convinced that the key to human learning is not the conditioned response but, rather, motivation aroused by external stimuli, the speaker has initiated researches on curiosity-manipulation behavior as related to learning in monkeys (7, 10, 12). The justification for the use of monkeys is that we have more monkeys than children. Furthermore, the field is so unexplored that a systematic investigation anywhere in the phyletic scale should prove of methodological value. The rhesus monkey is actually a very incurious and nonmanipulative animal compared with the anthropoid apes, which are, in turn, very incurious nonmanipulative animals compared with man. It is certainly more than coincidence that the strength and range of curiosity-manipulative motivation and position within the primate order are closely related.

We have presented three studies which demonstrate that monkeys can and do learn to solve mechanical puzzles when no motivation is provided other than presence of the puzzle. Furthermore, we have presented data to show that once mastered, the sequence of manipulations involved in solving these puzzles is carried out relatively flawlessly and extremely persistently. We have presented what we believe is incontrovertible evidence against a second-order drive interpretation of this learning.

A fourth study was carried out recently by Gately at the Wisconsin laboratories. Gately directly compared the behavior of two groups of four monkeys presented with banks of four identical mechanical puzzles, each utilizing three restraining devices. All four food- plus puzzle-rewarded monkeys solved the four identical puzzles, and only one of the four monkeys motivated by curiosity alone solved all the puzzles. This one monkey, however, learned as rapidly and as efficiently as any of the food-rewarded monkeys. But I wish to stress an extremely important observation made by Gately and supported by quantitative records.

When the food-rewarded monkeys had solved a puzzle, they abandoned it. When the nonfood-rewarded animals had solved the puzzle, they frequently continued their explorations and manipulations. Indeed, one reason for the nonfood-rewarded monkeys' failure to achieve the experimenter's concept of solution lay in the fact that the monkey became fixated in exploration and manipulation of limited puzzle or puzzle-device components. From this point of view, hunger-reduction incentives may be regarded as motivation-destroying, not motivation-supporting, agents.

Twenty years ago at the Vilas Park Zoo, in Madison, we observed an adult orangutan given two blocks of wood, one with a round hole, one with a square hole, and two plungers, one round and one square. Intellectual curiosity alone led it to work on these tasks, often for many minutes at a time, and to solve the problem of inserting the round plunger in both holes. The orangutan never solved the problem of inserting the square peg into the round hole, but inasmuch as it passed away with perforated ulcers a month after the problem was presented, we can honestly say that it died trying. And in defense of this orangutan, let it be stated that it died working on more complex problems than are investigated by most present-day learning theorists.

Schiller[1] has reported that chimpanzees solve multiple-box-stacking problems without benefit of food rewards, and he has presented observational evidence that the joining of sticks resulted from manipulative play responses.

The Cebus monkey has only one claim to intellectual fame—an ability to solve instrumental problems that rivals the much publicized ability of the anthropoid apes (11, 18). It can be no accident that the Cebus monkey, inferior to the rhesus on conventional learning tasks, demonstrates far more spontaneous instrumental-manipulative responses than any old-world form. The complex, innate external-stimulus motives are variables doubtless as important as, or more important than, tissue tensions, stimulus generalization, excitatory potential, or secondary reinforcement. It is the oscillation of sticks, not cortical neurons, that enables the Cebus monkey to solve instrument problems.

No matter how important may be the analysis of the curiosity-manipulative drives and the learning which is associated with them, we recognize the vast and infinite technical difficulties that are inherent in the attack on the solution of these problems—indeed, it may be many years before we can routinely order such experiments in terms of latin squares and factorial designs, the apparent *sine qua non* for publication in the *Journal of Experimental Psychology* and the *Journal of Comparative and Physiological Psychology*.

There is, however, another vast and important area of external-stimulus incentives important to learning which has been explored only superficially and which can, and should, be immediately and systematically attacked by rodentologists and primatologists alike. This is the area of food incentives—or, more broadly, visuo-chemo variables—approached from the point of view of their function as motivating agents per se. This function, as the speaker sees it, is primarily an affective one and only secondarily one of tissue-tension reduction. To dispel any fear of subjectivity, let us state that the affective tone of food incentives can probably be scaled by preference tests with an accuracy far exceeding any scaling of tissue tensions. Our illusion of the equal-step intervals of tissue tensions is the myth that length of the period of deprivation is precisely related to tissue-tension intensity, but the recent experiments by Koch and Daniel (19) and Horenstein (13) indicate that this is not true, thus beautifully confirming the physiological findings of thirty years ago.

Paired-comparison techniques with monkeys show beyond question that the primary incentive variables of both differential quantity and differential quality can be arranged on equal-step scales, and there is certainly no reason to believe that variation dependent upon subjects, time, or experience is greater than that dependent upon physiological hunger.

In defense of the rat and its protagonists, let it be stated that there are already many experiments on this lowly mammal which indicate that its curiosity-investigatory motives and responsiveness to incentive variables can be quantitatively measured and their significant relationship to learning demonstrated. The latent learning experiments of Buxton (2), Haney (9), Seward, Levy, and Handlon (27), and others have successfully utilized the exploratory drive of the rat. Keller (16) and Zeaman and House (35) have utilized the rat's inherent aversion to light, or negative heliotropistic tendencies, to induce learning. Flynn and Jerome (8) have shown that the rat's avoidance of light is an external-incentive motivation that may be utilized to obtain the solution of complex learned performances. For many rats it is a strong and very persistent form of motivation. The importance of incentive variables in rats has been emphasized and re-emphasized by Young (33), and the influence of incentive variables on rat learning has been demonstrated by Young (33), Zeaman (34), Crespi (5), and others. I am not for one moment disparaging the value of the rat as a subject for psychological investigation; there is very little wrong with the rat that cannot be overcome by the education of the experimenters.

It may be argued that if we accept the theses of this paper, we shall be returning to an outmoded psychology of tropisms, instincts, and hedonism. There is a great deal of truth to this charge. Such an approach might be a regression were it not for the fact that psychology now has adequate techniques of methodology and analysis to attack quantifiably these important and neglected areas. If we are ever to have a comprehensive theoretical psychology, we must attack the problems whose solution offers hope of insight into human behavior, and it is my belief that if we face our problems honestly and without regard to, or fear of, difficulty, the theoretical psychology of the future will catch up with, and eventually even surpass, common sense.

REFERENCES

 1. Birch, H. C. The relation of previous experience to insightful problem solving. *J. comp. Psychol.*, 1945, *39*, 15–22.
 2. Buxton, C. E. Latent learning and the goal gradient hypothesis. *Contr. psychol. Theor.*, 1940, *2*, No. 2.
 3. Cannon, W. B. *The wisdom of the body.* New York: Norton, 1932.
 4. Carmichael, L. An experimental study in the prenatal guinea-pig of the origin and development of reflexes and patterns of behavior in relation to the stimulation of specific receptor areas during the period of active fetal life. *Genet. Psychol. Monogr.*, 1934, *16*, 337–491.
 5. Crespi, L. P. Quantitative variation of incentive and performance in the white rat. *Amer. J. Psychol.*, 1942, *55*, 467–517.
 6. Crozier, W. J. The study of living organisms. In C. Murchison (Ed.), *The foundations of experimental psychology.* Worcester, Mass.: Clark Univ. Press, 1929.
 7. Davis, R. T., Settlage, P. H., & Harlow, H. F. Performance of normal and brain-operated monkeys on mechanical puzzles with and without food incentive. *J. genet. Psychol.*, 1950, *77*, 305–311.
 8. Flynn, J. P., & Jerome, E. A. Learning in an automatic multiple-choice box with light as incentive. *J. comp. physiol. Psychol.*, 1952, *45*, 336–340.
 9. Haney, G. W. The effect of familiarity on maze performance of albino rats. *Univer. Calif. Publ. Psychol.*, 1931, *4*, 319–333.
10. Harlow, H. F. Learning and satiation of response in intrinsically motivated complex puzzle performance by monkeys. *J. comp. physiol. Psychol.*, 1950, *43*, 289–294.
11. Harlow, H. F. Primate learning. In C. P. Stone (Ed.), *Comparative psychology.* (3rd Ed.) New York: Prentice-Hall, 1951.
12. Harlow, H. F., Harlow, Margaret K., & Meyer, D. R. Learning motivated by a manipulation drive. *J. exp. Psychol.*, 1950, *40*, 228–234.
13. Horenstein, Betty. Performance of conditioned responses as a function of strength of hunger drive. *J. comp. physiol. Psychol.*, 1951, *44*, 210–224.
14. Jennings, H. S. *Behavior of the lower organisms.* New York: Columbia Univer. Press, 1906.
15. Jensen, K. Differential reactions to taste and temperature stimuli in newborn infants. *Genet. Psychol. Monogr.*, 1932, *12*, 361–476.
16. Keller, F. S. Light-aversion in the white rat. *Psychol. Rec.*, 1941, *4*, 235–250.
17. Kinsey, A. C., Pomeroy, W. B., & Martin, C. E. *Sexual behavior in the human male.* Philadelphia: W. B. Saunders, 1948.

18. Klüver, H. *Behavior mechanisms in monkeys.* Chicago: Univer. Chicago Press, 1933.
19. Koch, S., & Daniel, W. J. The effect of satiation on the behavior mediated by a habit of maximum strength. *J. exp. Psychol.*, 1945, *35*, 162–185.
20. Langworthy, O. R. The behavior of pouch-young opossums correlated with the myelinization of tracts in the nervous system. *J. comp. Neurol.*, 1928, *46*, 201–248.
21. Loeb, J. *Forced movements, tropisms and animal conduct.* Philadelphia: Lippincott, 1918.
22. Maslow, A. H. A theory of human motivation. *Psychol. Rev.*, 1943, *50*, 370–396.
23. Meyer, D. R. Food deprivation and discrimination reversal learning by monkeys. *J. exp. Psychol.*, 1951, *41*, 10–16.
24. Miller, N. E. Learnable drives and rewards. In S. S. Stevens (Ed.), *Handbook of experimental psychology.* New York: Wiley, 1951.
25. Pavlov, I. P. *Conditioned reflexes* (translated by G. V. Anrep). London: Oxford Univer. Press, 1927.
26. Richter, C. P. Animal behavior and internal drives. *Quart. Rev. Biol.*, 1927, *2*, 307–343.
27. Seward, J. P., Levy, N., & Handlon, J. H., Jr. Incidental learning in the rat. *J. compl. physiol. Psychol.*, 1950, *43*, 240–251.
28. Sheffield, F. D., & Roby, T. B. Reward value of a non-nutrient sweet taste. *J. comp. physiol. Psychol.*, 1950, *43*, 471–481.
29. Strassburger, R. C. Resistance to extinction of a conditioned operant as related to drive level at reinforcement. *J. exp. Psychol.*, 1950, *40*, 473–487.
30. Thorndike, E. L. *Animal intelligence.* New York: Macmillan, 1911.
31. Watson, J. B. *Behavior: An introduction to comparative psychology.* New York: Holt, 1914.
32. Yerkes, R. M., & Dodson, J. D. The relation of strength of stimulus to rapidity of habit formation. *J. comp. Neurol. Psychol.*, 1908, *18*, 459–482.
33. Young, P. T. Food-seeking drive, affective process, and learning. *Psychol. Rev.*, 1949, *56*, 98–121.
34. Zeaman, D. Response latency as a function of amount of reinforcement. *J. exp. Psychol.*, 1949, *39*, 466–483.
35. Zeaman, D., & House, Betty J. Response latency at zero drive after varying numbers of reinforcements. *J. exp. Psychol.*, 1950, *40*, 570–583.

NOTE

[1] Personal communication.

8

The Nature of Love

Harry F. Harlow

Love is a wondrous state, deep, tender, and rewarding. Because of its intimate and personal nature it is regarded by some as an improper topic for experimental research. But, whatever our personal feelings may be, our assigned mission as psychologists is to analyze all facets of human and animal behavior into their component variables. So far as love or affection is concerned, psychologists have failed in this mission. The little we know about love does not transcend simple observation, and the little we write about it has been written better by poets and novelists. But of greater concern is the fact that psychologists tend to give progressively less attention to a motive which pervades our entire lives. Psychologists, at least psychologists who write textbooks, not only show no interest in the origin and development of love or affection, but they seem to be unaware of its very existence.

The apparent repression of love by modern psychologists stands in sharp contrast with the attitude taken by many famous and normal people. The word "love" has the highest reference frequency of any word cited in Bartlett's book of *Familiar Quotations*. It would appear that this emotion has long had a vast interest and fascination for human beings, regardless of the attitude taken by psychologists; but the quotations cited, even by famous and normal people, have a mundane redundancy. These authors and authorities have stolen love from the child and infant and made it the exclusive property of the adolescent and adult.

Thoughtful men, and probably all women, have speculated on the nature of love. From the developmental point of view, the general plan is

Harlow, H. F. The nature of love. *Amer. Psychol.*, 1958, *13*, 673–685. Copyright 1958 by the American Psychological Association. Reprinted by permission of the publisher and author.

quite clear: The initial love responses of the human being are those made by the infant to the mother or some mother surrogate. From this intimate attachment of the child to the mother, multiple learned and generalized affectional responses are formed.

Unfortunately, beyond these simple facts we know little about the fundamental variables underlying the formation of affectional responses and little about the mechanisms through which the love of the infant for the mother develops into the multifaceted response patterns characterizing love or affection in the adult. Because of the dearth of experimentation, theories about the fundamental nature of affection have evolved at the level of observation, intuition, and discerning guesswork, whether these have been proposed by psychologists, sociologists, anthropologists, physicians, or psychoanalysts.

The position commonly held by psychologists and sociologists is quite clear: The basic motives are, for the most part, the primary drives—particularly hunger, thirst, elimination, pain, and sex—and all other motives, including love or affection, are derived or secondary drives. The mother is associated with the reduction of the primary drives—particularly hunger, thirst, and pain—and through learning, affection or love is derived.

It is entirely reasonable to believe that the mother through association with food may become a secondary-reinforcing agent, but this is an inadequate mechanism to account for the persistence of the infant-maternal ties. There is a spate of researches on the formation of secondary reinforcers to hunger and thirst reduction. There can be no question that almost any external stimulus can become a secondary reinforcer if properly associated with tissue-need reduction, but the fact remains that this redundant literature demonstrates unequivocally that such derived drives suffer relatively rapid experimental extinction. Contrariwise, human affection does not extinguish when the mother ceases to have intimate association with the drives in question. Instead, the affectional ties to the mother show a lifelong, unrelenting persistence and, even more surprising, widely expanding generality.

Oddly enough, one of the few psychologists who took a position counter to modern psychological dogma was John B. Watson, who believed that love was an innate emotion elicited by cutaneous stimulation of the erogenous zones. But experimental psychologists, with their peculiar propensity to discover facts that are not true, brushed this theory aside by demonstrating that the human neonate had no differentiable emotions, and they established a fundamental psychological law that prophets are without honor in their own profession.

The psychoanalysts have concerned themselves with the problem of the nature of the development of love in the neonate and infant, using ill and aging human beings as subjects. They have discovered the overwhelming importance of the breast and related this to the oral erotic tendencies developed at an age preceding their subjects' memories. Their theories range from a belief that the infant has an innate need to achieve and suckle at the breast to beliefs not unlike commonly accepted psychological theories. There are exceptions, as seen in the recent writings of John Bowlby, who attributes importance not only to food and thirst satisfaction, but also to "primary object-clinging," a need for intimate physical contact, which is initially associated with the mother.

As far as I know, there exists no direct experimental analysis of the relative importance of the stimulus variables determining the affectional or love responses in the neonatal and infant primate. Unfortunately, the human neonate is a limited experimental subject for such researches because of his inadequate motor capabilities. By the time the human infant's motor responses can be precisely measured, the antecedent determining conditions cannot be defined, having been lost in a jumble and jungle of confounded variables.

Many of these difficulties can be resolved by the use of the neonatal and infant macaque monkey as the subject for the analysis of basic affectional variables. It is possible to make precise measurements in this primate beginning at two to ten days of age, depending upon the maturational status of the individual animal at birth. The macaque infant differs from the human infant in that the monkey is more mature at birth and grows more rapidly; but the basic responses relating to affection, including nursing, contact, clinging, and even visual and auditory exploration, exhibit no fundamental differences in the two species. Even the development of perception, fear, frustration, and learning capability follows very similar sequences in rhesus monkeys and human children.

Three years' experimentation before we started our studies on affection gave us experience with the neonatal monkey. We had separated more than 60 of these animals from their mothers 6 to 12 hours after birth and suckled them on tiny bottles. The infant mortality was only a small fraction of what would have obtained had we let the monkey mothers raise their infants. Our bottle-fed babies were healthier and heavier than monkey-mother-reared infants. We know that we are better monkey mothers than are real monkey mothers thanks to synthetic diets, vitamins, iron extracts, penicillin, chloromycetin, 5% glucose, and constant, tender, loving care.

During the course of these studies we noticed that the laboratory-raised babies showed strong attachment to the cloth pads (folded gauze diapers) which were used to cover the hardware-cloth floors of their cages. The infants clung to these pads and engaged in violent temper tantrums when the pads were removed and replaced for sanitary reasons. Such contact-need or responsiveness had been reported previously by Gertrude van Wagenen

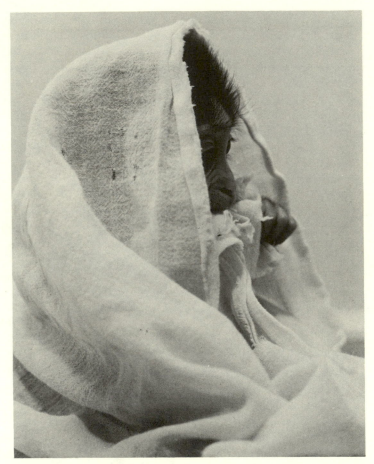

Figure 8-1   Response to gauze pad by six-month-old monkey used in another study.

for the monkey and by Thomas McCulloch and George Haslerud for the chimpanzee and is reminiscent of the devotion often exhibited by human infants to their pillows, blankets, and soft, cuddly stuffed toys.... An unusual and strong attachment of a six-month-old infant to the cloth pad is illustrated in Figure 8-1. The baby, human or monkey, if it is to survive, must clutch at more than a straw.

   We had also discovered during some allied observational studies that a baby monkey raised on a bare wire-mesh cage floor survives with difficulty, if at all, during the first five days of life. If a wire-mesh cone is introduced, the baby does better; and, if the cone is covered with terry cloth, husky, healthy, happy babies evolve. It takes more than a baby and a box to make a normal monkey. We were impressed by the possibility that, above and beyond the bubbling fountain of breast or bottle, contact comfort might be a very important variable in the development of the infant's affection for the mother.

At this point we decided to study the development of affectional responses of neonatal and infant monkeys to an artificial, inanimate mother, and so we built a surrogate mother which we hoped and believed would be a good surrogate mother. In devising this surrogate mother we were dependent neither upon the capriciousness of evolutionary processes nor upon mutations produced by chance radioactive fallout. Instead, we designed the mother surrogate in terms of modern human-engineering principles....We produced a perfectly proportioned, streamlined body stripped of unnecessary bulges and appendices. Redundancy in the surrogate mother's system was avoided by reducing the number of breasts from two to one and placing this unibreast in an upper-thoracic, sagittal position, thus maximizing the natural and known perceptual-motor capabilities of the infant operator. The surrogate was made from a block of wood, covered with sponge rubber, and sheathed in tan cotton terry cloth. A light bulb behind her radiated heat. The result was a mother, soft, warm, and tender, a mother with infinite patience, a mother available twenty-four hours a day, a mother that never scolded her infant and never struck or bit her baby in anger. Furthermore, we designed a mother-machine with maximal maintenance efficiency since failure of any system or function could be resolved by the simple substitution of black boxes and new component parts. It is our opinion that we engineered a very superior monkey mother, although this position is not held universally by the monkey fathers.

Before beginning our initial experiment we also designed and constructed a second mother surrogate, a surrogate in which we deliberately built less than the maximal capability for contact comfort. This surrogate mother is illustrated in Figure 8-2. She is made of wire-mesh, a substance entirely adequate to provide postural support and nursing capability, and she is warmed by radiant heat. Her body differs in no essential way from that of the cloth mother surrogate other than in the quality of the contact comfort which she can supply.

In our initial experiment, the dual mother-surrogate condition, a cloth mother and a wire mother were placed in different cubicles attached to the infant's living cage as shown in Figure 8-2. For four newborn monkeys the cloth mother lactated and the wire mother did not; and, for the other four, this condition was reversed. In either condition the infant received all its milk through the mother surrogate as soon as it was able to maintain itself in this way, a capability achieved within two or three days except in the case of very immature infants. Supplementary feedings were given until the milk intake from the mother surrogate was adequate. Thus, the

Figure 8-2   Wire and cloth surrogate mothers.

experiment was designed as a test of the relative importance of the variables of contact comfort and nursing comfort. During the first 14 days of life the monkey's cage floor was covered with a heating pad wrapped in a folded gauze diaper, and thereafter the cage floor was bare. The infants were always free to leave the heating pad or cage floor to contact either mother, and the time spent on the surrogate mothers was automatically recorded. Figure 8-3 shows the total time spent on the cloth and wire mothers under the two conditions of feeding. These data make it obvious that contact comfort is a variable of overwhelming importance in the development of affectional responses, whereas lactation is a variable of negligible importance. With age and opportunity to learn, subjects with the lactating wire mother showed decreasing responsiveness to her and increasing responsiveness to the nonlactating cloth mother, a finding completely contrary to any interpretation of derived drive in which the mother-form becomes conditioned to hunger-thirst reduction. The persistence of these differential responses throughout 165 consecutive days of testing is evident in Figure 8-4.

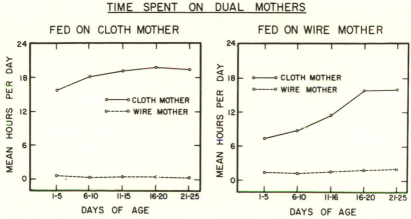

Figure 8-3   Time spent on cloth and wire mother surrogates.

One control group of neonatal monkeys was raised on a single wire mother, and a second control group was raised on a single cloth mother. There were no differences between these two groups in amount of milk ingested or in weight gain. The only difference between the groups lay in

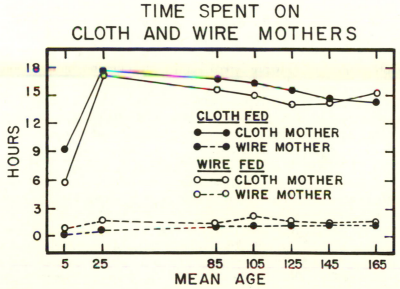

Figure 8-4   Long-term contact time on cloth and wire mother surrogates.

the composition of the feces, the softer stools of the wire-mother infants suggesting psychosomatic involvement. The wire mother is biologically adequate but psychologically inept.

We were not surprised to discover that contact comfort was an important basic affectional or love variable, but we did not expect it to overshadow so completely the variable of nursing; indeed, the disparity is so great as to suggest that the primary function of nursing as an affectional variable is that of insuring frequent and intimate body contact of the infant with the mother. Certainly, man cannot live by milk alone. Love is an emotion that does not need to be bottle- or spoon-fed, and we may be sure that there is nothing to be gained by giving lip service to love.

A charming lady once heard me describe these experiments; and, when I subsequently talked to her, her face brightened with sudden insight: "Now I know what's wrong with me," she said, "I'm just a wire mother." Perhaps she was lucky. She might have been a wire wife.

We believe that contact comfort has long served the animal kingdom as a motivating agent for affectional responses....

One function of the real mother, human or subhuman, and presumably of a mother surrogate, is to provide a haven of safety for the infant in times of fear and danger. The frightened or ailing child clings to its mother, not its father; and this selective responsiveness in times of distress, disturbance, or danger may be used as a measure of the strength of affectional bonds. We have tested this kind of differential responsiveness by presenting to the infants in their cages, in the presence of the two mothers, various fear-producing stimuli such as the moving toy bear illustrated in Figure 8-5. A typical response to a fear stimulus is shown in Figure 8-6, and the data on differential responsiveness are presented in Figure 8-7. It is apparent that the cloth mother is highly preferred over the wire one, and this differential selectivity is enhanced by age and experience. In this situation, the variable of nursing appears to be of absolutely no importance: the infant consistently seeks the soft mother surrogate regardless of nursing condition.

Similarly, the mother or mother surrogate provides its young with a source of security, and this role or function is seen with special clarity when mother and child are in a strange situation. At the present time we have completed tests for this relationship on four of our eight baby monkeys assigned to the dual mother-surrogate condition by introducing them for three minutes into the strange environment of a room measuring six feet by six feet by six feet (also called the "open-field test") and containing multiple stimuli known to elicit curiosity-manipulatory responses in baby monkeys. The subjects were placed in this situation twice a week for eight weeks with no mother surrogate present during alternate sessions and the cloth mother present during the others. A cloth diaper was always available as one of the stimuli throughout all sessions.

Figure 8-5 Typical fear stimulus.

After one or two adaptation sessions, the infants always rushed to the mother surrogate when she was present and clutched her, rubbed their bodies against her, and frequently manipulated her body and face. After a few additional sessions, the infants began to use the mother surrogate as a source of security, a base of operations. As is shown in Figures 8-8 and 8-9, they would explore and manipulate a stimulus and then return to the mother before adventuring again into the strange new world. The behavior of these infants was quite different when the mother was absent from the room. Frequently they would freeze in a crouched position, as is illustrated in Figure 8-10. Emotionality indices such as vocalization, crouching, rocking, and sucking increased sharply. Total emotionality score was cut in half when the mother was present. In the absence of the mother some of

Figure 8-6 Typical response to cloth mother surrogate in fear test.

the experimental monkeys would rush to the center of the room where the mother was customarily placed and then run rapidly from object to object, screaming and crying all the while. Continuous, frantic clutching of their bodies was very common, even when not in the crouching position. These monkeys frequently contacted and clutched the cloth diaper, but this action never pacified them. The same behavior occurred in the presence of the wire mother. No difference between the cloth-mother-fed and wire-mother-fed infants was demonstrated under either condition. Four control infants never raised with a mother surrogate showed the same emotionality scores when the mother was absent as the experimental infants showed in the absence of the mother, but the controls' scores were slightly larger in the presence of the mother surrogate than in her absence.

Some years ago Robert Butler demonstrated that mature monkeys enclosed in a dimly lighted box would open and reopen a door hour after

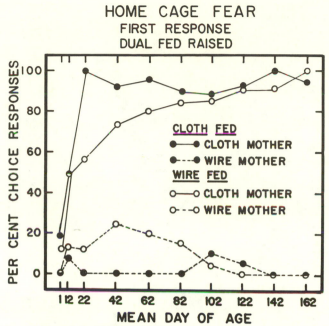

Figure 8-7 Differential responsiveness in fear tests.

hour for no other reward than that of looking outside the box. We now have data indicating that neonatal monkeys show this same compulsive visual curiosity on their first test day in an adaptation of the Butler apparatus which we call the "love machine," an apparatus designed to measure love. Usually these tests are begun when the monkey is 10 days of age, but this same persistent visual exploration has been obtained in a three-day-old monkey during the first half-hour of testing. Butler also demonstrated that rhesus monkeys show selectivity in rate and frequency of door-opening to stimuli of differential attractiveness in the visual field outside the box. We have utilized this principle of response selectivity by the monkey to measure strength of affectional responsiveness in our infants in the baby version of the Butler box. The test sequence involves four repetitions of a test battery in which four stimuli—cloth mother, wire mother, infant monkey, and empty box—are presented for a 30-minute period on successive days. The first four subjects in the dual mother-surrogate group were given a single test sequence at 40 to 50 days of age, depending upon the availability of the apparatus, and only their data are presented. The second set of four subjects is being given repetitive tests to obtain information relating to the development of visual exploration. The apparatus is illustrated in Figure 8-11. The data obtained from the first

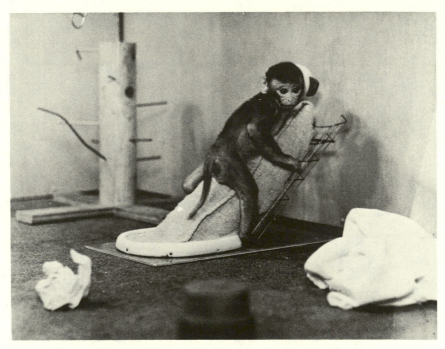

Figure 8-8   Response to cloth mother in the open-field test.

four infants raised with the two mother surrogates show approximately equal responding to the cloth mother and another infant monkey, and no greater responsiveness to the wire mother than to an empty box. Again, the results are independent of the kind of mother that lactated, cloth or wire. The same results are found for a control group raised, but not fed, on a single cloth mother. Contrariwise, no differential responsiveness to cloth and wire mothers by a second control group, which was not raised on any mother surrogate. We can be certain that not all love is blind.

The first four infant monkeys in the dual mother-surrogate group were separated from their mothers between 165 and 170 days of age and tested for retention during the following 9 days and then at 30-day intervals for six successive months....In keeping with the data obtained on adult monkeys by Butler, we find a high rate of responding to any stimulus, even the empty box. But throughout the entire 185-day retention period there is a consistent and significant difference in response frequency to the cloth mother contrasted with either the wire mother or the empty box, and no consistent difference between wire mother and empty box.

Affectional retention was also tested in the open field during the first 9 days after separation and then at 30-day intervals, and each test condition was run twice at each retention interval. The infant's behavior differed

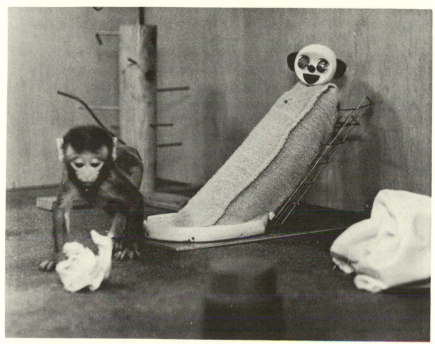

Figure 8-9   Object exploration in the presence of cloth mother.

from that observed during the period preceding separation. When the cloth mother was present in the post-separation period, the babies rushed to her, climbed up, clung tightly to her, and rubbed their heads and faces against her body. After this initial embrace and reunion, they played on the mother, including biting and tearing at her cloth cover; but they rarely made any attempt to leave her during the test period, nor did they manipulate or play with the objects in the room, in contrast with their behavior before maternal separation. The only exception was the occasional monkey that left the mother surrogate momentarily, grasped the folded piece of paper (one of the standard stimuli in the field), and brought it quickly back to the mother. It appeared that deprivation had enhanced the tie to the mother and rendered the contact-comfort need so prepotent that need for the mother overwhelmed the exploratory motives during the brief, three-minute test sessions. No change in these behaviors was observed throughout the 185-day period. When the mother was absent from the open field, the behavior of the infants was similar in the initial retention test to that during the preseparation tests; but they tended to show gradual adaptation to the open-field situation with repeated testing and, consequently, a reduction in their emotionality scores.

Figure 8-10   Response in the open-field test in the absence of the mother surrogate.

In the last five retention test periods, an additional test was introduced in which the surrogate mother was placed in the center of the room and covered with a clear Plexiglas box. The monkeys were initially disturbed and frustrated when their explorations and manipulations of the box failed to provide contact with the mother. However, all animals adapted to the situation rather rapidly. Soon they used the box as a place of orientation for exploratory and play behavior, made frequent contacts with the objects in the field, and very often brought these objects to the Plexiglas box. The emotionality index was slightly higher than in the condition of the available cloth mothers, but it in no way approached the emotionality level displayed when the cloth mother was absent. Obviously, the infant monkeys gained emotional security by the presence of the mother even though contact was denied.

Affectional retention has also been measured by tests in which the monkey must unfasten a three-device mechanical puzzle to obtain entrance into a compartment containing the mother surrogate. All the trials are initiated by allowing the infant to go through an unlocked door, and in half the trials it finds the mother present and in half, an empty compartment. The door is then locked and a ten-minute test conducted. In tests given

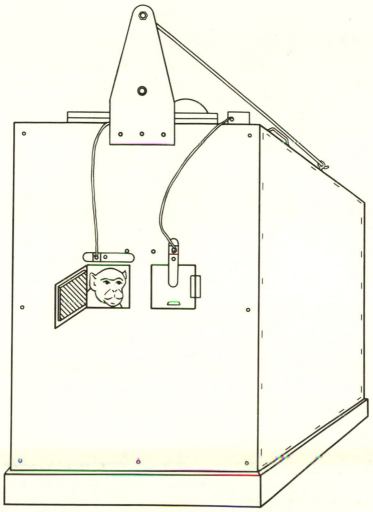

Figure 8-11   Visual exploration apparatus.

prior to separation from the surrogate mothers, some of the infants had solved this puzzle and others had failed. The data show that on the last test before separation there were no differences in total manipulation under mother-present and mother-absent conditions, but striking differences exist between the two conditions throughout the post-separation test periods. Again, there is no interaction with conditions of feeding.

The over-all picture obtained from surveying the retention data in unequivocal. There is little, if any, waning of responsiveness to the mother throughout this five-month period as indicated by any measure. It becomes perfectly obvious that this affectional bond is highly resistant to forgetting and that it can be retained for very long periods of time by relatively infrequent contact reinforcement. During the next year, retention tests will be conducted at 90-day intervals, and further plans are dependent upon the results obtained. It would appear that affectional responses may show as much resistance to extinction as has been previously demonstrated for learned fears and learned pain, and such data would be in keeping with those of common human observation.

The infant's responses to the mother surrogate in the fear tests, the open-field situation, and the baby Butler box and the responses on the retention tests cannot be described adequately with words. For supplementary information we turn to the motion picture record. (At this point a 20-minute film was presented illustrating and supplementing the behaviors described thus far in the address.)

We have already described the group of four control infants that had never lived in the presence of any mother surrogate and had demonstrated no sign of affection or security in the presence of the cloth mothers introduced in test sessions. When these infants reached the age of 250 days, cubicles containing both a cloth mother and a wire mother were attached to their cages. There was no lactation in these mothers, for the monkeys were on a solid-food diet. The initial reaction of the monkeys to the alterations was one of extreme disturbance. All the infants screamed violently and made repeated attempts to escape the cage whenever the door was opened. They kept a maximum distance from the mother surrogates and exhibited a considerable amount of rocking and crouching behavior, indicative of emotionality. Our first thought was that the critical period for the development of maternally directed affection had passed and that these macaque children were doomed to live as affectional orphans. Fortunately, these behaviors continued for only 12 to 48 hours and then gradually ebbed, changing from indifference to active contact on, and exploration of, the surrogates. The home-cage behavior of these control monkeys slowly became similar to that of the animals raised with the mother surrogates from birth. Their manipulation and play on the cloth mother became progressively more vigorous to the point of actual mutilation, particularly during the morning after the cloth mother had been given her daily change of terry covering. The control subjects were now actively running to a cloth mother when frightened and had to be coaxed from her to be taken from the cage for formal testing.

Objective evidence of these changing behaviors...[shows]the amount of time these infants spent on the mother surrogates. Within 10 days mean contact time is approximately nine hours, and this measure remains relatively constant throughout the next 30 days. Consistent with the results on the subjects reared from birth with dual mothers, these late-adopted infants spent less than one and one-half hours per day in contact with the wire mothers, and this activity level was relatively constant throughout the test sessions. Although the maximum time that the control monkeys spent on the cloth mother was only about half that spent by the original dual mother-surrogate group, we cannot be sure that this discrepancy is a function of differential early experience. The control monkeys were about three months older when the mothers were attached to their cages than the experimental animals had been when their mothers were removed and the retention tests begun. Thus, we do not know what the amount of contact would be for a 250-day-old animal raised from birth with surrogate mothers. Nevertheless, the magnitude of the differences and the fact that the contact-time curves for the mothered-from-birth infants had remained constant for almost 150 days suggest that early experience with the mother is a variable of measurable importance.

The control group has also been tested for differential visual exploration after the introduction of the cloth and wire mothers. By the second test session a high level of exploratory behavior had developed, and the responsiveness to the wire mother and the empty box is significantly greater than that to the cloth mother. This is probably not an artifact since there is every reason to believe that the face of the cloth mother is a fear stimulus to most monkeys that have not had extensive experience with this object during the first 40 to 60 days of life. Within the third test session a sharp change in trend occurs, and the cloth mother is then more frequently viewed than the wire mother or the blank box; this trend continues during the fourth session, producing a significant preference for the cloth mother.

Before the introduction of the mother surrogate into the home-cage situation, only one of the four control monkeys had ever contacted the cloth mother in the open-field tests. In general, the surrogate mother not only gave the infants no security, but instead appeared to serve as a fear stimulus. The emotionality scores of these control subjects were slightly higher during the mother-present test sessions than during the mother-absent test sessions. These behaviors were changed radically by the fourth post-introduction test approximately 60 days later. In the absence of the cloth mothers the emotionality index in this fourth test remains near the earlier level, but the score is reduced by half when the mother is present, a result strikingly similar to that found for infants raised with the dual mother-surrogates from birth. The control infants now show increasing object exploration and play behavior, and they begin to use the mother as a base of operations, as did the infants raised from birth with the mother surrogates. However, there are still definite differences in the behavior of the two groups. The control infants do not rush directly to the mother and clutch her violently; but instead they go toward, and orient around her, usually after an initial period during which they frequently show disturbed behavior, exploratory behavior, or both.

That the control monkeys develop affection or love for the cloth mother when she is introduced into the cage at 250 days of age cannot be questioned. There is very reason to believe, however, that this interval of delay depresses the intensity of the affectional response below that of the infant monkeys that were surrogate-mothered from birth onward. In interpreting these data it is well to remember that the control monkeys had had continuous opportunity to observe and hear other monkeys housed in adjacent cages and that they had had limited opportunity to view and contact surrogate mothers in the test situations, even though they did not exploit the opportunities.

During the last two years we have observed the behavior of two infants raised by their own mothers. Love for the real mother and love for the surrogate mother appear to be very similar. The baby macaque spends many hours a day clinging to its real mother. If away from the mother when frightened, it rushes to her and in her presence shows comfort and composure. As far as we can observe, the infant monkey's affection for the real mother is strong, but no stronger than that of the experimental monkey for the surrogate cloth mother, and the security that the infant gains from the presence of the real mother is no greater than the security it gains from a cloth surrogate. Next year we hope to put this problem to final, definitive, experimental test. But, whether the mother is real or a cloth surrogate, there does develop a deep and abiding bond between mother and child. In one case it may be the call of the wild and in the other the McCall of civilization, but in both cases there is "togetherness."

In spite of the importance of contact comfort, there is reason to believe that other variables of measurable importance will be discovered. Postural support may be such a variable, and it has been suggested that, when we build arms into the mother surrogate, 10 is the minimal number required to provide adequate child care. Rocking motion may be such a variable, and we are comparing rocking and stationary mother surrogates and inclined planes. The differential responsiveness to cloth mother and cloth-covered inclined plane suggests that clinging as well as contact is an affectional variable of importance. Sounds, particularly natural, maternal sounds, may operate as either unlearned or learned affectional variables. Visual responsiveness may be such a variable, and it is possible that some semblance of visual imprinting may develop in the neonatal monkey. There are indications that this becomes a variable of importance during the course of infancy through some maturational process.

John Bowlby has suggested that there is an affectional variable which he calls "primary object following," characterized by visual and oral search of the mother's face. Our surrogate-mother-raised baby monkeys are at first inattentive to her face, as are human neonates to human mother faces. But by 30 days of age ever-increasing responsiveness to the mother's face appears—whether through learning, maturation, or both—and we have reason to believe that the face becomes an object of special attention.

Our first surrogate-mother-raised baby had a mother whose head was just a ball of wood since the baby was a month early and we had not had time to design a more esthetic head and face. This baby had contact with the blank-faced mother for 180 days and was then placed with two cloth mothers, one motionless and one rocking, both being endowed with painted, ornamented faces. To our surprise the animal would compulsively rotate both faces 180 degrees so that it viewed only a round, smooth face and never the painted, ornamented face. Furthermore, it would do this as long as the patience of the experimenter in reorienting the faces persisted. The monkey showed no sign of fear or anxiety, but it showed unlimited persistence. Subsequently it improved its technique, compulsively removing the heads and rolling them into its cage as fast as they were returned. We are intrigued by this observation, and we plan to examine systematically the role of the mother face in the development of infant-monkey affections. Indeed, these observations suggest the need for a series of ethological-type researches on the two-faced female.

Although we have made no attempts thus far to study the generalization of infant-macaque affection or love, the techniques which we have developed offer promise in this uncharted field. Beyond this, there are few if any technical difficulties in studying the affection of the actual, living mother for the child, and the techniques developed can be utilized and expanded for the analysis and developmental study of father-infant affection.

Since we can measure neonatal and infant affectional responses to mother surrogates, and since we know they are strong and persisting, we are in a position to assess the effects of feeding and contactual schedules; consistency and inconsistency in the mother surrogates; and early, intermediate, and late maternal deprivation. Again, we have here a family of problems of fundamental interest and theoretical importance.

If the researches completed and proposed make a contribution, I shall be grateful; but I have also given full thought to possible practical applications. The socioeconomic demands of the present and the threatened socioeconomic demands of the future have led the American woman to displace, or threaten to displace, the American man in science and industry. If this process continues, the problem of proper child-rearing practices faces us with startling clarity. It is cheering in view of this trend to realize that the American male is physically endowed with all the really essential equipment to compete with the American female on equal terms in one essential activity: the rearing of infants. We now know that women in the working classes are not needed in the home because of their primary mammalian capabilities; and it is possible that in the foreseeable future neonatal nursing will not be regarded as a necessity, but as a luxury—to use Veblen's term—a form of conspicuous consumption limited perhaps to the upper classes. But whatever course history may take, it is comforting to know that we are now in contact with the nature of love.

NOTE

The researches reported in this paper were supported by funds supplied by Grant No. M-722, National Institutes of Health, by a grant from the Ford Foundation, and by funds received from the Graduate School of the University of Wisconsin.

9

Nature of Love—Simplified

Harry F. Harlow and Stephen J. Suomi

The cloth surrogate and its wire surrogate sibling entered into scientific history as of 1958 (Harlow, 1958). The cloth surrogate was originally designed to test the relative importance of body contact in contrast to activities associated with the breast, and the results were clear beyond all expectation. Body contact was of overpowering importance by any measure taken, even contact time.

However, the cloth surrogate, beyond its power to measure the relative importance of a host of variables determining infant affection for the mother, exhibited another surprising trait, one of great independent usefulness. Even though the cloth mother was inanimate, it was able to impart to its infant such emotional security that the infant would, in the surrogate's presence, explore a strange situation and manipulate available physical objects (see Figure 9-1) or animate objects (see Figure 9-2). Manipulation of animate objects leads to play if these animate objects are age-mates, and play is the variable of primary importance in the development of normal social, sexual, and maternal functions, as described by Harlow and Harlow (1965). It is obvious that surrogate mothers, which are more docile and manipulative than real monkey mothers, have a wide range of experimental uses.

SIMPLIFIED SURROGATE

Although the originate surrogates turned out to be incredibly efficient dummy mothers, they presented certain practical problems. The worst of

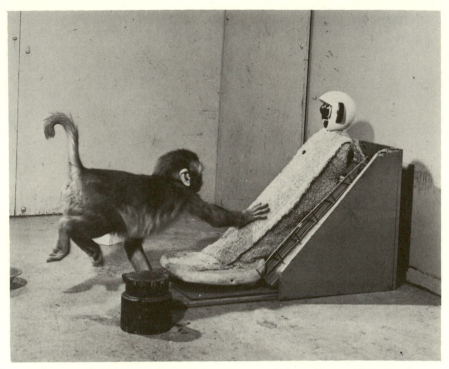

Figure 9-1   Infant monkey security in presence of cloth surrogate.

the problems was that of cleanliness. Infant monkeys seldom soil their real mothers' bodies, though we do not know how this is achieved. However, infant monkeys soiled the bodies of the original cloth surrogates with such efficiency and enthusiasm as to present a health problem and, even worse, a financial problem resulting from laundering. Furthermore, we believed that the original cloth surrogate was too steeply angled and thereby relatively inaccessible for cuddly clinging by the neonatal monkey.

In the hope of alleviating practical problems inherent in the original cloth surrogate, we constructed a family of simplified surrogates. The simplified surrogate is mounted on a rod attached to a lead base 4 inches in diameter, angled upward at 25°, and projected through the surrogate's body for 4 inches, so that heads may be attached if desired. The body of the simplified surrogate is only 6 inches long, 2½ inches in diameter, and stands approximately 3 inches off the ground. Figure 9-3 shows an original cloth surrogate and simplified surrogate placed side by side.

As can be seen in Figure 9-4, infants readily cling to these simplified surrogates of smaller body and decreased angle of inclination. Infant monkeys do soil the simplified surrogate, but the art and act of soiling is

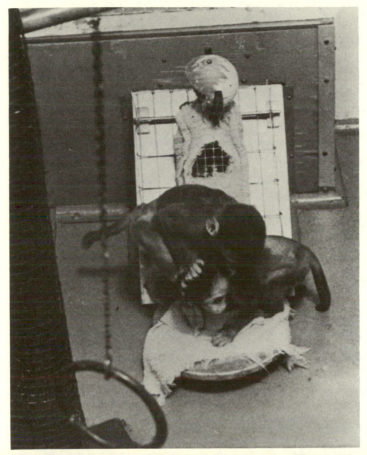

Figure 9-2 Infant play in presence of cloth surrogate.

very greatly reduced. Terry cloth slipcovers can be made easily and relatively cheaply, alleviating, if not eliminating, laundry problems. Thus, the simplified surrogate is a far more practical dummy mother than the original cloth surrogate.

SURROGATE VARIABLES

Lactation

Although the original surrogate papers (Harlow, 1958; Harlow & Zimmermann, 1959) were written as if activities associated with the breast, particularly nursing, were of no importance, this is doubtless incorrect.

Figure 9-3 Original surrogate and simplified surrogate.

There were no statistically significant differences in time spent by the babies on the lactating versus nonlactating cloth surrogates and on the lactating versus nonlactating wire surrogates, but the fact is that there were consistent preferences for both the cloth and the wire lactating surrogates and that these tendencies held for both the situations of time on surrogate and frequency of surrogate preference when the infant was exposed to a fear stimulus. Thus, if one can accept a statistically insignificant level of confidence, consistently obtained from four situations, one will properly conclude that nursing is a minor variable but one of more than measurable importance operating to bind the infant to the mother.

To demonstrate experimentally that activities associated with the

Figure 9-4 Infant cuddling simplified surrogate.

breasts were variables of significant importance, we built two sets of differentially colored surrogates, tan and light blue; and using a 2 × 2 Latin square design, we arranged a situation such that the surrogate of one color lactated and the other did not. As can be seen in Figure 9-5, the infants showed a consistent preference for the lactating surrogate when contact comfort was held constant. The importance of the lactational variable probably decreases with time. But at least we had established the hard fact that hope springs eternal in the human breast and even longer in the breast, undressed.

Facial Variables

In the original surrogates we created an ornamental face for the cloth surrogate and a simple dog face for the wire surrogate. I was working with few available infants and against time to prepare a presidential address for the 1958 American Psychological Association Convention. On the basis of sheer intuition, I was convinced that the ornamental cloth-surrogate face would become a stronger fear stimulus than the dog face when fear of the unfamiliar matured in the monkeys from about 70 to 110 days (Harlow & Zimmermann, 1959; Sackett, 1966). But since we wanted each surrogate to have an identifiable face and had few infants, we made no effort to balance faces by resorting to a feebleminded 2 × 2 Latin square design.

Subsequently, we have run two brief unpublished experiments. We tested four rhesus infants unfamiliar with surrogate faces at approximately 100 days of age and found that the ornamental face was a much stronger

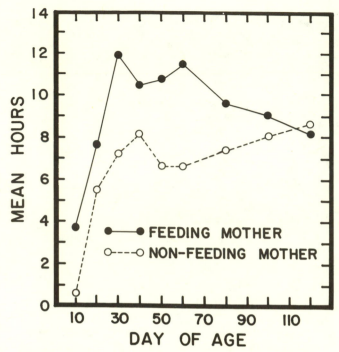

Figure 9-5   Infant preference for lactating surrogate.

fear stimulus than the dog face. Clearly, the early enormous preference for the cloth surrogate over the wire surrogate was not a function of the differential faces. Later, we raised two infants on cloth and two on wire surrogates, counterbalancing the ornamental and dog faces. Here, the kind of face was a nonexistent variable. To a baby all maternal faces are beautiful. A mother's face that will stop a clock will not stop an infant.

The first surrogate mother we constructed came a little late, or phrasing it another way, her baby came a little early. Possibly her baby was illegitimate. Certainly it was her first baby. In desperation we gave the mother a face that was nothing but a round wooden ball, which displayed no trace of shame. To the baby monkey this featureless face became beautiful, and she frequently caressed it with hands and legs, beginning around 30–40 days of age. By the time the baby had reached 90 days of age we had constructed an appropriate ornamental cloth-mother face, and we proudly mounted it on the surrogate's body. The baby took one look and screamed. She fled to the back of the cage and cringed in autistic-type posturing. After some days of terror the infant solved the medusa-mother problem in a most ingenious manner. She revolved the face 180° so that she always faced a bare round ball! Furthermore, we could rotate the maternal face dozens of times and within an hour or so the infant would turn it around 180°. Within a week the baby resolved her unfaceable problem once and for all. She lifted the maternal head from the body, rolled it into the corner, and abandoned it. No one can blame the baby. She had lived with and loved a faceless mother, but she could not love a two-faced mother.

These data imply that an infant visually responds to the earliest version of mother he encounters, that the mother he grows accustomed to is the mother he relies upon. Subsequent changes, especially changes introduced after maturation of the fear response, elicit this response with no holds barred. Comparisons of effects of babysitters on human infants might be made.

Body-Surface Variables

We have received many questions and complaints concerning the surrogate surfaces, wire and terry cloth, used in the original studies. This mountain of mail breaks down into two general categories: that wire is aversive, and that other substances would be equally effective if not better than terry cloth in eliciting a clinging response.

The answer to the first matter in question is provided by observation: Wire is not an aversive stimulus to neonatal monkeys, for they spend much time climbing on the sides of their hardware-cloth cages and exploring this substance orally and tactually. A few infants have required medical treatment from protractedly pressing their faces too hard and too long against the cage sides. Obviously, however, wire does not provide contact comfort.

In an attempt to quantify preference of various materials, an exploratory study[1] was performed in which each of four infants was presented with a choice between surrogates covered with terry cloth versus rayon, vinyl, or rough-grade sandpaper. As shown in Figure 9-6, the infants demonstrated a clear preference for the cloth surrogates, and no significant preference difference between the other body surfaces. An extension of this study is in progress in which an attempt is being made to further quantify and rank order the preference for these materials by giving infants equal exposure time to all four materials.

Motion Variables

In the original two papers, we pointed out that rocking motion, that is, proprioceptive stimulation, was a variable of more than statistical significance, particularly early in the infant's life, in binding the infant to the mother figure. We measured this by comparing the time the infants spent

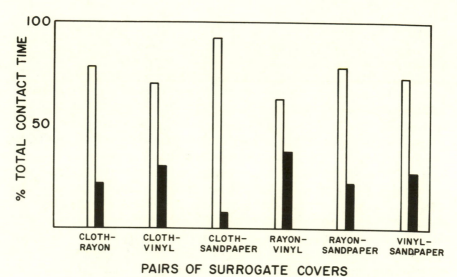

Figure 9-6   Effect of surface on surrogate contact.

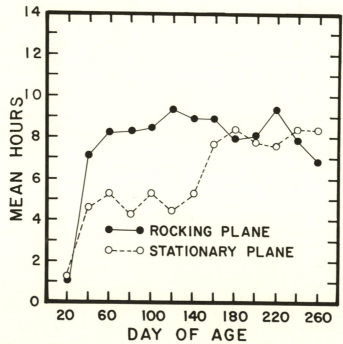

Figure 9-7   Infant contact to stationary and rocking planes.

on two identical planes, one rocking and one stationary (see Figure 9-7) and two identical cloth surrogates, one rocking and one stationary (see Figure 9-8).

Temperature Variables

To study another variable, temperature, we created some "hot mamma" surrogates. We did this by inserting heating coils in the maternal bodies that raised the external surrogate body surface about 10° F. In one experiment, we heated the surface of a wire surrogate and let four infant macaques choose between this heated mother and a room-temperature cloth mother. The neonatal monkeys clearly preferred the former. With increasing age this difference decreased, and at approximately 15 days the preference reversed. In a second experiment, we used two differently colored cloth surrogates and heated one and not the other. The infants preferred the hot surrogate, but frequently contacted the room-temperature surrogate for considerable periods of time.

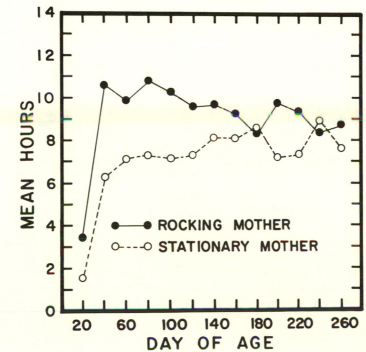

Figure 9-8   Infant contact to stationary and rocking surrogates.

More recently, a series of ingenious studies on the temperature variable has been conducted by Suomi, who created hot- and cold-running surrogates by adaptation of the simplified surrogate. These results are important not only for the information obtained concerning the temperature variable but also as an illustration of the successful experimental use of the simplified surrogate itself.

The surrogates used in these exploratory studies were modifications of the basic simplified surrogate, designed to get maximum personality out of the minimal mother. One of these surrogates was a "hot mamma," exuding warmth from a conventional heating pad wrapped around the surrogate frame and completely covered by a terry cloth sheath. The other surrogate was a cold female; beneath the terry cloth sheath was a hollow shell within which her life fluid—cold water—was continuously circulated. The two surrogates are illustrated in Figure 9-9, and to the untrained observer they look remarkably similar. But looks can be deceiving, especially with females, and we felt that in these similar-looking surrogates we had really simulated the two extremes of womanhood—one with a hot body and no head, and one with a cold shoulder and no heart. Actually, this is an exaggeration, for the surface temperature of the hot surrogate was only 7° F. above room temperature, while the surface temperature of the cold surrogate was only 5° F. below room temperature.

In a preliminary study, we raised one female infant from Day 15 on the warm surrogate for a period of four weeks. Like all good babies she quickly and completely became attached to her source of warmth, and during this time she exhibited not only a steadily increasing amount of surrogate contact but also began to use the surrogate as a base for exploration. At the end of this four-week period, we decided that our subject had become spoiled enough and so we replaced the warm surrogate with the cold version for one week. The infant noticed the switch within two minutes, responding by huddling in a corner and vocalizing piteously. Throughout the week of bitter maternal cold, the amount of surrogate contact fell drastically; in general, the infant avoided the surrogate in her feeding, exploratory, and sleeping behaviors. Feeling somewhat guilty, we switched surrogates once more for a week and were rewarded for our efforts by an almost immediate return to previously high levels of surrogate contact. Apparently, with heart-warming heat, our infant was capable of forgiveness, even at this tender age. At this point, we switched the two surrogates daily for a total of two weeks, but by this time the infant had accepted the inherent fickle nature of her mothers. On the days that her surrogate was warm, she clung tightly to its body, but on the days when the body was cold, she generally ignored it, thus providing an excellent example of naive behaviorism.

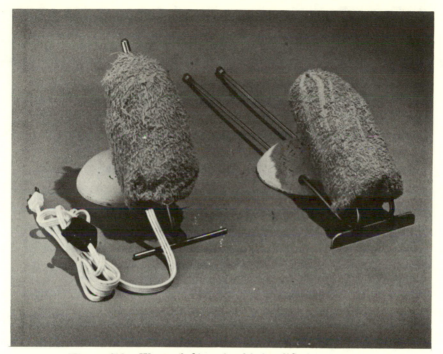

Figure 9-9 Warm (left) and cold simplified surrogates.

With a second infant we maintained this procedure but switched the surrogates, so that he spent four weeks with the cold surrogate, followed by one week with the warm, an additional week with the cold, and finally a two-week period in which the surrogates were switched daily. This infant became anything but attached to the cold surrogate during the initial four-week period, spending most of his time huddling in the corner of his cage and generally avoiding the surrogate in his exploratory behavior (see Figure 9-10). In succeeding weeks, even with the warm surrogate, he failed to approach the levels of contact exhibited by the other infant to the cold surrogate. Apparently, being raised with a cold mother had chilled him to mothers in general, even those beaming warmth and comfort.

Two months later both infants were exposed to a severe fear stimulus in the presence of a room-temperature simplified surrogate. The warm-mother infant responded to this stimulus by running to the surrogate and clinging for dear life. The cold-mother infant responded by running the other way and seeking security in a corner of the cage. We seriously doubt that this behavioral difference can be attributed to the sex difference of our subjects. Rather, this demonstration warmed our hopes and chilled our

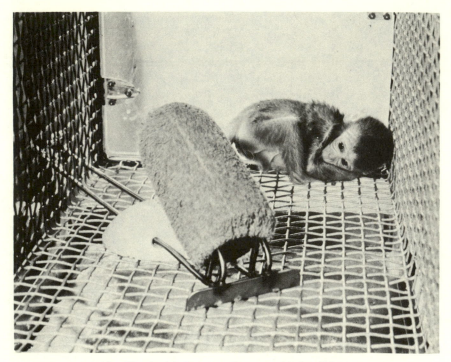

Figure 9-10   Typical infant reaction to cold simplified surrogate.

doubts that temperature may be a variable of importance. More specifically, it suggested that a simple linear model may not be adequate to describe the effects of temperature differences of surrogates on infant attachment. It is clear that warmth is a variable of major importance, particularly in the neonate, and we hazard the guess that elevated temperature is a variable of importance in the operation of all the affectional systems: maternal, mother-infant, possibly age-mate, heterosexual, and even paternal.

PROSPECTIVES

Recently we have simplified the surrogate mother further for studies in which its only function is that of providing early social support and security to infants. This supersimplified surrogate is merely a board 1½ inches in diameter and 10 inches long with a scooped-out, concave trough having a maximal depth of ¾ inch. The supersimplified surrogate has an angular deviation from the base of less than 15°, though this angle can be increased by the experimenter at will. The standard cover for this supremely simple surrogate mother is a size 11, cotton athletic sock, though covers of various qualities, rayon, vinyl (which we call the "linoleum lover"), and sandpaper, have been used for experimental purposes.

> Linoleum lover, with you I am through
> The course of smooth love never runs true.

This supersimplified mother is designed to attract and elicit clinging responses from the infant during the first 15 days of the infant's life.

We have designed, but not yet tested, a swinging mother that will dangle from a frame about 2 inches off the floor and have a convex, terry cloth or cotton body surface. Observations of real macaque neonates and mothers indicate that the infant, not the mother, is the primary attachment object even when the mother locomotes, and that this swinging mother may also elicit infantile clasp and impart infant security very early in life. There is nothing original in this day and age about a swinger becoming a mother, and the only new angle, if any, is a mother becoming a swinger.

Additional findings, such as the discovery that six-month social isolates will learn to cling to a heated simplified surrogate, and that the presence of a surrogate reduces clinging among infant-infant pairs, have substantiated use of the surrogate beyond experiments for its own sake. At present, the heated simplified surrogate is being utilized as a standard apparatus in studies as varied as reaction to fear, rehabilitation of social isolates, and development of play. To date, additional research utilizing the cold version of the simplified surrogate has been far more limited, possibly because unused water faucets are harder to obtain than empty electrical outlets. But this represents a methodological, not a theoretical problem, and doubtless solutions will soon be forthcoming.

It is obvious that the surrogate mother at this point is not merely a historical showpiece. Unlike the proverbial old soldier, it is far from fading away. Instead, as in the past, it continues to foster not only new infants but new ideas.

REFERENCES

Harlow, H. F. The nature of love. *American Psychologist*, 1958, *13*, 673–685.

Harlow, H. F., & Harlow, M. K. The affectional systems. In A. M. Schrier, H. F. Harlow, & F. Stollnitz (Eds.), *Behavior of nonhuman primates.* Vol. 2. New York: Academic Press, 1965.

Harlow, H. F., & Zimmermann, R. R. Affectional responses in the infant monkey. *Science*, 1959, *130*, 421–432.

Sackett, G. P. Monkeys reared in visual isolation with pictures as visual input: Evidence for an innate releasing mechanism. *Science*, 1966, *154*, 1468–1472.

NOTES

This research was supported by United States Public Health Service Grants MH-11894 and FR-0167 from the National Institutes of Health to the University of Wisconsin Primate Laboratory and Regional Primate Research Center, respectively.

[1] We wish to thank Carol Furchner, who conducted this experiment and the described experiment in progress.

10

The Nature of Complex, Unlearned Responses

Harry F. Harlow and Clara Mears

We are very fond of the title of our chapter "The Nature of Complex, Unlearned Responses," because it illustrates one of our violent aversions. Let us try to expiate sin.

Everyone knows that nature abhors a vacuum, but there is one thing that nature abhors more than a vacuum, and that is a logical *dichotomy*. Yet, when people speak and try to think, they automatically think in such dichotomies: hot and cold, day and night, black and white, men and women, God and the Devil, heaven and hell, and, above all, learned and innate or heredity and environment. Fortunately, the pituitary gland escaped. Everyone knows that all behaviors, both learned and unlearned, are localized in the pituitary!

In the title of our chapter, we unwittingly created two dichotomies in the two successive words, *complex* and *unlearned. Complex* infers its opposite, simple, and *unlearned* its opposite, learned.

After choosing our topic, we prepared to research its history at the University of Arizona libraries, but the University of Arizona apparently heard about our intentions and immediately closed the libraries for 45 days. Fortunately, the senior author had taught comparative psychology for 30 years, from 1930 to 1960, and knew most of the history of the theories of unlearned, innate, or unconditioned responses. We also were aware that for the past quarter of a century these terms had been religiously avoided as thoroughly as scientists can act religiously.

Harlow, H. F., & Mears, C. E. The nature of complex, unlearned responses. In M. Lewis & L. A. Rosenblum (Eds.), *The development of affect*. New York: Plenum Press, 1978, pp. 257–274.

The first facts and theories about unlearned responses existed under the rubric of *tropisms*, defined as differential responses to unequal stimulation of the two sides of bilaterally symmetrical animals. Tropisms were supposedly the unlearned responses made by organisms ranging from mealworms to man. Almost 100 years ago, biological scientists who were interested in converting the simplest behaviors to complicated mathematics studied tropisms. Even psychologists recognize that tropisms are not important forms of mammalian behaviors until they themselves fall victim to the mathematical compulsion to thus express the meaningless. Tropisms were obviously scientific data since they could be described in terms of mathematical formulas, whether the stimuli were external or internal or both. For example, stimulation of the right side of the slug *tenebrio* is followed by head turning to the left, and this act can be simplified and described by a mathematical equation.

Note, for example, the beauty of this mathematical formula (Crozier, 1929):

$$-\frac{ds}{dt} = k_1 S_0 - K_1 x - K_2 S_0 x^2 + K_2 x^3$$

Of course, the responses being measured, the genuflection of the anterior segments of mealworms, were maudlin and meaningless movements, but maudlin movements acquire mysterious meaning if they can be expressed mathematically. Furthermore, men have tropisms if they are blindfolded and left to ice skate on frozen vastnesses in northern Minnesota. These responses are called circus responses and they are a form of tropism. Human tropistic circus responses can also be produced by having blindfolded men ride motorcycles over the white sand dunes of the Sahara.

Even sighted men engage in circus responses if they are totally lost in forest vastness. These responses can also be elicited in dogs and other normal animals by removal of either the left or the right hemisphere of the brain. Remove the right hemisphere and the animal circles to the left, and remove the left hemisphere and the animal circles to the right (Loeb, 1918).

The origin of theories of complex, unlearned behaviors trace back to instinct theory. Instinct theory was described and observed in detail by Fabre (1918) with various species of wasps, especially the giant wasp, *Specius speciosus*. Fabre doubted that these responses could be explained in terms of evolution, and even though Eisele (1975) believes that they can be traced back to evolution, he doubts that this will ever be accomplished by any living human being.

The early psychologists, including James, McDougall, and Watson, properly accepted instincts as the basis for all of the present misconnotations.

J. B. Watson, one of the most ardent of the instinct theorists and also one of the most ingenious instinct investigators, defined instinct as "a series of concatenated movements unfolding serially to appropriate stimulation" (1914). With Lashley, Watson conducted two long and detailed researches on the noddy and sooty tern on the island of the Dry Tortugas. Watson, in his own comment, described his personal level of scholarship, saying "I do not read books. I write them." Lashley once told the senior author that had Watson and he not exhausted their supply of cigarettes and whiskey while on the Dry Tortugas, they would probably not only have remained on the island, but they also might have remained instinct theorists.

Being an instinctivist came instinctively to Watson because for almost 15 years of his academic life, he had no inkling of the real significance of Pavlovian conditioned responses. In his 1914 writings, he thought of conditioned responses as just one of four different techniques for measuring sensory limens in subhuman animals. By 1919, Watson had still not abandoned instinct theory, nor had he entirely escaped from any of the fabled 13. There were no detailed accounts of conditioning and no references to conditioning or conditioned reflexes in his 1919 book. He was still far more impressed by Bechterev than by Pavlov.

By 1919, Watson had discovered a new category of unlearned behavior, the emotions. At that time, he thought of emotions and instincts as being very similar, save for the fact that emotions were more related to visceral and instincts to skeletal muscle responses. Watson's emotions were not complex unlearned responses as instincts had been. He described his three new instinct allies, fear, anger, and love, as relatively discrete, limited, and almost reflexlike responses. Fear was produced by loud sounds and loss of support, rage by hampering of bodily movements, and love by stimulation of the erogenous zones. Watson and Raynor, for whom he did feel some emotion, not fear, succeeded in conditioning little Albert, an 11-month-old infant, to the fear of a rat. Neither Albert nor Watson was ever quite the same again.

As scientifically expressed, neither Watson's emotions nor his instincts could be clearly considered complex, unlearned responses. Complex instincts were espoused by William James, Thorndike, and McDougall. McDougall believed, in addition, that every instinct carried with it some emotional aura.

In the early 1920s, Watson began to bite the hand that fed him and to deny and deride instinct theory. This was the beginning of the great black-and-white era. What was innate could not be tainted by learning, and upon innate rudiments of behavior, monolithic superstructures of learning were amassed. Instinctivists, whose instincts covered the waterfront, were just as exclusive as were the extreme behaviorists. Black was black and white was white.

Three unconditioned response theorists dominated psychological thinking on unlearned responses and these three were Pavlov, Guthrie, and Skinner. Pavlov's contributions to complex unlearned behaviors were nil. Guthrie was more broadminded and finally realized that the unconditional stimuli underlying complex learning were more than simple reflexes. Guthrie was well ahead of his time and was the first psychologist to turn down an academic offer from Harvard, which has since become one of the three greatest universities in Massachusetts.

Any survey of the nature of complex unlearned responses would be more or less incomplete if one did not mention Fred Skinner. Although Skinner never mentions unconditioned stimuli, it is clear that he conceives of unlearned responses as any responses that any animal naturally makes, the theory of "doing what comes naturally." Thus, Skinner discovered that a peck of pigeons makes a bushel of research.

Actually, Skinner's research would have destroyed the Japanese navy had the American navy not already destroyed it. Skinner had the ingenious idea of having pigeons guide guided missiles by differential pecking. Skinner approached this problem a peck at a time while hiding his light under a bushel.

After World War II ended, the navy continued these researches, and after Harlow joined the army as a civilian in 1949–1950, they generously offered to give him all of the million dollars worth of equipment as well as the pigeons and to ship everything out to the University of Wisconsin. He had no interest in keeping the navy shipshape and therefore declined the offer. Besides, Harlow had decided that Skinner's research on guided missiles was misguided. Fortunately, Skinner subsequently went farther and with greater accuracy.

When Skinner discovered some animals that didn't do naturally what he wanted them to do, he conveniently discovered the technique of "shaping," which took care of his problem. The fact that shaping by other names was just as sweet did not alter the fact that it had been previously discovered by a series of psychologists during the last half-century. It was even independently discovered by Tinbergen, whose wife used it as a therapeutic technique not yet adopted by psychiatrists. Guthrie and Horton (1946) did an original and brilliant experimental study incorporating the shaping principle as early as 1946. They created a puzzle box whose door opening was activated by a bar hung from the ceiling. When the cat in the box brushed any part of its body against the bar, the door obligingly opened. Guthrie and Horton traced the progress of the cats, watching the aimless characteristic of the behavior gradually disappear. Eventually, the cat purposefully and immediately approached and activated the bar.

In Skinner's recently evolved theories relating to unlearned behavior, one of his categories is that of "precise, fixed, but persistent" reflex-type behavior. These are not the Pavlovian acute and transient unconditioned responses. They are not only precise and repetitive but, what is more important, they are persistent behaviors. The classic example is pigeon pecking, which has a long and honorable history. Pigeons will persistently peck at any bright and precise object, and if all bright and precise objects are removed, the pigeons will persistently peck anyway. They apparently realize that a single peck does not provide a peck of pickled peppers. Just as the pigeon's peck paid off, so did Skinner's persistent research.

The other and more important type of Skinnerian unconditioned responses is that designed to serve an experimenter's predestined destiny. The classic example is lever pressing. Just as Archimedes planned to move the world with a lever, so did Skinner plan to move psychology. Since rats and some very stupid primates do not automatically make *persistent* lever-pressing responses, Skinner used his technique of shaping according to the naval doctrine of "shape up or ship out."

Although conditioning became the learning byword for the neobehaviorists of the 1950s and 1960s, their learning apparatus changed from the unconditioned response to maze manipulations. The original maze was the Hampton Court maze, but since rats did not shape readily to the HC maze, new and simpler mazes came into use, particularly the multiple T mazes and Y mazes (Hull, 1952). Having started, however, the shaping process ran its inevitable course, and the multiple T and Y mazes shrank down to single T and single Y units. Eventually, these single T and Y units were simplified into straight-alley mazes, which enabled Logan to measure incentives (Logan, 1960). Previously, Tolman and Miles learned to "shape" elevated maze learning by running rats on straight-alley mazes, and most maze runners ran rats on a straight-alley maze to shape subsequent multiple blind-alley maze performance.

"It matters not how straight the gate." Both Hull and Spence became so enchanted with their "shaping" straight-alley techniques that they subsequently abandoned attempts to study the real learning of mazes by rats. Not only were the rats shaped up, but so were the experimenters. This was beautifully illustrated by the demise of maze learning. Psychologists shaped their animals by running them down straight alleys for shaping purposes. Eventually, psychologists found that running the animals down straight alleys enabled them to measure such variables as speed of running from one end of the straight alley to the other and also equally unimportant *complicated* motivational variables such as food and water deprivation. However, there was a real advantage and probably a real tragedy produced by these shaping procedures. Hull and Spence made the unfortunate discovery that the variables underlying meaningless straight-alley learning could be reduced, and we really mean reduced, to mathematical formulas (Spence, 1956):

$$_sH_R = ICO\ (1-e^{-kw})\,e^{-jT'}(1-lc^{-lN})$$

A description of one weekly colloquium of the Harvard psychology department in a biographical sketch of von Bekesy, a Nobel Prize winner, aptly sums up the importance of reducing pseudolearning to mathematical formulas. The guest colloquium speaker was desperately dull in discussing his mathematical theory of behavior. At the conclusion of his lay lecture, the audience responded at equally great length and with equally fatuous comments.

> When at long last it was all over, Bekesy led me directly to the blackboard in his office, picked up a piece of chalk and said, 'This is the most important but least known equation in all of the social sciences. Always remember it, for, as you have just seen, it completely describes a great deal of human behavior.' And then—summing up the whole afternoon neatly—he wrote: $0 + 0 = 0$. (Ratliff, 1976)

While giving due credit to the futile and foolish theories of the famous behavior theorists, we must accept the fact that none of these men even approached a study of the mechanisms underlying complex unlearned behaviors. By *complex behaviors,* we mean such behaviors as play, aggression, love in its many-faceted forms, language, and thinking.

There are three criteria useful in the determination of complex, unlearned responses:

1. *In orderly fashion, they follow developmental maturation stages.* Complex unlearned behavior may start early or late, but the completion of maturation is always relatively late. If you study the developmental stages and sequences, it will be obvious that none of them could possibly have escaped the taint and tar brush of limited or even unlimited learning. Learning is inescapable at all times after the very start of complex unlearned behaviors.

2. *They are complex in nature, based as they are upon multiple variables.* Complex unlearned behaviors are not conglomerates of many innate elements, but there will be more than one variable, since primate behavior is by nature not simple enough to explain by only one factor. No matter how many or how few the unlearned variables, there may be countless learned ways of expressing these unlearned behaviors.

3. *Complex, unlearned behaviors are extremely persistent over long periods of time or even through life itself.* Of complex unlearned behaviors, the love systems and especially the infant-mother relationships most readily illustrate these three criteria, probably because the surrogate mother experiments lent themselves to extensive, definitive findings. The love of the

infant for the mother and the maternal love for the infant each pass through developmental stages based primarily upon the gradual maturation of the child, both in mastering its physical environment and in understanding its cultural environment. Research with the surrogate mother established the complexity of these loves based on the multiple variables of contact comfort, warmth, rocking motion, and nursing (Harlow, 1958). Numerous recent studies have found that mothers respond lovingly in their own fashion to these same variables and that, in addition, communication plays an important part in the loves of both. Communication adds to the complexity of the maternal-infant affectional system, based as it also is on multiple variables that include eye contact, smiling, touch, and gesture, plus varied auditory stimulation even before spoken language becomes added to the list. Research on these variables formed the bases for many of the presentations in the present symposium.

Maternal and infant love have been found to be very persistent in the face of many odds, including the commercialism of Mother's Day. Oddly enough, infant love in many cases proves to be even more persistent than the long belabored maternal love. It persists even when the infant is completely ignored or actually battered by the abnormal motherless mother (Harlow, Harlow, Dodsworth, & Arling, 1966).

Peer love and heterosexual love form a progression in the maturation of the first four of the love systems. The basic mechanism of peer love is social play, though peer bonds may form even before social play burgeons (Harlow & Harlow, 1969). Peer love depends also upon adequate, antecedent maternal affection. To this requirement heterosexual love adds adequate, antecedent peer relations. This trilogy is bound together by the contact comfort provided originally by the mother. The appreciation and acceptance of bodily contact through maternal love bonds prepares the young for enjoyment of the physical contact attendant upon peer play. Peer play is the proving ground for social and sexual roles that encompass preparation for heterosexual love. Without pleasant prior peer play and affection, the blushing bride or nonblushing unmarried is likely to insist upon physical privacy, which has drawbacks in promoting happy, heterosexual hugs.

The persistence of peer love is obvious from the long-lived friendships between peers of the same or opposite sexes. These friendships often outlast one, two, or even three heterosexual loves. Whether or not one accepts the persistence of heterosexual love depends entirely upon whether or not one demands the legalization of same.

There is one love, that of the forgotten man, the father, which deserves individual attention because most paternal behavior has been presumed to be largely learned. The father has been quietly accumulating attention in his own experimental right. Of course, the father has for decades been recognized for his protection of family and friends, especially of feral family and friends. The more successfully the father protects, the more likely he is to have successors, and this is one good argument for the unlearned nature of paternal protective behavior. It seems, however, that many human fathers feel more than just protective affection for their offspring, as Lamb (1975) has been proving first while at Yale and now at Wisconsin. Fathers may even play with their young ones more frequently and in a different fatherly fashion than does the ever-loving mother.

Psychological theories concerning the complex responses of many other behaviors, particularly those of play, aggression, and language, have remained troubled and muddled. Since evidence is being compiled from two primate species, and the macaque does not possess verbal apparatus anatomically adequate for spoken language, we are in this paper considering just the first two of these behaviors, play and aggression.

Just as the love of the infant for the mother was for years liquefied in maternal libations, so was play, the delight of childhood, engulfed in obscurity along with its prerequisite, childhood. Accurate records of the developmental childhood years were nonexistent during the Middle Ages, but we do know that during the 18th and 19th centuries the Industrial Revolution forced countless children, as well as their parents, into not very gainful employment. Even before the height of the industrial developments, England began to feel the force of the Puritan religious movement, which then moved, along with the Puritans, to the American continent. The Puritan fathers, who slept sanctimoniously in their straight and narrow beds, gave religious sanction to the work ethic and discouraged play along with pleasure. The development of play and games went into not a recess but a long recession.

In the United States, the first child labor laws, with New York State taking the lead, were passed at the beginning of the 20th century, but for many more years, the theories of play reflected the need to justify the very existence of childhood and play. There is still some acceptance of Groos' (1898) theory that play provides exercise for direct training for adulthood. There is even more discussion of the psychoanalytic concept of play as a receptacle for either disguising or acting out emotional conflicts. Play for pleasure and for play's sake have been tacitly recognized in studies of game preferences, but the pith of play has remained a mystery.

Harlow became interested in social play as the underlying mechanism in peer love and the proving ground for social and sexual roles. In his search for an antecedent to social play, he postulated that curiosity and exploration might form the unlearned basis but was never experimentally convinced. This theory is so obviously wrong and so hopelessly inept that it gained ready acceptance from a number of psychologists. However, as Hutt (1966) pointed out, there may have been chaos added to confusion because two different types of exploration have been considered as one.

Mears had for a number of years been interested in the role of physical activity in maintaining positive personal adjustment. She had also noted that few studies of play in young children had been conducted outdoors where the child has freedom physically and permission parentally to run and to jump, to climb and to swing, with pervasive pleasure. The element of pleasure in animal play has long been recognized and described in human play by Blurton-Jones (1967) in the rough-and-tumble play of nursery-school children.

Mears (see Mears & Harlow, 1975) proposed that exploration of one type, comparable to the "specific" form of Hutt, was connected with play but just as much with many other behaviors, since it was responsible for the initiation of new behaviors. She also postulated, however, that the fundamental play form, primary and basic to social play, was a group of behaviors termed *self-motion play* or *peragration,* the motion of a body through space. We suspect that the term *peragration* was originally used to refer to the motion of heavenly bodies through heavenly space, but as many bodies have been referred to as heavenly, prosaic license has been exercised. Rosenblum (1961), in his categories of feedback object play and activity play among rhesus monkeys, presented the picture most nearly resembling self-motion play but with some fundamental differences (Mears, 1978).

Mears and Harlow (1975) conducted a three-month developmental study of the play of eight rhesus macaques from the average ages of 90 to 180 days. All behaviors were recorded with the exception of basic intake and output of food and drink. Five categories of peragration were specifically investigated, and three of these proved to be of significance. These were self-motion play, individual or nonsocial, both with and without the use of apparatus. Social self-motion play developed significantly only when apparatus was involved. Peragration is best illustrated by the activities of swinging, rocking, water or snow skiing, leaping, running, and jumping. A total list of appropriate behaviors would be extensive, but all would be dependent upon the motion of the whole body.

Self-motion play was found to exist as an entity separate from ordinary locomotion and from visual and tactile exploration, both of which started at different levels of frequency than peragration and then maintained an almost level plateau of frequency, whereas self-motion play spiraled upward at an amazingly significant rate to a level of frequency more than six times as great.

Peragration could be either a social or an individual behavior, but it developed earlier and to a greater extent as a solitary, nonsocial activity, a play form basic and primary in the maturational hierarchy. Both with and without the use of extensive motion apparatus in the playroom, self-motion individual play held significant sway, whereas social play required apparatus to raise the developmental rate to a significant level.

The pervasive and powerful persistence of self-motion play in human life is evidenced by the progressive stages of rocking behavior from rocking in mother's arms, in the cradle, and on the rocking horse to the merry-go-round, rock and roll, and the rocking chair with the approaching glimpse of the Rock of Ages.

Experimentally we also had confirmation of the persistence of peragration (Mears, 1978). Two matched groups of rhesus were separated after the developmental study, four to remain in the original equipped playroom with ladders, platforms of different heights, swinging rings, bars, and revolving apparatus to encourage peragration. The other four shared a playroom with all of the motion equipment removed except for the long bar with the swinging rings. This bar was moved to within 5 cm of the ceiling, which was approximately 260 cm above the floor. The chains of the swinging rings were wound tight around the bar, immobilizing the rings.

During the 90 days of this experiment, not only the persistence but the extent of the preference for self-motion play was evident. Peragration without the use of any apparatus, leaping and jumping in the air, running, somersaulting, and tumbling significantly increased in the deprived playroom, both in individual and in social play. This increase was significant both in comparison with their own prior play and with the play of the four matched rhesus still playing in the original playroom. These two groups had shown no significant difference in performance on any self-motion behaviors before, during, or at the end of the original developmental experiment.

An unexpected jackpot was won when one of the infant male monkeys in the deprived playroom literally reached motivational heights, as illustrated in the series of Figures 10-1–10-6. For days and weeks, he sat in the pictorially documented pose, on his surrogate, looking longingly at the bar and rings no longer accessible by way of platforms, ladders, and leaps as shown in Figure 10-1. He also gazed at a 2-cm projection, two-thirds of the distance up the wall, on which one end of the long bar had rested. This tiny knob was some 160 cm up the sidewall and only 1 cm wide. Day after day, the infant made leaps at the wall, going higher and higher, until he finally caught hold of the little knob (Figures 10-2 and 10-3). From there on, he climbed the walls, both sideways and up, around the corner, most of the time with his back to the wall (see Figures 10-4 and 10-5). First, his finger was on the bar, then his feet and his body above it, as shown in Figure 10-6. He had won and sat scrunched against the ceiling but lord of all he surveyed. This act he repeated many times during the remaining

Figure 10-1   Aiming high.

weeks, in spite of the fact that the bar and the rings did not have the same end result as before. The mastery mechanism that had been suggestively evident during the play of the eight infants now received an experimental stamp of approval.

As a bonus, the liveliest female of the group proceeded to follow the master in a slow repeat performance. If two could look smug with their backs tight to a ceiling, these two did. The performance reminded an onlooker of the face of a human child taking, with every effort of every muscle of her body, the first few tottering but exhilarating steps. The monkeys gave the testers an experimentally corroborated vision of early self-actualization in their physical mastery of the environment.

Figure 10-2   Practice leap.

Knowing the appeal and the augmentation of apparatus, as well as the persistence of self-motion play, we decided to test further the relationship between individual and social peragration. In the very same playroom that had been the scene of lively play, we put each monkey, one hour at a time, once a week, all alone, to test its prowess with the lovely apparatus at its disposal. Did they take advantage of their opportunities? Not at all. They acted like miserable urchins, just sat all by themselves and screeched, then just moped and screeched some more. The rhesus would just as soon and even sooner play all alone when all of the fine, furry friends were around, but would it play without them around? No. There was a possibility that they were suffering from the separation syndrome, but each rhesus had its surrogate present when alone in the playroom and also had spent the major part of most days alone in the quadrant of the quad cage for over a year. Not being loris or lemur, they had not been able to see the other members of the quadrant at night either.

The intensity of the behavior when they were placed alone in the playroom would suggest that the monkeys were very much aware of the presence of their peers even when not playing with them, and although

Figure 10-3   Halfway house.

they did not regularly choose to play with them, they were not about to play without them. Through self-motion play, these primates learned through the primarily individual patterns of peragration to accommodate themselves to the physical environment and to discover their relation to it. At the same time, the presence of others was not an extraneous fact. The young animal was becoming agreeably accustomed to the presence of conspecifics even before social play became prevalent, and we name this phenomenon *social support*. Those individuals, both monkey and human, who gain self-confidence in the physical environment have made vital progress toward social role readiness. The individual without this background is often faced with the simultaneous demands and challenges of both the physical and the social environments, with resultant confusion and feelings of inadequacy.

The development of lively self-motion play well illustrates the course of development of complex, unlearned behaviors and the increasing complexity of these behaviors through both learning and maturation. Early peragration permits not only exploration of the different facets of the environment but, primarily and most potently, the understanding of one's own body in relation to the many elements of air, water, and land, the

Figure 10-4   Climbing the walls.

capabilities and limitations of oneself. Because the individual gains confidence in learning what the body can and cannot accomplish in space, with proper experience and reinforcement, as the physical capabilities mature, pleasure in accomplishment becomes not only possible but probable and more prevalent.

The only key to the analysis of these complex responses is that of tracing them developmentally, both ontogenetically and phylogenetically. One can understand the maturational meaning of one kind or class of involved behaviors only if one also knows the maturational meaning of different but related behavior.

Unfortunately, adequate data on the ontogenetic development of affection, aggression, and play exist on only two animal species: man and macaque monkeys. However, these two reinforce each other because of the striking similarity in the order of maturational development of many complex behaviors of both. Of course, one must allow for the fact that the monkey at birth has a human anatomical age of 1 year as measured by carpal bone development, and the macaque monkey matures four to five times as fast as the human child on such diverse measures as intelligence and sexual maturity.

Figure 10-5   Goal gradient.

Take, for example, the maturation of aggression. The control of aggression is basically dependent on the fact that the primary love or affectional systems mature before aggression rears or raises its ugly head. Maternal love and infant-mother love in the macaque monkey are present at parturition or very shortly after parturition. Even agemate affection is firmly founded at 6 months of age. Contrariwise, aggression toward external objects is not firmly established until the second year of life in normal, socially raised monkeys. Self-aggression does not mature until age 4. Love is an early-maturing behavior and aggression a late-maturing behavior.

When love does not have a chance to operate with its protective power—for example, in monkeys raised in social isolation—aggression may, under the circumstances, take advantage of the opportunity presented and fill the void. This fact was dramatically illustrated in the case of rhesus infants raised in complete social isolation for six months, without either maternal or peer affection. Mitchell (Harlow, Dodsworth, & Harlow, 1965) found that these isolates, when tested at 2–3½ years of age, displayed aggression even to 1-year-old infants, as no self-respecting socially raised rhesus would.

Figure 10-6 Lord of all.

Failure to recognize the importance of the relative times of the maturation of aggression and love and the appearance of the protective mechanisms resulting from antecedent love led Lorenz (1966) to create his almost remarkably inadequate theory of aggression, with concomitant recommendations of ineffective techniques of aggression control. Lorenz recognized the great difference between predation (aggression against members of other species) and conspecific aggression between members of the same species. He believed that intraspecific aggression was minimized by "appeasement gestures or ritual submission," but the thought never crossed his mind to search for the developmental variables, the very mechanism that in reality held introspecies aggression to a minimum. One cannot research the mother-infant relationships of the macaque without seeing the mother teach the baby, through her own behavior, the use of threat gestures toward the stranger as opposed to the friendly behavior to conspecific members of the nuclear family.

Berkowitz (1962) has successfully challenged Lorenz's hydraulic drive theory, which puts a lot of water behind the dam without knowing from whence the damn water came. He has also refuted the effectiveness of releasing the energy of aggression through general release of energy as a catharsis. Lorenz (1966) suggested release through channelized sports and educated laughter. If aggression is to have a sporting chance of being controlled, it should not be laughed away. Lorenz's theory of aggression and its control beautifully illustrates the futility of theories of either learned or unlearned complex behavior without adequate ontogenetic or phylogenetic information. In a happy burst of delayed insight, Lorenz stated in the final paragraph of his famous book. *On Aggression,* that "the bond of personal love and friendship was the epochmaking invention...[enabling] two or more members of an aggressive species to live peacefully together and to work for a common end." Too little and too late.

Knowledge of the maturation of the primary and basic forms of self-motion play show how early and in what fashion peer love may gain ascendancy. The way is paved for social play and the development of positive and pleasant social relationships. When added to the positive affect of effective maternal love, aggression does not have a chance among conspecifics.

In early study of innate behaviors, investigators insisted that unlearned behavior must be simple to be free of learning. This inexorable and inevitable demand for simplicity caused decades of confusion even though the study of single-alley mazes did reduce the need for complex thinking.

The self-defeating theories of all-black unlearned and all-white learned behaviors have gradually been replaced, not by a dull gray merging of the two theories but by a realistic theory of interaction between the unlearned and the learned, a theory with which complex unlearned responses come easily to terms. Such behaviors were long thought to be inaccessible to experimentation, but the wealth of scientific research on the early years of primate infancy, both human and subhuman, vitiates this negative stance.

REFERENCES

Berkowitz, L. *Aggression.* New York: McGraw-Hill, 1962.

Blurton-Jones, N. G. In D. Morris (Ed.), *Primate ethology.* Chicago: Aldine, 1967, pp. 347–368.

Crozier, W. J. The study of living organisms. In C. Murchison, (Ed.), *The foundations of experimental psychology.,* London: Oxford University Press, 1929, Chapter 2.

Eisele, L. *All the strange hours: The excavation of a life.* New York: Scribner's, 1975.

Fabre, J. H. *The wonders of instinct.* London: T. Fisher University, 1918.

Groos, K. *The play of animals: Play and instinct.* New York: Appleton, 1898.

Guthrie, E. R., & Horton, R. *Cats in a puzzle box.* New York: Rinehart, 1946.

Harlow, H. F. The nature of love. *American Psychologist,* 1958, *13,* 673–685.

Harlow, H., Dodsworth, R., & Harlow, M. Total isolation in monkeys. *Proceedings of the National Academy of Science,* 1965, *54*(1), 90–97.

Harlow, H. F., & Harlow, M. K. The affectional systems. In A. M. Schrier, H. F. Harlow, & F. Stollnitz (Eds.), *Behavior of non-human primates* (Vols. 1 and 2), New York: Academic Press, 1965, 287–334.

Harlow, H. F., & Harlow, M. K. Age mate or peer affectional system. In P. S. Lehrman, R. A. Hinde, & E. Shaw (Eds.), *Advances in the study of behavior* (Vol. 2). New York: Academic Press, 1969.

Harlow, H. F., Harlow, M. K., Dodsworth, R. S., & Arling, G. L. Maternal behavior of rhesus monkeys deprived of mothering and peer associations in infancy. *Proceedings of the American Philosophical Society,* 1966, *40*, 58–66.

Hull, C. L. *A behavior system.* New Haven: Yale University Press, 1952.

Hutt, C. Exploration and play in children. *Symposium Zoological Society London,* 1966, *18*, 61–81.

James, W. *The principles of psychology,* New York: Holt, 1890.

Lamb, M. E. Fathers: Forgotten contributors to child development. *Human Development,* 1975, *18*, 245–265.

Loeb, J. *Forced movements, tropisms, and animal conduct.* Philadelphia: Lippincott, 1918.

Logan, F. *Incentive.* New Haven: Yale University Press, 1960.

Lorenz, K. *On aggression.* New York: Harcourt Brace & World, 1966.

McDougald, W. *Introduction to social psychology.* London: Methuen, 1908.

Mears, C. E., & Harlow, H. F. Play: Early & Eternal, *Proceedings National Academy Sciences,* May 1975, *72*(5), 1878–1882.

Mears, C. Play and development of cosmic confidence. *Developmental Psychology,* July 1978, *14*(4), 371–378.

Miles, W. R. The narrow path elevated maze for studying rats. *Proceedings Society Experimental Biology and Medicine,* 1927, *24*, 454–456.

Pavlov, I. *Conditioned responses: An investigation of the physiological activity of the cerebral cortex.* London: Oxford University Press, 1927.

Ratliff, F., & Von Bekesy, G. *Bibliographic memoirs* (Vol. 48). Washington, D.C.: National Academy of Sciences, 1976.

Rosenblum, L. Unpublished doctoral thesis. University of Wisconsin, 1961.

Spence, K. W. *Behavior theory and conditioning.* New Haven: Yale University Press, 1956.

Watson, J. B. *Behavior: An introduction to comparative psychology,* New York: Holt, 1914.

Watson, J. B. *Psychology from the standpoint of a behaviorist.* Philadelphia: Lippincott Co., 1919.

Watson, J. B. *Behaviorism.* New York: Norton, 1924.

PART FOUR
AFFECTIONAL STRESS

11

The Maternal Affectional System of Rhesus Monkeys

Harry F. Harlow, Margaret K. Harlow, and Ernst W. Hansen

As adequate data accumulate from field studies and laboratory investigations, it becomes increasingly apparent that the affectional ties which exist among members of subhuman primate social groups play extremely important roles as social organizational forces. Indeed, these are doubtless the primary forces that hold monkeys or apes together as a social group and give the various subgroups their proper place and status.

In a monkey society individuals and the group make mutual contributions, real or potential. Separated from associates, the individual's chance of survival is precarious and its opportunity for genetic contribution is nonexistent. The orderly functioning of social organizations enables individual monkeys to meet basic needs for food, water, sleep, and sex with maximal efficiency. These physical needs, however, are only one set of forces determining monkey social organization. In fact, it is more than likely that the resolution of biological needs is largely a result, not a cause, of social organization. The basic mechanisms for primate social structuring are the complex affectional relationships among the members of the societies, and the continuance of these societies is dependent more upon love than lust, more upon happiness than hunger.

Because of the importance of the affectional systems to social structure and to individual animals, each affectional system must be studied in

Harlow, H. F., Harlow, M. K., & Hansen, E. W. The maternal affectional system of rhesus monkeys. In H. L. Rheingold (Ed.), *Maternal Behavior in Mammals.* New York: Wiley, 1963, pp. 254–281, copyright © 1963. Reprinted by permission of John Wiley and Sons.

detail. Each system is expressed through multiple behavior patterns, each system develops in a series of orderly stages, and each possesses underlying variables and mechanisms that differ considerably in nature, number, and importance.

There are at least five affectional systems: (1) the affection of the infant for the mother—the infant-mother affectional system; (2) the affectional relationships between infants or between juveniles—the infant-infant or peer affectional system; (3) the affectional relationship between adolescent and adult males and females—the heterosexual affectional system; (4) the affection of the mother for her infant—the mother-infant affectional system; and (5) the affection of adult males for infants and juveniles—the father-infant affectional system.

In this chapter we are concerned with the analysis of a single affectional system in rhesus monkeys, the maternal affectional system, but because the physical and psychological bonds between mother and infant are so intimate, it is not possible to explore or describe mother-infant affection independently of the responses of the infant to the mother. Thus we cannot limit ourselves to a description of how maternal behaviors affect infants; we must also discuss how infant behaviors affect the expression of maternal behavior.

The analysis here of the monkey mother's affectional system has been made by a series of observations and experiments, some complete and some in progress, conducted within the laboratory. A large part of our basic information concerning the development of the maternal affectional system has been obtained in a situation which we call the playpen, illustrated in Figure 11-1. Essentially the playpen apparatus consists of a series of four living cages and a play area subdivided into four individual play cells, each of which abuts a large living cage. A 3.5-inch × 5.5-inch opening cut into the wall of each living cage and the adjoining play cell allows free passage of the infant while effectively restricting the mother to the living cage. The apparatus is constructed of stainless-steel wire mesh, which permits full view of the animals and thereby facilitates continuous, detailed observations. Each playpen unit is housed in an individual room approximately 14 feet square with a one-way vision screen in the corridor wall. Thus supplementary observations can be made from the corridor without alerting the animals, although the primary observations have been made inside the test room.

Three different groups of four babies and their mothers were intensively studied in the playpen situation. Two groups were composed of four multiparous monkey mothers and their infants, taken from our breeding colony, and the third, of four infants living with inanimate cloth surrogate mothers (Harlow, 1958). All mothers and infants were placed in the living cages within 24 hours of the infant's birth. The surrogate

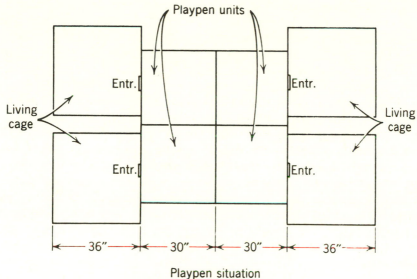

Playpen situation

Figure 11-1 Playpen situation.

mothers had round or square faces and cloth bodies of different colors so that the human observer, and presumably the monkey infants, could differentiate the individual cloth surrogates as easily as they could the real monkey mothers. The four infants in mother-group 1 were males with an age spread of 27 days; it was necessary to take the animals as they came, and the monkey mothers gave birth to infants without regard to experimental design. The sex split for the infants in both mother-group 2 and surrogate-group 1, however, was two males and two females each. The role of mother-group 2 was primarily to provide supplementary information about the sex variable after 9½ months of age, when the animals became available following participation in an infant-separation study reported by Seay, Hansen, and Harlow (1962). Although they had lived in a playpen situation from birth, their early treatment differed somewhat from that of the other two groups (for details, see Seay, et al., 1962, or Hansen, 1962).

During days 16 to 180 the partitions between pairs of play cells were removed for two 1-hour sessions a day, 5 days a week, permitting the babies to interact with one another and with either or both mothers. Cage positions were shifted weekly on a predetermined schedule so that each infant interacted with every other infant an equal number of weeks. Observations were made of both mother and infant behaviors.

Two observers scored the behaviors exhibited during separate 30-minute test sessions, and time of day and order of testing were balanced for all subjects. Subsequently, throughout the second half-year of the infants' lives, the monkeys were allowed to interact 1 hour a day in pairs and 40 minutes a day as a group of four.

The mother and the infant behaviors in the two-animal interaction sessions were measured in terms of the occurrence, within 15-second intervals, of behaviors included in an inventory of 96 items. This was accomplished by using a system of symbols to record sequential behaviors. There were discrete master symbols for each of 13 major behavior categories: play, sex, mother contact, cradling, maternal protection, maternal punishing, grooming, breast contact, clasping, threatening, exploration-manipulation, disturbance, and vocalization. Specific behaviors within these categories were indicated by variations either within the master symbol or appended to it. There were also special symbols for 12 discrete items of behavior: approach, withdrawal, food-stealing, lip-smacking, signals to return, fear, grimacing, nonspecific contact, facilitation, self-mouthing, scratching, yawning, and convulsive jerking. A description of the major behavioral categories which provided the data utilized herein is reported elsewhere (Hansen, 1962, Appendix I). The reliability for most of the major behaviors was above .90 as determined by the product-moment correlations of the daily scores of two individual observers scoring the same animal during 20 half-hour sessions.

Because of the complexity of behaviors exhibited in the four-animal interactions, observation was restricted to 24 behaviors (Hansen, 1962). The reliability for these measures was slightly depressed but, with few exceptions, above .85.

No attempt is made to present data here on all the recorded items. In fact, the data recorded for many of these behaviors were so scanty as to be of only limited or specialized usefulness (for further details see Hansen, 1962).

THE STAGES OF MATERNAL BEHAVIOR

The maternal affectional system, like the other affectional systems, can be described more adequately in terms of sequential stages. The three principal maternal stages are those of attachment and protection, ambivalence, and separation or rejection. The stage of attachment and protection is characterized by maternal responses which are almost totally positive, including cradling, nursing, grooming, restraining when the infant attempts to leave, and retrieving when the infant does escape. The stage of ambivalence includes both positive and negative responses, which eventually become almost equally in frequency. Negative responses include mouthing or biting, cuffing or slapping, clasp-pulling the fur, and rejecting the infant's attempts to attain or maintain physical contact. The stage of separation, as the name implies, results in the termination of physical contact between mother and infant.

The various stages in the development of the maternal affectional system, and this is true for all the affectional systems, do not appear suddenly in terms of hours or days and are not sharply and discretely defined. On the contrary, they are characterized by extensive temporal overlapping. Thus the stage of ambivalence contains many components of the previous stage, and special events, such as any threat or danger, may cause the infant to seek its mother's protection, and may reestablish the mother as a totally affectionate and protective monkey for long periods of time.

On the other hand, separative mechanisms are also clearly developing throughout this stage both on the part of the mother and the infant until separation is complete. In the wild the mother may actively protect the infant in emergencies even after physical separation, suggesting a temporal lag between nearly complete physical separation and nearly complete psychological separation, although it is likely that the specificity of protective behaviors decreases during this interval.

The temporal delineation of all the stages depends on the operation of such multiple variables as the nature of the physical and social environment; the life history of the animal; previous pregnancies and experience with infants; endocrinological factors; and even the behavioral criteria chosen or the time of day that the data are collected.

It should be noted that the maternal affectional system differs from most of the other affectional systems in that it is cyclical, recurring with full intensity with the advent and maturing of each new baby. It is probable that maternal affectional responding is never completely absent in the rhesus female, particularly after the birth of her first baby. However, the variables underlying the maternal affectional system differentially affect the attitude and behavior of females and provide for considerable individuality in maternal responsiveness.

The Stage of Maternal Attachment and Protection

During the stage of maternal attachment and protection, the mother monkey spends a great deal of time holding the baby close to the ventral surface of her body or cradling it loosely in her arms and legs, but still providing it with active contactual support. The developmental course of intimate infant-mother bodily contact is illustrated in Figure 11-2 in terms of ventral contacts. It will be noted that the frequency of these responses, although initially high, progressively decreased after the first month and became relatively infrequent by the third month. Undoubtedly this resulted

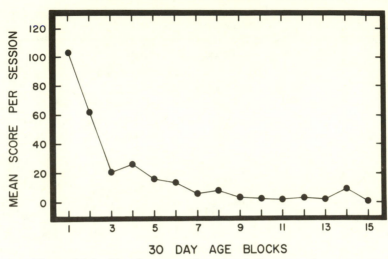

Figure 11-2 Development of mother-infant ventral contacts.

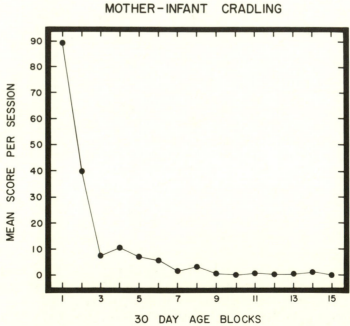

Figure 11-3 Development of mother-infant cradling.

160

NIPPLE CONTACTS

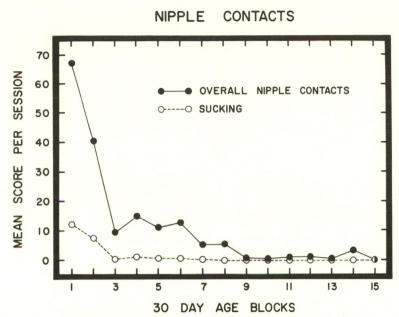

Figure 11-4 Nutritional and non-nutritional nipple contacts.

in part from the greater mobility of the infant, but it also reflects a gradual waning in the strength of the first developmental stage of maternal affectional responding. An almost identical developmental course is followed by the cradling response, shown in Figure 11-3. Thus, the powerful infantile reflexes, which early in life lock the infant to the mother's body (Harlow, 1960), are supported and complemented by reciprocal maternal behaviors.

Nonnutritional and nutritional contacts with the nipple followed a comparable developmental course (Figure 11-4), and nipple contacts during the infant-interaction sessions were relatively infrequent after the third month. These data, as well as most of our other measures of mother-infant interactions, are in part a reflection of the measurement situation, and limited diurnal observations of mother-infant interactions during periods when the infants were not permitted to interact with each other support this view. In effect, the infants used the time offered by the interaction sessions to romp and play with other infants and only occasionally returned to the mothers. Indeed, after the first few months the only time that they consistently returned to the mother and attached to the nipple was when they were frightened. The frightened infant clasps the mother's body with its arms and mouths her nipple, but in this situation mouthing the nipple may be only one component of the total infant-mother contact-clinging pattern and is not necessarily nutritionally directed. Thus mother-infant contact measurements are in part a reflection of infant-mother dependency on the one hand and the development of infant-infant interactions on the other.

In late evening and early morning hours overall breast contacts and nutritive sucking were more frequent than during the infant play sessions. Lactation continued for a considerable period of time, and seven of the eight monkey mothers continued to lactate for 18 months postpartum as determined by manual palpation of their nipples.

An extremely powerful social response observed throughout the monkey kingdom is that of grooming, and this response actually increased throughout the first 30 days as the mothers probably became more socially aware of, and responsive to, their infants as shown in Figure 11.5....Perhaps these data represent an intensification of the specific psychological bond between the mother and the infant. After this initial increase, there was a sharp reduction paralleling that reported for bodily contacts and cradling.

Maternal affection and protection were also measured by restraining-retrieving responses, a pattern which increased during the first 40 days and then decreased sharply....Restraining and retrieving are dependent upon and consequent to the infant's voluntary attempts to break contact with the mother, and the developing locomotor ability of the infant is an important factor in the increasing frequency of restraints and retrievals during the first 30 days or more.

The sharp decrease at 45 to 50 days is not, however, directly ascribable to the behavior of the infant. During this period, the infants actually increased their attempts—and successes—in breaking away from the mother and engaging in infant-infant interactions. The change in restrain-retrieve responses was a function of the mother's making progressively fewer attempts to restrict her infant's activities. In place of restraining and retrieving responses, escapes now elicited little more from the mother than a pattern of watchful waiting.

During the first 3 months, monkey mothers sometimes retrieved infants, when beyond reach, by two intriguing communication mechanisms, categorized as the "silly grin response" and the "affectional present." The silly grin was seen as a rare but particularly striking behavior pattern exhibited at least once by all four mothers in mother-group 1 during the first 3 months. In 12 of the 22 observed occurrences, the silly grin was successful in bringing about an *immediate* return of the infant to its mother regardless of the infant's position or orientation. Since many kinds of responses were available to the infants at this time, the probability is extremely remote that return to the mother was a product of chance. In

POSITIVE RESPONSES TO OWN INFANT

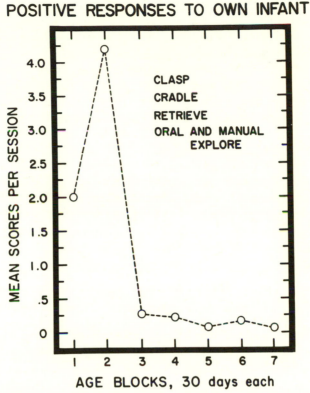

CLASP
CRADLE
RETRIEVE
ORAL AND MANUAL
EXPLORE

MEAN SCORES PER SESSION

AGE BLOCKS, 30 days each

Figure 11-5 Maternal positive responses toward own infant.

experiments outside the playpen situation, these behaviors occurred only when an infant had been separated from its mother, and both mother and infant appeared extremely disturbed. On one occasion this response was seen twenty-two times within a given 10-minute period after the insertion of a Plexiglas screen between the mother and the infant.

The second communication mechanism used for retrieving at a distance occurred more frequently than the silly grin during the corresponding period of time and consisted of a posturing which was, at times, indistinguishable from the female present pattern. Because of its apparent differential function, however, the term affectional present was applied to this category. Of 96 occurrences of this pattern, 56 were successful in bringing about an *immediate* return to the mother regardless of the position or orientation of the infant. Both mechanisms for retrieving at a distance, like the contact-retrieving responses, practically disappeared after 90 days.

As already implied, the initial stage of the maternal affectional system is one in which the mother is constantly vigilant for any impending danger. The mothers at first frequently threatened the observers...in the stable and safe playpen situation, but these responses rapidly dropped to a low level. We believe that this decrease reflects, in part, adaptation and, in part, an actual decrease in maternal vigilance.

Most normal monkey mothers show affection and protection toward infants not their own ("other-infants") during the first few weeks or months after parturition, and this was objectively measured as a ratio of positive to negative responses exhibited toward other-infants.... The initial contacts between the playpen mothers and the first other infant to enter their cages occurred from 19 to 27 days postpartum. These initial interactions were nearly totally positive and consisted of cradling, grooming, and exploring. However, the stage of maternal acceptance of other infants was brief, and the infants rapidly learned that physical associations with most other-mothers quickly changed from positive to punitive.

The Stage of Maternal Ambivalence

As the initial stage of attachment and protection wanes, the stage of maternal ambivalence gradually develops. There are many criteria that could be used to assess this transition, and one of these, maternal punishment, is plotted in Figure 11-6. Maternal punishment was almost nonexistent during the first 2 months of life and seldom occurred during the third month. During the 4th and 5th months, punishment increased to a maximum frequency. It is evident that punishment decreased after 5 months, but not because of a decrease in the mother's readiness to punish. It was more likely a function of the infant's improved ability to avoid punishment. The infants learned to approach their own mothers warily, and they progressively decreased the frequency of behavior which elicited punishment.

Although we have little objective evidence that babies learned how to avoid being punished by their own mothers, we do have data indicating their mastery of skills in avoiding the punishment meted out by other-mothers. Thus, in the four-animal interaction sessions, mothers made 784 attempts to punish other-infants and succeeded in only 62, or 7.7%. During the first half of these sessions, punishment was effective on 12.1% of the attempts, and in the second half on only 4.1%, a statistically significant difference.

The delineation of the stage of maternal ambivalence can also be made in terms of an overall index of maternal responsiveness to both own and other-infants. This has been done for the data presented in Figure 11-7. Positive responses to other-infants predominated during the 1st month, positive and negative responses were essentially equal during the 2nd month, and negative responses predominated thereafter. Thus, if one

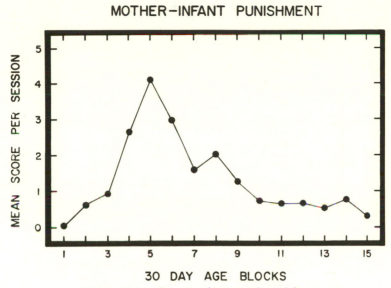

Figure 11-6 Course of maternal punishment.

arbitrarily takes the .50 value as a measure of maternal ambivalence and some arbitrary ratio (for example, .10) for separation, ambivalence appeared within the second month toward other-infants and not until the 9th month toward the mothers' own infants. Separation appeared at 4 months toward other-infants and did not appear with respect to the mothers' own infants during the 15 months of development included in this study.

The stage of maternal ambivalence is characterized by both positive and negative responses. The negative responses consisted largely of threatening and punishing behaviors. Punishment during the early months of the infant's life was typically mild and highly relevant to its behavior. The stimulation which most frequently elicited maternal punishment during this stage involved vigorous tugging at the mother's hair. Excessive biting or mouthing of the nipples may also have been important, but definitive data were not obtained. Contrariwise, punishment during the stage of maternal ambivalence often occurred when the experimenters observed no infantile behavior that might have provoked maternal wrath. Moreover, punishment responses became increasingly harsh as a function of time, and this was especially evident in the category labeled rejecting. The rejecting responses in this stage consisted of vigorously terminating or prohibiting contact and took the form of shaking the infant loose from the body or even stiff-arming the infant when it attempted to initiate contact. One mother developed the stiff-arm pattern with maximal finesse,

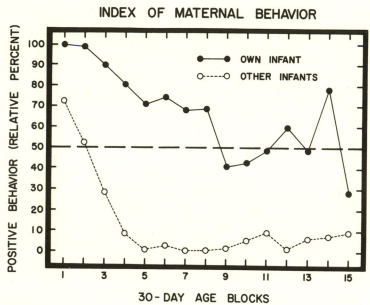

Figure 11-7 Maternal responsiveness to own and other infants.

at times sending her infant sprawling head over heels as though abiding by the advice of Lewis Carroll.

> Speak roughly to your little boy,
>   And beat him when he sneezes;
> He only does it to annoy,
>   Because he knows it teases.

There was, it should be noted, marked variation in the extent and severity of the punishment exhibited by individual mothers. In this, as well as in every measure of maternal behavior used, marked individual differences were obtained.

The Stage of Maternal Separation or Rejection

We know from observations of macaques, baboons, and langurs in the wild that there is a stage when the mother physically, and later psychologically, separates from her infant. As the responses of the mother become increasingly punitive during the stage of maternal ambivalence, the mother-infant bonds become more tenuous. Nevertheless, we did not see true physical or psychological separation of the mother from her own infant in the laboratory during the 21 and 18 months we studied monkey-mother groups 1 and 2, respectively, It is even possible that if we had continued this study for a longer period, sexual relationships might have developed between the mothers and their male infants.

In the feral state, physical separation between the rhesus mother and her own infant takes place with the appearance of the next baby, generally a year later. Even so, the displaced infant is frequently seen in physical proximity to the mother for an additional period of time before psychological emancipation becomes complete. In the case of the Japanese macaque *(Macaca fuscata)*, it has been reported that female offspring may remain close to the mother even after they become mothers themselves, but most males leave by the end of the second year. The exceptional males are those with dominant mothers (Imanishi, 1957). Although we did not see the stage of separation between the mothers and their own infants in our laboratory study, we were able to observe complete alienation between the adult females and infants not their own, and there is every reason to believe that there is much overlap in the separation mechanisms of mother and own-infant and mother and other-infant.

VARIABLES INFLUENCING MATERNAL BEHAVIOR

Maternal affection is a function of multiple variables involving internal incentive stimulation, various experiential factors, and multiple endocrinological forces. External incentives are those relating to the infant and involve contact-clinging, warmth, sucking, and visual and auditory cues. Experiential variables influencing maternal behavior probably embrace the mother's entire experience, but it is likely that her early experience is of special importance as are her relationships with each individual infant she bears and the cumulative experiences gained from raising successive infants. In free-ranging colonies, observations of other mothers with infants probably play a role. Endocrinological factors are both those relating to pregnancy and parturition and those associated with the resumption of the normal ovulatory cycle.

The analysis of monkey maternal affection must be made primarily in terms of the mother's day-to-day actions and interactions with real monkey babies. Unfortunately, the mother-infant relationships are so intimate and complex that analysis is difficult. A final determination of the operating variables and their relative importance must await the accumulation of a large body of experimental data in which all major variables are subjected to rigid controls.

External Incentive Variables

On the basis of direct observations we would postulate that contact-clinging is the primary variable that binds mother to infant and infant to mother. Maternal affection is at a maximum during close ventral-ventral contacts between mother and infant, and maternal affection appears to wane progressively as the frequency of this type of bodily interchange decreases.

Intimate ventral-ventral clinging responses between mother and child gradually decreased and were partially replaced by less intimate patterns involving contact but not clinging. It is not possible to assess the degree to which this resulted from a decreased incentive value of contact to the infant or to the mother, nor can we at the present time isolate the role of sucking or thermal variables. As long as the baby maintained intimate contact with the mother, maternal affection was at a maximum, and there was high correlation between the decrease of intimate contact and the development of maternal ambivalence.

The enormous importance of intimate contact-clinging of an infant to mother is illustrated by the feral rhesus monkey mother physically separating herself from the previous infant when the stimulation of neonatal contact-clinging is reinstated by a new infant. The contact-clinging incentive must be so strong that it overrides both the relatively weak physical ties and all acquired experiential variables associated with the older infant.

Although direct observation of monkey mother and neonate gives no information concerning the relative importance of contact and nursing, some suggestive information has been obtained. The baby of a rhesus mother was removed from her a few hours after birth and the mother was given the opportunity to adopt a kitten. The adoption was complete as long as the mother clung to the kitten and successful nursing was initiated. Unfortunately, the kitten could not cling and, as the mother gradually intermittently relaxed her clasping responses and moved about the cage, the infant fell from her body. For several days the mother repeatedly retrieved the kitten and reattached it to the breast. However, as this act of involuntary separation was repeated over and over again, the mother indicated increased frustration, increased latency in retrieving, and eventually abandoned the kitten. Thus nursing, although probably an important variable, does not appear to be a variable sufficient in and of itself to maintain monkey maternal affection.

Bodily contact is such an important variable that it may elicit the full pattern of maternal behavior in a nonnursing monkey mother. We have observed the behavior of two multiparous rhesus monkeys (299 and 385) whose own infants were removed on the day of birth. After a separation interval of 9 and 4 months, respectively, these females were given the opportunity to adopt infant monkeys.

The procedure in the case of female 385 was to separate a 78-day-old infant from its real mother by inserting a Plexiglas screen between them and to give the infant access to the cage of the prospective adopting mother. After the infant's real mother was removed from the room, the infant immediately ran to and contacted female 385. Overtly normal patterns of motherhood appeared and were maintained until the infant was forcibly removed 3 months later.

A different procedure was used with female 299. A 38-day-old infant was placed in an open-field test situation and the female subsequently introduced. During the first few minutes after the female entered, the infant oriented and moved toward her several times but could make no contact because she was seated on a shelf 3 feet above the floor. The infant, noticeably disturbed, alternately cried and screeched, while the female frequently looked at the infant. After this brief delay, the female suddenly dropped to the floor, picked up the infant, and held it for the remainder of the session and during transport back to her cage. She was not observed to release it for 3 days. Again, entirely normal mother-infant relationships were established and maintained until the pair was separated by the experimenter some months later.

In both cases, the behavior of the infants was similar in that they actively sought out the female. We do not know the relative importance of the variables which underlie the original acceptance of the infant by the females, but many variables, including visual and auditory factors and previous maternal experience, probably play important roles.

We believe that the maintenance of the normal mother-infant relationships that ensued was primarily attributable to the incentive value of contact both to the mother and to the infant. The fact that normal mother-infant relationships were established while neither mother was lactating (insofar as observed—we made no test because we had not anticipated the eventual results) indicates that lactation is not an essential variable for eliciting normal mother-infant relationships. Both infants sucked at the breast and, although we cannot precisely delineate the temporal factors involved, the females subsequently produced milk in quantity. A detailed chemical analysis indicated that the nitrogen and calcium content was appropriate and the milk biochemically normal.

The one case in which attempted adoption failed was equally informative. The baby of mother 294 was removed after 34 days, and 3 days later she was given a 38-day-old infant for adoption. This infant (B20) had been separated from its mother a few hours after birth and housed in a wire-mesh cage adjacent to that of 294. During the first month of life, while living alone, B20 developed a bizarre, autistic pattern of self-clutching, rocking, and penis-mouthing. When placed in mother 294's cage, the infant folded itself into a tight ball and screamed when contacted by the female. During the daily 30-minute exposures, the mother vacillated between approach and avoidance, made some body and hand contacts, and, from the fourth day on, occasionally groomed the infant. However, the infant never responded contactually to the mother, and the potential foster mother never responded adequately to the infant. These observations suggest that the appearance and vocalizations of an infant monkey, by themselves, are inadequate for eliciting and maintaining maternal affectional responses. We are convinced that the mother did not adopt simply because the baby made no effort whatsoever to cling to, clasp, or contact her. Indeed, the baby resisted all maternal approaches. An infant that does not feed back will not be fed. Further evidence that the fault was the infant's lies in the fact that this mother subsequently adopted a congenitally blind infant that had been mercilessly abused for 2 weeks by its own mother, one of the so-called motherless mothers that had never known a monkey mother of her own.

The contact variable's importance to the mother is illustrated by the form of infant-retrieving responses during the first few months. In this period of time the infant is not merely brought into the cage, but is placed by the mother on her ventral surface. Within the first few weeks this behavior is primarily maternal, but as a function of time the infant plays an increasingly larger cooperative role until it is frequently impossible to isolate maternal and infantile components. We frankly cannot assess the differential contribution to this pattern of the various stimulus-incentive components of contact-clinging, warmth, nursing, and visual-auditory cues. Although the retrieving responses rapidly diminished in frequency after 40 days, they could still be elicited consistently by any sudden stimulus change, sudden movements by the observers, or the presence of intruders. However, these acts of retrieval appeared qualitatively different in that placement of the infant on the mother's ventral surface was seldom a result of maternal positioning but was initiated by the infant.

Temporary reestablishment of the intimate contact-clinging responses more than 200 days after parturition was observed in an experimental study by Seay, Hansen, and Harlow (1962). Four rhesus infants were separated from their mothers at approximately 210 days by inserting transparent Plexiglas panels between the living cages and the play cells of the playpen apparatus. After 3 weeks the panels were removed and all the infants went to their appropriate mothers. In three of the four cases, intimate ventral-ventral clinging was immediately reestablished. In the remaining case, the mother appeared totally indifferent and the infant was unable to "retrieve" the mother for more than 24 hours. After this delay, however, the infant made ventral-ventral contact and there followed a resurgence of the mother-infant tie.

Although we have emphasized contact variables, we recognize the important role of other exteroceptive stimuli in regulating maternal behavior. It is more than likely that motherhood specifically attunes and sensitizes the female to specific infantile vocalizations and visual cues.

An experiment by Cross and Harlow (1963) gives presumptive evidence that the sight and sound of a neonatal monkey are significant incentives to monkey mothers. Three groups of five monkeys each were placed in a Butler-type exploration box (Butler, 1953) with the option of viewing either an infant or a juvenile monkey.... A multiparous group, which had given birth to their last infants 2 to 4 months prior to this experiment and had had their babies removed during the first day, showed a clear-cut preference for baby-viewing throughout the experiment. The group of nulliparous adult females showed no preference whatsoever. The most interesting group consisted of females that gave birth to babies during the course of this experiment. These babies were removed from their mothers after 3 days, and the mothers were returned to the apparatus for additional testing. Before the birth of their babies, these females showed no preference for infant-viewing; following birth, a sudden rise in preference for baby-viewing developed. Although the basis for this is not clear, the most likely explanation is that the transient contact experience enhanced monkey-baby incentive values.

The foregoing data indicate that exteroceptive incentives provided by the sight of the baby and the sounds that monkey babies utter are measurable variables in eliciting maternal affection. We doubt they have the power apparently intrinsic to contact-clinging, but vision and audition are probably additional primary modalities through which learned affectional responses develop. In other words, these modalities serve as both unconditioned and conditioned channels in the formation and expression of maternal bonds.

Although there is reason to believe that baby-viewing stimulates maternal behavior, there is also contradictory evidence. Viewing divorced from contactual responding soon wanes. In the separation study of Seay et al., mothers deprived of contact with their babies increased their visual responses to the infant, measured before, during, and after separation, from a mean of slightly over one visual response per 30-minute period during the week before separation to a mean of over three responses during the first week of separation. This increment was largely a function of the behavior of two of the four mothers.... It is also apparent that in the subsequent 2 weeks of separation, visual responses decreased. The viewing data, taken together, suggest that the sight of the baby is secondarily reinforcing, deriving from learning that is reinforced by other rewarding properties of the baby and its behavior.

In a current study of two mothers and their infants there is also a suggestion that auditory cues provided by the baby may arouse a mother even though she cannot herself act to relieve the distressed baby. A multiparous mother with strong maternal behavior and a primiparous "motherless" mother and their babies share a half-playpen unit. It has been noted that when the primiparous mother fails to contact her screeching baby, the multiparous mother threatens the neglectful mother. Since there are no threats when the screeching baby is held by its mother, we believe the behavior reflects a frustrated maternal response, not a response to an aversive sound.

Experiential Variables

The maternal affectional system, waxing and waning with the birth and growth of each particular baby, is unlike most other affectional systems. Doubtless, maternal affection is influenced by several families of experiential variables: (1) the experience associated with each baby that it observes or produces, (2) the accumulative effects of multiple motherhood, and (3) the mother's personal life history.

The Variables of Individual Infant-Raising

Traumatic experiences happening to a particular mother-infant combination can alter the expression of maternal behaviors, but this is probably specific to the particular infant involved. On one occasion we were forced to separate a mother and her 36-day-old infant for 3 days to treat the baby's infected hand. After the infant was returned to its mother, we observed a resurgence of the intimate contact responses which characterized the mother-infant pairs during the first month of life, and this augmentation of contact endured more than a month. The results of our separation study (Seay et al., 1962) also indicated that, in general, mother-infant separation was followed by a resurgence of intimate physical contact characteristic of an earlier developmental stage.

Maternal overprotection and infantile overdependence were produced by allowing individual infants to live with their mothers a period of 7 months in standard 30-inch × 30-inch × 30-inch living cages. During this time the infants were raised by affectionate, normal, multiparous mothers. The mother-infant pairs were then placed in the home cages of a two-unit playpen situation in order to study infant-infant interactions. Observation was simple and totally reliable—there were no infant-infant interactions. One infant never left the home cage during 12 weeks of observations, and, although the second infant did enter its play cell, it made no social overtures to the other mother-infant combination. It is probable that the early restricted living conditions imposed upon these animals resulted in maternal overprotection and infant overattachment which inhibited the development of infant-infant interrelationships at this point in time.

There are, however, several uncontrolled variables in this pilot investigation. Not only had the infants had no opportunity to interact with other infants, but they also had been denied opportunity to explore a larger, more challenging world than that of the living cages prior to the playpen placement. Furthermore, the new situation was strange to the animals and may have enhanced infantile dependence and maternal overprotection. It is also possible that there is a critical time—some lapse of weeks or months—during which conditions favoring the development of maternal ambivalence must occur if this stage of maternal behavior is to appear. Unless the baby has frequent opportunities to leave and return to the mother during the first year of life, it may reach the point of no voluntary separation.

The Variables of Multiple Motherhood

It is the general impression of primatologists that multiparous females are more effective mothers than primiparous, although the absence of supporting or negative data indicates our lack of knowledge concerning this variable. There is neither scientific support for this general statement nor information about the degree to which it might apply to particular stages of maternal responding or to individual mothers.

At present we are making an experimental attack on the problem by comparing in the playpen situation the behaviors of two groups of four primiparous and four multiparous females and their babies. Although most of the data remain to be analyzed, we have been pleasantly surprised by the very efficient maternal behaviors of the primiparous mothers and the normal social behaviors exhibited by their infants. Typical of the comparisons of maternal responses are those for cradling and retrieving (Figures 11-8 and 11-9). In both instances, the response showed a similar course of development in the primiparous and multiparous groups, and differences were in no instance significant.

The Variables of Early Experience

Another kind of experiential variable that can have an enormous influence on maternal affectional responding is the mother's personal life history. This was dramatically illustrated when we traced the maternal behaviors of a group of five so-called motherless mother macaques which had never

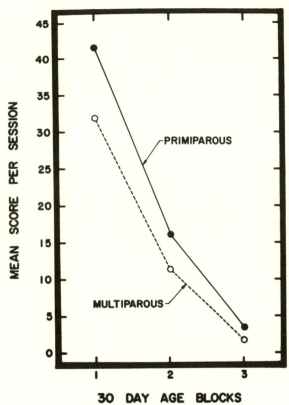

Figure 11-8 Infant cradling responses by primiparous and multiparous mothers.

known a real monkey mother of their own, had been denied the opportunity
to develop normal infant-infant affectional patterns, and subsequently had
had only limited physical association with other monkeys.

All five females were totally hopeless mothers, and none of the infants
would have survived without artificial feeding in the first days or weeks of
life. Two mothers were essentially indifferent to their infants; three were
violently abusive. Indeed, the last infant was separated when it became
apparent that otherwise it would not live. The maternal inadequacies of
these animals cannot be attributed to faulty responding by the babies.
Early in life the babies repeatedly offered visual and auditory cues normally
appropriate for eliciting maternal responses (Figure 11-10), and as soon as
the first four infants were physically able to initiate approach and body-
contact responses, they made repeated attempts to attach to the mothers,
only to be repulsed and rejected....So strong were these contact-seeking
responses in two infants that they withstood brutal and continuous abuse

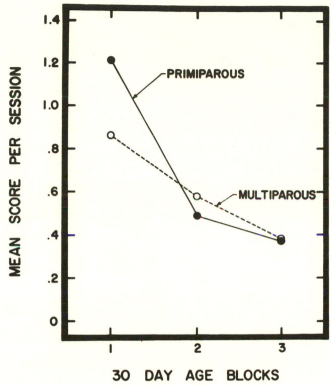

Figure 11-9 Infant retrieving responses by primiparous and multiparous mothers.

by the mothers until they attained the breasts for reasonable periods of time.

These data not only show that monkey mothering can be drastically altered by experiential factors, but they also indicate the importance of social learning for the normal expression of maternal behavior. Unfortunately for the interpretation of the results, these motherless mothers had been denied both monkey mothering and any adequate opportunity to develop normal social relationships with other monkeys. Although we strongly suspect that inadequate infant-infant experience played an overwhelmingly important role in contributing to their maternal inadequacies, we cannot, as yet, make any definitive statement.

It is conceivable that specific factors of inadequate early experience produce specific types of inadequate mothering. For example, failure of normal gratification of contact-clinging in infancy may make it impossible for the adult female to show normal contact relationships with her own infant. Likewise, maternal brutality may stem from inadequate social

Figure 11-10   Infant cues to elicit maternal responding.

experience with other infants within the first year of life. Our data do not suggest any such correlations. Rather, they suggest that maternal affection in the monkey is a highly integrated, global system, not a series of isolated components that vary independently. On this basis it seems plausible that the expression of adequate, normal, maternal affection depends more upon general social experience than upon specific experiences.

Our data to date indicate a relationship between normal and abnormal maternal behavior and the adequacy of previous heterosexual behavior. Thus none of the motherless-mother animals ever showed normal female sex posturing and responding. They were impregnated, not through their own effort, but because of the patience, persistence, and perspicacity of our breeding males. Although we do not regard heterosexual inadequacy as a cause of maternal inadequacy, we believe both are products of a common factor or factors. By and large, feral-raised female monkeys are adequate sexually and maternally. Occasionally, a feral-raised mother shows no interest in her offspring and even destroys them. The one such inadequate feral female we have closely observed engaged in the procreative act with enthusiasm but was uninterested in the end product, killing one infant and maltreating a subsequent baby, forcing separation to preserve life. We, of course, have no knowledge of this female's prelaboratory life history and are in no position to make any assessment of possible hormonal disturbances.

We have stressed the primacy of infant-infant affectional development for normal maternal behavior on the basis of indirect evidence. Almost all of our infant monkeys given the opportunity to interact intimately with other infants during the first half-year of life have developed normal adult-type sexual responsiveness, whether raised without mothers, with cloth-surrogate mothers, with motherless mothers, or with normal mothers. Only one female among the scores denied infant-infant interactions during the first half-year of life has shown normal adult-type sex behavior, and this population includes males and females, monkeys raised alone in bare cages and monkeys raised with wire- or cloth-surrogate mothers. We predict that rearing conditions that produce normal sexual behavior patterns will also produce normal maternal behavior patterns. Unfortunately, we must wait at least two more years to validate this hypothesis since there is a time lag between preadolescent sexual play and motherhood.

So far in our description and analysis of the variables influencing maternal behavior we have largely limited ourselves to the first stage of maternal affectional development, the stage of attachment and protection. The variables that bind the mother to the infant are most accessible to analysis when the maternal bond is at its peak.

Obviously, as the mother passes through the succeeding stages of ambivalence and separation, previously operating variables must fade and disappear, and fade and disappear at different rates. Entirely new variables may appear and have pervasive effects as one passes from one stage to another. Thus the resumption of the estrous cycle involves a change in endocrinological variables which may play important roles in guiding the expression of maternal behaviors.

We can make reasonable hypotheses concerning the variables which operate in the stage of attachment and protection and reasonable estimates concerning their relative importance. Thus contact-clinging, which may also involve warmth, is a primary variable for the initiation and maintenance of this stage just as it is in the infant-mother affectional system (Harlow, 1958). Nursing is apparently a variable of measurable importance in both affectional systems but not an essential variable. Relatively specific visual and auditory variables play a supplementary role—they are additional sensory modalities through which learned affectional responses are mediated.

Unfortunately, we have less information and can only speculate about the variables and changes in variables which give rise to the stage of maternal ambivalence and mother-infant separation. . . . During the first few months, the mother's need for intimate contact exceeds the infant's, producing maternal protection. This early protectiveness becomes apparent when the infant attains sufficient strength and agility to make repetitive attempts to leave the mother. Maternal protection is manifested by the high frequency of restrain-retrieve responses and the communicative responses for retrieval at a distance.

Subsequently, the intensity of maternal and infantile contact needs is reversed until the infant's needs exceed the mother's. . . . Beyond this point, the stage of ambivalence exists, and the infant's attempts to make physical contact are rebuffed with increasing frequency and severity. As attachment abates, ambivalence arises and anticipates alienation.

> From here on mother does not care
>   For baby fingers in her hair;
> A touch that once went to her heart
>   Now merely makes the hair depart.

Changes in both mother and child normally tend to produce gradual separation. We make the assumption that not only are there endocrinological factors influencing the mother and causing the waning of affectional responding, but there are behavioral changes in the infant which contribute to the same end. Thus we believe that maturational factors intrinsic to every infant tend to dilute the infant-mother affectional tie. The infant gradually changes from a reflex, clinging, cuddling individual to one that moves about freely, squirms when held, inflicts physical discomfort, and reaches out physically and intellectually to the world around it. As the world expands from one consisting only of the mother's face and body, the infant progressively becomes an organism which fails to feed back basic incentives which tie the mother to the infant. With each step of development, the infant is less reinforced by the mother and the mother by the infant; in both cases the net result is the same. The mother is more capable of accepting ensuing progeny and the infant of breaking the maternal bonds that would otherwise inhibit social development.

The inevitable stages of maturation shape and reshape the mother-infant bonds in monkeys. The process of growth, augmented by continuously accompanying learned processes, creates and destroys the ties between individual mothers and infants. However, the capacity for maternal affection is not destroyed, and with the next baby comes a reinstatement of the cycle. For the separated infant, other affectional systems become preeminent and ensure successful social adaptation within the culture of its particular primate group.

SUMMARY

The maternal affectional system is one of a number of affectional systems exhibited by rhesus monkeys. Its course has been studied in the laboratory by observing rhesus mothers with their infants from birth until 18 or 21 months of age in a special apparatus designed to provide both living quarters and infant play facilities. Supplementary studies have been directed toward isolating variables determining the mother-infant relationship.

Maternal behavior in the rhesus monkey is characterized by sequential stages designated as attachment and protection, ambivalence, and separation or rejection. During attachment and protection, the earliest phase, the mother has close physical contact with the infant and responds to it positively, holding it close to her much of the time and restricting its free locomotion in large degree. Negative responses such as rejecting some of the infant's approaches and punishing it for encroachments gradually appear. These, nevertheless, mark the start of the ambivalence stage, characterized by positive and negative responses to the infant. Finally, physical separation takes place, although this stage did not appear by 21 months in the laboratory situation. Generally, physical separation in the natural environment appears with the birth of a new baby, which reinstates the maternal cycle with the newborn now the center of the mother's attention and the older offspring occupying the periphery.

The variables operating to determine maternal roles in rhesus monkeys can be grouped into external incentives, experiential factors, and endocrinological forces. External incentives are those relating to the infant, such as contact-clinging, warmth, sucking, baby vocalizations, and the baby's visual properties. Experiential variables influencing the mother's responses to the baby include her early experiences, especially with age-mates, and probably cumulative experiences from raising earlier offspring or observing other females caring for babies. The exact contribution of the hormonal system prevalent in the postparturient period awaits experimental attack.

REFERENCES

Butler, R. A. (1953), Discrimination learning by rhesus monkeys to visual-exploration motivation. *J. comp. physiol. Psychol., 46*, 95–98.

Cross, H. A., and H. F. Harlow (1963), Observation of infant monkeys by female monkeys. *Percept. mot. Skills, 16*, 11–15.

Hansen, E. W. (1962), The development of infant and maternal behavior in the rhesus monkey. Unpublished doctoral dissertation, University of Wisconsin.

Harlow, H. F. (1958), The nature of love. *Amer. Psychologist, 13*, 673–685.

Harlow, H. F. (1960), Primary affectional patterns in primates. *Amer. J. Ortho-psychiat.*, *30*, 676–684.

Imanishi, K. (1957), Social behavior in Japanese monkeys, *Macaca fuscata. Psychologia*, *1*, 47–54.

Seay, B., E. W. Hansen, and H. F. Harlow (1962), Mother-infant separation in monkeys. *J. Child Psychol. Psychiat.*, *3*, 123–132.

NOTE

The researches reported in this paper were supported by funds supplied by Grants M-722 and HE-6287, National Institutes of Health, and by a grant from the Ford Foundation.

12

Age-Mate or Peer Affectional System

Harry F. Harlow

Probably the most pervading and important of all the affectional systems in terms of long-range personal-social adjustment is the age-mate or peer affectional system. This system begins through interaction between infants and children and continues throughout preadolescence, adolescence, and adulthood. Age-mate or peer affectional relationships may exist between members of the same sex or members of opposite sexes but, as we shall see, there are certain basic physical and behavioral differences conducive to sexual separation insofar as the age-mate affectional system is concerned.

The age-mate affectional system begins when the intimate physical bonds between the mother and child weaken and the infant is permitted to wander beyond the range of the maternal body and maternal arms. We have already discussed this maternal stage of tolerance to infant separation (see Harlow *et al.*, 1963), but the separation is normally as much or more a function of the infant's behavior as it is a function of changes by the mother.

DEVELOPMENTAL STAGES

Stages of Inanimate Object Play

No doubt the primary motive underlying the formation of the age-mate affectional system is the curiosity of the infants themselves toward all

---

Harlow, H. F. Age-mate or peer affectional system. In D. S. Lehrman, R. A. Hinde, and E. Shaw (Eds.), *Advances in the study of behavior*, Vol. 2. New York: Academic Press, 1969, pp. 333–383.

objects in the external world. Curiosity motivation toward inanimate objects develops in monkeys through a series of four stages: (1) the reflex stage, (2) the exploratory stage, (3) the object utilization stage, and (4) the object aggressive stage.

Reflex Stage

The first of these stages, the reflex stage, involves automatic investigatory responses elicited by exteroceptive stimuli of contact, sound, and vision which orient head and body responses toward the stimulation source and facilitate eye, head, and body postural and locomotor responses which in turn direct the animal toward the arousing stimulus. These are doubtless infantile forms of the investigatory reflexes described by Pavlov (1927) and the postural reflexes described by Magnus (1924).

Exploratory Stage

As soon as adequate locomotor capabilities have matured, the infant monkey enters into the second stage, the exploratory stage, during which the infant seeks and contacts external stimulating objects. Object exploration becomes oral, contactual, and manipulatory as these motor mechanisms mature. The oral manipulatory mechanisms are functional at birth, and the locomotor mechanisms enable the infant monkey to move about in space with considerable facility by 10–15 days of age (Hines, 1942). Actually, limited locomotor ability is possible even before this time (see Mowbray and Cadell, 1962; Zimmermann, personal communication). The hand and finger prehension capabilities develop at a much faster rate in macaques than in men; the grasp reflex in the fingers comes under voluntary control by 15 days of age, and crude manipulation of objects is operant by 51 days of age, according to Jensen (1961). Precise, human-type finger-thumb approximations develop relatively slowly in the macaque and precise pincer grasp homologous to that of the human being does not appear until approximately Day 185. Actually, it is doubtful if rhesus monkeys ever achieve the human level of perfection of digital dexterity.

It should be stressed that there is nothing mysterious about the development of curiosity-motivated exploration responses in monkeys and men, and doubtless this is true for many or most mammals. This category of responses automatically appears if three basic conditions are met: physical maturity, availability of objects, and personal security. The animal must have physically matured to the point that it can perceive and orient to appropriate stimuli and conduct appropriate motor responses. Thus, the fact, function, and nature of the manipulatory responses are dependent upon the maturation of appropriate oral, manual, and digital skills which have been assiduously traced in man (Halverson, 1931), described for the chimpanzee (Riesen and Kinder, 1952), and at least outlined for macaque monkeys. A second condition is the sheer availability of appropriate manipulable objects which are ever present in the normal environment of all primates but can be either withheld or made available in the laboratory. A third condition is that of personal security, since curiosity is clearly depressed or inhibited by fear or disturbance as demonstrated by Montgomery (1955) for rats and Harlow and Zimmermann (1959) for infant monkeys. Such a position was clearly presented in the classic review on levels of motivation by Maslow (1943).

Object Utilization Stage

During the third stage of inanimate object play, the object utilization stage, the macaque monkey actively displaces objects, explores all their aspects, and even moves objects about or translocates them in space, as is shown in Figure 12-1. A further extension of this stage is seen when the infant macaque incorporates the objects of the physical world to assist him in his own playful activity. Laboratory examples are the use of flying rings for cage or playroom locomotion, as seen in Figure 12-2, or the use of mobile tree limbs or vines to achieve similar functions in the feral environment.

Object Aggressive Stage

The fourth stage of inanimate object play, the object aggressive stage, involves aggressive manipulation by the monkeys in which the physical object may be damaged or destroyed, apparently for no other motive than the sheer joy and pleasure inherent in object-directed and object-vented aggression. Nonhuman primates frequently express this object-directed aggressive exploration or aggressive play by tearing physical objects to shreds with their teeth. Almost any plaything left in a monkey cage "to dust returneth," or at least to debris, even when assailed by monkeys under a year of age. As the temporal muscles and canine teeth develop, particularly in the adolescent or adult male macaque, even a solid oak platform placed in a cage is gradually reduced to splinters. Such objects do not appear to have frustrating properties as frustration is commonly defined, since the objects often facilitate rather than hinder the monkeys in their daily play activities. The oak planks are destroyed because the act of destructive aggression apparently has self-reinforcing or rewarding properties. At an appropriate developmental stage it is fun to chew on any and all objects, animate or inanimate, whether or not they possess any obvious frustrating properties or interfere with activities in progress.

Figure 12-1   Rhesus monkey carrying plastic ball.

Stages of Age-Mate Affection

We advocated a fourfold stage for the development of inanimate object play, and we believe that four similar stages of age-mate affection may be described: (1) a reflex stage of peer affection, or at least peer interaction, (2) an exploratory stage of peer interaction, (3) a peer utilization stage, which we also describe as the stage of social play, and (4) a stage of aggressive play. There are multiple similarities between the development of simple object play and the development of age-mate affection. The latter may be thought of as a complex form of animate object curiosity-exploration, in which other animals, commonly members of one's own species, operate in much the same way as inanimate objects to elicit

Figure 12-2 Use of flying ring by rhesus infant.

persistent curiosity-exploratory-manipulatory responses (Rosenblum, 1961; Harlow, 1962).

Reflex Stage of Peer Affection

The first stage of age-mate affection, the reflex or investigatory response stage, is one in which the sounds and movements of age mates attract the attention of the stimulated neonate or infant. Evidence for this reflex stage of age-mate affection has already been obtained on the basis of relatively casual observation of the behavior of monkeys during the first 15–30 days in which they were placed 20 minutes per day in our original playroom situation (Playroom I) illustrated in Figure 12-3. Early in life there was a strong tendency for the infants to locomote or explore in close proximity to each other (see Figure 12-4), and when one left the group to investigate a more distant part of the environment, the other three would frequently reorient and follow. Unfortunately, this social following behavior had not been predicted, was not systematically observed, nor objectively scored. Furthermore, we have little or no data indicating the

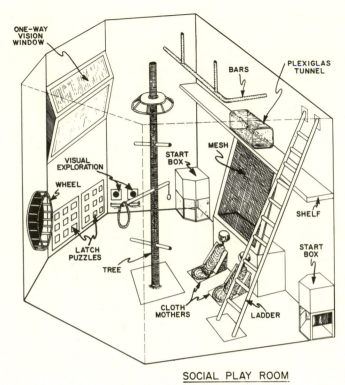

SOCIAL PLAY ROOM

Figure 12-3   Playroom.

normal transition from the reflex stage to the subsequent stages of individual peer exploration and play.

The reflex stage of age-mate or peer affection probably never exists in the feral environment but is instead a fact or artifact of the laboratory, depending on one's laboratory or naturalistic bias. The normal monkey mother, particularly in the feral environment, seldom, if ever, gives her infant sufficient opportunity to interact with other infants during the first 30 days of life to permit either the existence or measurement of a reflex infant-infant affectional stage. The fact that such a stage does not exist in the wild must not be taken to mean that such a stage does not exist, that its development cannot be traced, and that the underlying neurophysiological variables cannot be measured.

Exploratory Stage of Peer Affection

The second stage of peer affection, the exploratory stage, which we have also described as the presocial stage, involves a much higher degree of

Figure 12-4 Infants maintaining close physical proximity in playroom situation at the reflex stage.

activity than is found during the reflex stage. During this second stage, the individual monkey infants explore the other infant monkeys of their social group while simultaneously exploring the specific physical objects of their external world. Actually, the responses involved in both object exploration and social exploration are very similar in pattern for all three identifiable components: (1) visual exploration, in which the animal orients closely to, and peers intently at, the object or other animal, (2) oral exploration, a gentle mouthing response (see Figure 12-5), and (3) tactual exploration, involving limited body contact or a transient clasp, either of a physical object or another animal. The duration of the individual responses of all these presocial responses is very brief, almost momentary. These simple transient patterns of exploration tend to decrease progressively for object exploration and drop rapidly for social exploration after peaking near 40 days (see Figure 12-6), as the more complex forms of social exploration and social play develop. These data were obtained from a group of infants in the playroom I situation with cloth surrogates present. The developmental trends for both object exploration and social exploration doubtless vary depending on the social situation employed, presence or absence of mothers or mother surrogates, and number and nature of available playmates.

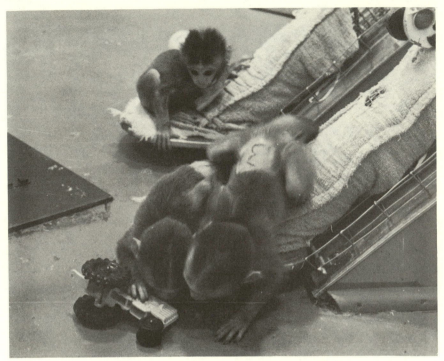

Figure 12-5   Infant oral manipulation.

Stage of Peer Utilization or Social Play

During the time the relatively gentle and transient social exploratory responses are waning, patterns of active social play are developing and superseding the preceding stage of peer affection. The stage of social play, which involves the active utilization of another monkey, rapidly comes to involve complex interactions between pairs of monkeys or larger social groups. Even though the stage of peer utilization may be thought of as paralleling the stage of object utilization, the interactions between monkeys become far more complex. Our data indicate that there are at least two basic social play patterns, which we have named rough-and-tumble play or contact play, and approach-withdrawal or noncontact play.

   The first of these two patterns which we have observed, and the pattern most easily described and measured, is that of rough-and-tumble play and is characterized by wrestling, rolling, pulling, and biting, usually by two animals. With increasing age the tempo, duration, and intensity of these rough-and-tumble sessions increase, but in spite of the relative fury of these bouts, there is seldom indication that any animal suffers pain or injury, at least during the first 6 months of life. As we shall see subsequently,

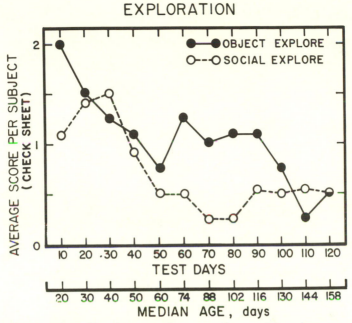

Figure 12-6 Developmental course of presocial exploratory stage of age-mate affection.

abnormal early social experience may distort and disturb the form of these play responses.

Rough-and-tumble play develops when a single monkey makes a unilateral attempt to initiate social play by approaching another monkey and pulling its hair or gently biting (Figure 12-7). Originally this behavior elicits no response from the partner but the frequency of reciprocated rough-and-tumble play steadily increases, particularly when two male infants are involved. Frequency and intensity of rough-and-tumble play are functions of many variables. In the playroom situation, as shown in Figure 12-8, it is clearly apparent by 30 days of age and has reached a near maximal level by 90 days of age. In the playroom situation the mother always was and always had been a cloth surrogate who could not restrain her infant in any manner, and the playroom sessions were limited to 20 minutes a day. Both of these conditions may be conducive to maximizing play.

We have also traced the development of rough-and-tumble play in our playpen situation illustrated in Figure 11-1 and described in detail by Hansen (1962) and Harlow *et al.* (1963). In this situation, one group of four infants was raised by real monkey mothers and another group of four by cloth surrogate mothers. The babies raised by real monkey mothers

Figure 12-7   Play-initiated response by infant rhesus.

were restrained from interacting with other infants during the first month by their mothers, and the babies raised by surrogates were allowed no unrestricted interaction with other infants for the first 15 days of life by the imposed experimental procedures. Even so, rough-and-tumble play, whose course is illustrated in Figure 12-9, was evident in both groups during their second month of life and attained an adequate or high level during the third.

A wealth of evidence has accumulated showing sex differences in rough-and-tumble play even during the first 180 days of life, in spite of the fact that rough-and-tumble play during this period is not aggressive and certainly is not abusive or cruel. During the first 6 months the females in the playroom situation showed a low incidence of threat responses and a

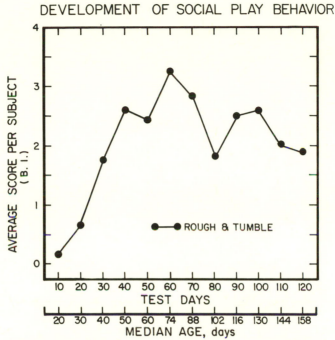

Figure 12-8 Development of rough-and-tumble play in playroom.

high incidence of passivity responses, and the converse was true for the males. Although frequency of rough-and-tumble play for sexes in the playroom situation was not graphed, male and female roles differed. Frequency of rough-and-tumble play by the males and females raised by real monkey mothers in the playpen situation was plotted by Hansen, and the data are presented graphically in Figure 12-10. At no point is there any overlapping between groups, and the differences are statistically significant.

The second form of social play, which is probably more advanced than that of rough-and-tumble play, has also been described, analyzed, and given the name approach-withdrawal play. This play pattern, in contrast to rough-and-tumble play, is characterized by less frequent bodily contact and involves rapid alternate chasing back and forth across the playroom or play area with frequent alternation of leader and follower...; or a pair of monkeys will choose a given point in a room, such as a particular platform, and make a series of repeated, socially oriented jumps to and from this place. Although this pattern is varied in form, it is nonetheless readily identifiable, as indicated by high reliability between independent observers. Initially, this play is short-lived and spatially very

ROUGH & TUMBLE PLAY

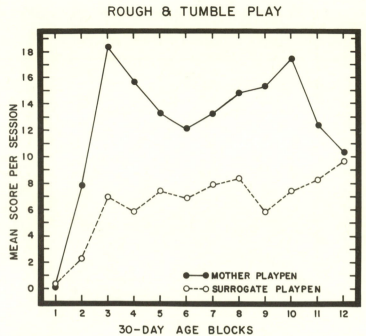

Figure 12-9 Development of rough-and-tumble play in play-room.

limited. As the pattern develops toward its full form, it increases in duration, with interactions longer than a minute not infrequently recorded, and it expands spatially, with interactions ranging from one corner of the room to another and from floor to ceiling. Frequently there are brief interruptions and then reelicitations to the entire pattern. Indeed, there are cases in which this pattern has appeared between members of a pair in each of the 1-minute recorded periods of a 30-minute test session. In these intense interactions, characterized by an almost frantic activity, the inanimate objects are not neglected but incorporated in the play sequences, and the brief breaks between may be filled with vigorous response to an inanimate object, such as clasping and carrying a block or ball, or violent swinging from a ring or rotating a wheel.

The development of the two basic patterns of rough-and-tumble and approach-withdrawal play in the playroom situation has been compared by Rosenblum (1961) and the data plotted in Figure 12-11. Although the appearance of rough-and-tumble play does precede that of approach-withdrawal play, the curves are similar in form and overlap to a very considerable extent. A similar developmental course of rough-and-tumble play and approach-withdrawal play has been plotted by Hansen for infant

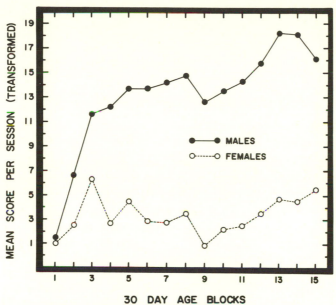

Figure 12-10 Frequency of rough-and-tumble play by males and females (raised by real mothers in the playpen situation) (see Hansen thesis, 1962, p. 75).

monkeys in the playpen situation, and the developmental courses of the two play patterns in the two test situations are similar.

During the second 6 months of life, as the infants develop increasing skill and strength, the tempo of the play patterns heightens and vigor and violence of the play become progressively augmented. Various names have been given to this changing play pattern, such as mixed play or interactive play. Whether it is classified as a new form of social play or a combination of contact and noncontact play may well be a matter of personal preference.

Stage of Aggressive Play

During the end of the first year of life or the beginning of the second, the play patterns between monkeys become more and more violent and the stage of aggressive play appears. The monkeys cry out in dismay from time to time as the wrestling, grabbing, and biting become rough-and-tumble for real and not merely for fun. Unfortunately, these changing play patterns have no distinct all-or-nothing quality and they lack the precise, stereotyped, repetitive, reliable, and differential qualities charac-

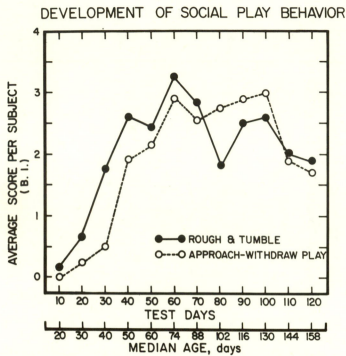

Figure 12-11   Development of rough-and-tumble play and
approach-withdrawal play patterns in playroom.

terizing aggressive patterns in such fish as sticklebacks and such birds as
sooty or noddy terns. Because of this, various investigators have disagreed
as to the exact time at which play becomes aggressive as contrasted to
nonaggressive. To complicate the matter, socially learned factors undoubtedly operate during the transition from nonaggressive to aggressive
play patterns, and this developmental trend is also influenced by early
experiential variables subsequently described in this paper, and by maternal
supervision and interference under feral conditions (Itani, 1963).

It might seem logical that the development of normal aggression or
aggressive play would terminate the age-mate or peer affectional system,
but this is in no sense true. In spite of the fact that the playrooms and the
playpens that we have employed for our social testing represent relatively
crowded living situations for social groups of four or more monkeys, we
have had no blood baths between such adolescent or near-adult groups
whose members had previously developed long-term age-mate or peer
affectional relationships.

We believe there are at least two factors that account for this phenomenon. Long before truly aggressive play matures, dominance relationships

have begun to develop, and the monkeys raised in our experimental social groups accept these relationships without recourse to lethal or near-lethal combat. Actually, dominance relationships may change within these groups over a course of years, and this is achieved without monkeys being maimed or mangled. Doubtless, social signs or gestural communications of dominance and submission serve as substitutes for combat, at least combat carried beyond the limits that would deny further positive social relationships.

There is also evidence that subhuman primates which develop intra-group affectional responses prior to the maturation of aggressive responses maintain feelings of affection for their group members for a long period of time, regardless of the social relationships that develop as a result of aggressive play. Actually, the development of primate social behavior cannot be understood adequately merely in terms of the differential developmental rates of affection and aggression. Temporally placed between these two is a stage of development of fear of unfamiliar environmental objects. The differential timing of these three basic behavior sequences of affection, fear, and aggression—the AFA developmental sequences—are factors of vast importance in the development of normal or abnormal primate social behaviors.

Although little appears in the scientific literature about the normal development of aggression, it is commonly assumed that affection and aggression are normal, and naturally opposing, behavioral categories. However, if one simultaneously traces the development of intraspecies affection and aggression, it becomes evident that these two modes of response are in no sense totally opposed in the normal development of social relationships between members of a single species. Studies of human children in nursery school situations reveal a positive correlation between the frequency of quarrelsomeness and friendship indices (Green, 1933), and it is probable that in children, as in our monkeys, playful interaction is basic not only to the formation of affection for members of one's species, but also to aggression, usually of a relatively controlled and gentle type. Members of interacting infant groups differ in size, strength, sex, and vigor, and play automatically results in the formation of dominance relationships independent of food, thirst, or sexual gratification.

EXTERNALLY DIRECTED AGGRESSION

Infant Aggression Against Mothers Not Their Own

The simultaneous interplay between the affectional and aggressive responses probably leads to the development of differential responsiveness to ingroup and outgroup members. Aggression toward the ingroup members is relatively transient and gentle, but the capability of channeling these aggressive responses, in a far more belligerent form, toward outgroup members has automatically developed. We have already described the differential responses of the mothers in the playpen situation (Hansen, 1962) toward their own infants and toward infants not their own.

However, we were unprepared to expect cooperative aggressive behavior by these "other" infants toward the mothers (not their own) which had treated them with less than consistent kindness. Unfortunately, since we had not expected these data, we did not have adequate behavior categories in our check-list system and as a result could prepare no figures tracing the developmental course of this behavior. Fortunately, descriptive notes were added to the objective measures recorded each day. We know that this mutual aggression by infants toward the "other-mothers" first appeared at or near the last quarter of the first year of playpen living, and the nature of other-mother aggression is adequately pictured in Figure 12-12. Two or three infants would line up in front of one of the other-mother's cages and threaten her. When the mother would attempt to reach out, snatch, and punish one of the offenders, she would leave herself in a relatively helpless position with one arm extended through the home cage wire front. At this moment one or two infants on the far side would reach in and snatch-grab the defenseless mother's body. These were not playful responses by the members of the infant aggressive team; the attacking infant or infants would often return with a handful of other-mother monkey hair, and the mother gave every indication of being severely discomfited by emitting cries of anguish and engaging in fits of rage. The exact mechanisms through which teamwork mother-heckling and hacking were achieved remain unknown, but these infants worked with all the efficiency of a pair or trio of adult, dominant male baboons defending a baboon troop in the wild against the threats of a marauding leopard.

Cooperative Aggression Against Other Species

An equally dramatic example of cooperative group aggression was observed, again largely on a chance basis, in a group of rhesus monkeys approximately 2½–3½ years old on the Madison Zoo monkey island. In 1962, the director of the Madison Zoo placed a number of 4- to 6-foot-long alligators in the moat surrounding the island, thus inhibiting these young monkeys from swimming in the moat during the hot summer weather.... A number of times the monkeys vented cooperative aggression against an alligator by lining up on the concrete wall surrounding the moat. As an alligator swam nearby, one or two of the waiting monkeys would grab the alligator's inner front limb, another pair would grab its near hind limb, and

Figure 12-12 Cooperative aggressive behavior by three infants toward mother not their own.

the team would pull the helpless reptile flat against the concrete wall of the moat while the other members of the waiting monkey clan would grab or bite the alligator's exposed side or belly. These observations are particularly interesting because psychologists have experienced great difficulty in producing cooperative behavior in monkeys (Wolfle and Wolfle, 1939; Mason and Hollis, 1962) and even in the more socially cooperative chimpanzees (see Crawford, 1937). Thus, attempts by psychologists to study cooperative behavior using conventional learning techniques have enjoyed limited success compared to the accidental successes reported above. This can only mean that the group experiential conditions, undoubtedly bound to ingroup affectional feelings, were inadequately understood, created, or controlled by the experimentalists working in this basically uncharted field.

Intraspecies Outgroup Aggression

The role of early age-mate affectional bonds in the formation and maintenance of cohesive group behaviors was also demonstrated by Hansen and Dodsworth (personal communication) at the Wisconsin Primate Laboratory. Hansen raised three groups of four rhesus monkeys each in three playpen units. They were subsequently combined and placed in a large playroom (Playroom II), and the within- and between-groups behavior was studied and analyzed. These three groups were: (1) a normal monkey mother-raised group of four male infants, (2) a surrogate mother-raised group of two male and two female infants, and (3) a delayed playpen group (first assembled at 9 months of age) of two male and two female mother-raised infants.

When the three groups, totalling 12 monkeys, were first put in Playroom II at 24–30 months of age, there were frequent, intermittent bursts of dominance struggling, centering about the behavior of the four animals comprising the surrogate-raised playpen group. This group included male No. A44, the most dominant monkey of the 12; a less dominant male, A48; a female "shrew," A45; and a small timid female, A47. The shrew moved freely about the room until threatened by some outgroup member. Then she would screech, a stimulus that evoked aggressive assault by A44 against the "offender" and frequently A48 and female A45 would join in the mauling sessions. The offender seldom attempted any defense and in no case was an offender ever really injured—typically, he or she was roughed-up but no blood was drawn.

The least dominant member of this group, female A47, soon learned that she was safe from aggression or assault by any member of the other two groups. When threatened or attacked by an outgroup member, immediate aid was secured also by a screech, and the offender was assaulted and punished by the dominant monkey, No. A44, and by the other two members of the group. Often monkey No. A47 would then join with the other members of her group in attacking her former assailant.

When the surrogate-raised group first engaged in cooperative aggression against individuals of the other two groups, half-hearted assistance was occasionally given to the "offender" by a member of his group, but these cooperative defense measures were rapidly abandoned because the attack was then turned upon them.

After several such skirmishes, the outgroup monkeys learned to respect the social rights of any and all members of the Hansen surrogate-raised group, and even during several sessions in which monkey No. A44 was removed from the room, the other monkeys continued to respect the rights of his group. Such protective behaviors by monkey mothers toward their own infants in the wild have frequently been reported, and it has been suggested that monkey infant personalities may be shaped in large part by the degree of safety, protection, and assurance their mothers can afford them (Imanishi, 1963). The degree of maternal protection given rhesus infants by their own mothers was reported in detail by Hansen (1962).

It is obvious that age-mate or peer affection among monkeys does not cease with infancy but continues to operate as an extremely important variable influencing the nature and frequency of the interpersonal relations involved in the heterosexual affectional system, the maternal affection system, and doubtless the paternal affectional system. Unfortunately, the field studies provide only limited data of a relatively uncontrolled nature relating to the effective developmental interactions between these affectional systems, and laboratory studies on these affectional system interactions have only recently been initiated.

AGE-MATE AFFECTIONAL VARIABLES

As we have already indicated, we believe there is considerable overlap between the variables that operate to release effectively the mother-infant and the infant-mother affectional relationships. In both cases, contact comfort, warmth, and activities associated with nursing are important positive variables operating early in the development of these affectional systems. Visual and auditory variables must also be important, but we cannot at the moment assess their relative roles in any quantitative manner since these variables have never been subjected to experimental manipulation at any stage in the development of either the mother-infant or infant-mother affectional system.

It is obvious that variables relating to nutritional needs do not operate in the development of the peer affectional system, and there is considerable experimental evidence (Harlow and Harlow, 1962) to show that contact comfort and presumably increased temperature are variables that inhibit rather than promote interinfant affectional development.

Contact Comfort as an Inhibitory Variable

When van Wagenen (1950) first described the importance of contact comfort as a primary variable in the development of infant-mother affection, she warned that this variable probably inhibited rather than supported the development of normal interactions between infants. Indeed, she wrote,

> All monkeys under a year should live alone in order to subvert the clinging reaction which is characteristic of the young monkey before it is completely rejected by its mother in favor of her next baby. This clinging reaction, undoubtedly initiated by the grasp reflex in the newborn, is unrelated to it physiologically—rather it is an expression of infantile emotional dependence. At the end of the year young animals can be placed three together in an adult cage without much fear of 'hugging,' for they have learned to live separately (p. 25).

Figure 12-13   Together-together monkeys paired at 30 days of age.

Studies on 2-Together-Together Monkeys

In spite of van Wagenen's gloomy predictions, which seemed completely reasonable to us, we finally raised a pair of 30-day-old rhesus infants (A17, A19) together in a living cage with no mother, real or surrogate. This initial pair of motherless infants rapidly went into a pattern of tight ventral-ventral clinging strikingly like that of the normal neonate-mother contact pattern or the neonate-surrogate mother contact pattern. The strength of this response, as is illustrated in Figure 12-13, was so intense that the two infants looked like a single, two-headed monkey, and we labelled these infants our "together-together" monkeys.

A series of observations employing an open field, a room approximately 6 × 6 × 6 feet (see Harlow and Zimmermann, 1959), was initiated in order to examine more closely the effects of this clinging response. Each member of the together-together pair was tested for five daily 3-minute periods under each of three conditions: with a partner, but confined in an 18 × 18 × 18 inch barred cage; with a strange monkey similarly confined; and with no monkey (and no barred cage) present. We found that there was a very high level of clinging responses and that these were predominantly directed toward the partner by Day 60 and totally directed toward the partner by Day 120. Disturbance measures indicated that in the presence of the partner the mean score was very low at both Day 60 and Day 120.

Beginning at Days 60 and 120, monkeys A17 and A19 were also tested in the Butler visual exploration box. They received three 30-minute daily trials for 12 consecutive days under each of four conditions: partner, stranger, cloth surrogate, or nothing in the stimulus chamber. The order of preference was to partner, stranger, cloth surrogate, and blank condition, and 4515, 3558, 2350 and 2250 responses were elicited, respectively. These data were consistent with the data obtained in the open field test.

After a period of 5–7 months of paired living, monkeys A17 and A19 were housed alone in our standard colony cages. When regular menstrual cycling was noted, we began our standard mating sessions with experienced adult males in the hope of impregnating and subsequently observing the maternal behavior of this first pair of together-together monkeys. Of the two, only one (A19) has had an infant to date and has been consistently mated in a normal manner. Monkey A19 was allowed to keep her infant for 1 week and her maternal behavior was judged to be adequate. The second monkey (A17) was originally mated and inseminated in the normal manner but was judged to be abnormal sexually and no further normal matings were initiated. To date she has aborted twice, and all subsequent matings have been performed with the use of the Eisele rack, a piece of equipment made of steel rods formed in such a manner as to hold the monkey in the normal rhesus sexual present position.

The data obtained on this single pair of together-together monkeys are in no sense definitive. The infants in a strange situation appeared to obtain some degree of security from the presence of the together-together associate. The development of play behavior was not measured, and the Butler box data give no unequivocal measure of affection between the members of the pair. The heterosexual data are equally indeterminate even though one of the two females exhibited normal sexual behavior—a rare phenomenon for monkeys raised under conditions of partial social isolation. The one female that conceived an infant showed normal maternal behavior, a phenomenon seldom or never seen in adult females denied any opportunity to form age-mate attachments (see Harlow *et al.*, 1965). Thus, there is

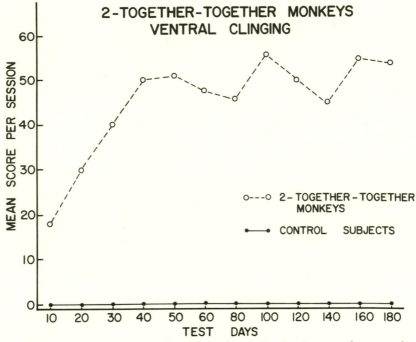

Figure 12-14 Frequency of mutual ventral clinging by together-together and control monkeys in the playroom situation (days 10–80).

presumptive evidence that prolonged together-together association has some socially ameliorating effects.

Subsequently we raised two pairs of 2-together-together monkeys from birth onward in our standard infant living cages, $18 \times 18 \times 24$ inches, and tested all four as a group in playroom I during a 20-minute standard test session 5 days a week for 180 days. Their behavior was compared with that of a group of four monkeys that lived continually with cloth surrogates except for the daily 20-minute sessions of playroom experience.

As one might expect, the pairs of 2-together-together monkeys exhibited an increasing amount of mutual clinging in the playroom situation paralleling the development of the together-together pattern in the small living cage. Thus, the play opportunities afforded by the stimulating playroom situation did not prevent the development of the together-together pattern, and the mutual clinging pattern dominated the behavior of the together-together monkeys even in the playroom from Days 10 to 180, as illustrated in Figure 12-14. By contrast, mutual ventral clinging was essentially nonexistent in the surrogate-raised monkeys in the same

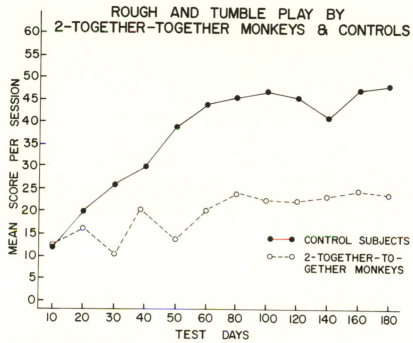

Figure 12-15 Frequency of rough-and-tumble play by together-together and control monkeys in the playroom situation.

test situation. The together-together monkeys seldom made any attempts to initiate play with each other during the 180-day test period. Play behavior by the together-together monkeys was severely depressed as compared to the play of the control group of four surrogate mother-raised and peer-experienced monkeys described in the preceding paragraph, and tested in playroom I throughout the same period (see Figure 12-15).

At approximately 180 days of age we shuffled the pairs of together-together monkeys, placing each of the members of the A pair with a member of the B pair for 2 weeks. Both new pairs immediately went into the ventral-ventral clinging pattern with their new partners, ... and there was no evidence of even transient bereavement or separation anxiety for the previous partner—unlike the clear-cut evidence for separation anxiety found when 180-day-old infants were separated from their real mothers (see Seay and Harlow, 1965). A half-year of completely intimate physical attachment had produced no specific, enduring, personal attachments.

After having been paired for 57 months, the two pairs of 2-together-together monkeys were separated and housed individually in standard

Figure 12-16   Characteristic "choo-choo pattern" of a 4-together-together monkey group.

laboratory cages. Subsequent to the appearance of regular menstrual cycles, these females were paired with adult males from Hansen's mother-raised playpen group and their sexual behavior observed. Two of the females showed normal heterosexual behavior and three were eventually inseminated. These data suggest that the together-together females possessed considerable capabilities of heterosexual expression, unlike monkeys that were totally peer-deprived for long periods of time.

Studies on 4-Together-Together Monkeys

We wondered if the intriguing and apparently partially adverse effects that early infant together-together pairing had on development of the age-mate affectional system would hold when infants were placed together from birth onward in groups of four instead of groups of two. For this reason we studied the behavior of a group of four monkeys, one male and three females, in their home cage and while interacting for 30 minutes daily in Playroom I for a 6-month period. This group, called our 4-together-together monkeys, quickly developed a pattern characterized by

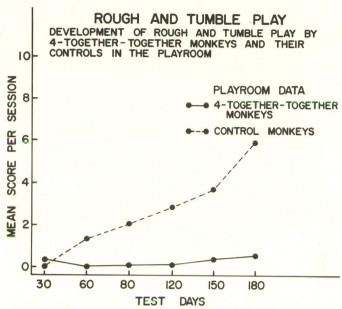

Figure 12-17 Rough-and-tumble play behavior by normal monkeys and 4-together-together monkeys

mutual dorsoventral clinging, illustrated in Figure 12-16, a pattern which we designated as the "choo-choo" effect.

As expected, when the group of 4-together-together monkeys were compared with a control group of four monkeys, two males and two females, raised on cloth surrogate mothers, we again found that the development of play in the control group was far more advanced than the greatly depressed development of play in the 4-together-together group in the playroom (Figure 12-17). The behavior of the 4-together-together monkeys was apparently less adversely affected in their living cage than in the playroom. However, their play behavior in the living cage differed from play development presented in Figure 12-17 only in a modest increase in play frequency during Days 120 to 180. As shown in Figure 12-18, the ventral clinging responses which undoubtedly inhibited play were not exhibited as prominently by the 4-together-together monkeys in their home cage as in the playroom.

Observations at 9 months of the 4-together-together group, in pairs and as a group of four, indicated that the sexual presentation of the females was normal in pattern and that the male of the group exhibited normal adult-type mounting behavior. Unfortunately, the male (R14) died when approximately 2 years of age, prohibiting subsequent investigation of his sex behavior.

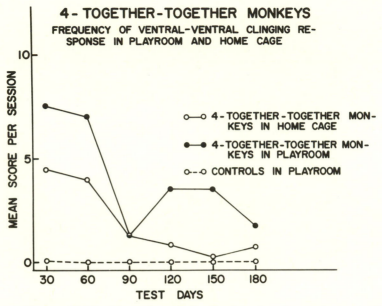

Figure 12-18 Ventral-ventral clinging by 4-together-together monkeys in home cage and in playroom.

Early Social Deprivation as an Inhibitory Variable

It has been known for a considerable time that monkeys subjected to protracted partial or total social deprivation make inadequate social and sexual adjustments to age mates when introduced to them, and that these inadequate social adjustments may be severe, prolonged, and even permanent (Mason, 1963; Mason and Sponholz, 1963; Rowland, 1964). However, the precise assessment of the effects of various periods of partial and total deprivation upon the age-mate or peer affectional system could not be quantified until adequate techniques for assessing such behaviors had been developed. The monkey open-field test first used in surrogate mother testing, as described by Harlow (1958) and by Harlow and Zimmermann (1959), offered limited capabilities, but the open field is less efficient than the playroom or playpen test situations which have been used repeatedly in testing normal infant-infant affectional development (Rosenblum, 1961; Hansen, 1962; Harlow and Harlow, 1962; Harlow *et al.*, 1966).

There are, of course, many types of partial social deprivation; indeed, there are as many or more types of partial social deprivation as there are kinds of social interactions. We have used the term *partial social deprivation* to refer to a situation in which monkeys are raised in bare wire cages

Figure 12-19   Partial social deprivation living conditions.

enabling them to see and hear other members of their species but not make physical contact with them. These cages, which are $12 \times 18 \times 24$ inches, are commonly stacked in adjoining racks as shown in Figure 12-19. There is only one animal living in a cage. We have limited data on a modified partial social isolation situation in which each animal lived alone but was separated from a neighbor by iron bars spaced 2 inches apart, center to center, so that it could physically interact manually with its neighbor. The limited data we obtained indicated that the infants from about 30 days onward engaged in manipulatory exploration of the neighbor, that these social responses tended to increase for a brief period of time, and then gradually waned. We conducted no definitive experiments using this situation, but the progressive disinterest that monkeys showed when so housed suggested that this minimal type of social interaction gave them no permanent social gain.

Partial social deprivation may also be achieved by raising monkeys with surrogate mothers or with real mothers, but denying them any physical interaction with age mates or any other animal for some prede-termined period. Whether or not there is any long-term social gain from raising baby monkeys with surrogates is open to question (Harlow *et al.*, 1965); a study by Alexander (see Alexander and Harlow, 1965) indicates that babies raised with their real mothers but denied age-mate interaction for various periods of time are far less socially handicapped than are babies raised under our condition of partial social isolation. We have spoken of these animals as our "mother-only" infants or our "mother-captive" infants, and it is quite clear that mothers are relatively effective substitutes for other infants, but that this effectiveness decreases with time. Partial social isolation may also be achieved by giving infant monkeys unlimited opportunity to interact with age mates, but denying them any mothering whatsoever.

Monkeys raised in total social isolation are allowed no interaction with other monkeys—or any other animal whatsoever—for some predetermined period. Total social isolation invariably implies a certain degree of sensory isolation also, but in our studies we attempted to hold this to a minimum by illuminating the isolation chambers 24 hours a day, not sound-shielding them, and by providing the infants with deliberately produced sensory deprivation such as the total social and opportunities to explore and manipulate physical stimuli on some prearranged schedule. Thus, total social isolation should be contrasted with deliberately produced sensory deprivation such as the total social and visual deprivation studies by Riesen (1961), and the proprioceptive deprivation studies by Nissen *et al.* (1951) in a single chimpanzee.

Effects of 6 Months of Semisocial Isolation

As we shall see, 3 months of total social isolation (Boelkins, 1963; Griffin, 1965) have little or no long-term social debilitating effects if the totally socially isolated monkeys are allowed subsequently to interact with groups of age mates. We may, therefore, presume that 3 months of semisocial isolation would impose no long-term deficit upon monkeys if they were subsequently allowed adequate interaction with age mates, and the social effects of 6 months of semisocial isolation therefore becomes a critical study.

In an unpublished study by Alexander, Seay, and Harlow the effects of 6 months of semisocial isolation were measured by comparing the social behavior of a group of four semisocial isolates with two groups of four rhesus monkeys that had experienced normal monkey mothering and had been given continuous social interaction with age mates. The semisocial isolates had been raised with cloth surrogate mothers, and even though data by Harlow (1958) and Harlow and Zimmermann (1959) show that infants so raised do form surrogate mother attachments, experiments by Harlow *et al.* (1965) suggest that cloth surrogate rearing, independent of infant interaction, leaves rhesus monkeys with an overall social deficit, i.e., cloth surrogate raising does not compensate for early infant-infant experience. Half of the normal monkeys in this study were raised by multiparous females and half by primiparous females (see Seay, 1964), but since no significant trends were disclosed in this investigation, the monkeys were treated as a group of eight. Supplementary data are also given on a group of four "motherless-mother" infants which had ample opportunity to socially interact during the first year of life. Motherless-mothers are by definition monkey mothers that had no mothers of their own and either no early peer experience or very limited peer experience. Their behavior while rearing their own infants has already been reported (Seay *et al.*, 1964).

The social behavior of the motherless-mother infants and the normal infants had been measured in the playpen situation before they reached 6 months of age; the present data were obtained in Playroom II, testing all infants as homogeneous groups of four in terms of antecedent rearing conditions. The data recorded are for 25 sessions of 25 minutes each, recorded over a 3-month period. The graphs presented below are for play, sex, aggression, and disturbance behavior. These categories are essentially combinations of categories devised by Hansen (1962). The behavior was recorded by observers utilizing a check sheet, recording the presence or absence of particular behaviors within successive 30-second intervals.

The disturbance data graphed in Figure 12-20 show that the normal infants made a remarkably effective adjustment to the new playroom situation even though no protective maternal figure of any kind was present. Thus, the normal infants showed little disturbance in the first 5-day block and essentially no disturbance thereafter. These data contrast sharply with those obtained for the semisocial isolate infants, whose disturbance data were high throughout all test sessions. The only surprising fact is the relatively high disturbance scores made by the motherless-mother infants.

The two normal groups exhibited almost no aggressive behavior during the 6- to 9-month test interval, whereas both the deprived and motherless-mother infants showed aggression peaking during the third test block and subsequently decreasing to the level of the normal infants. The aggressive behavior of the socially deprived infants was violent, vicious, and often prolonged, and involved physical damage and bloodletting to the point that the observers feared serious injury might result. We were unprepared to see these violent aggressive behaviors expressed in macaque infants under 9 months of age since group social studies by Hansen (1962) did not even disclose aggressive play until late in the first year or early in the second. Thus it would appear that semisocial isolation sensitizes infant monkeys for aggressive displays or, conversely stated,

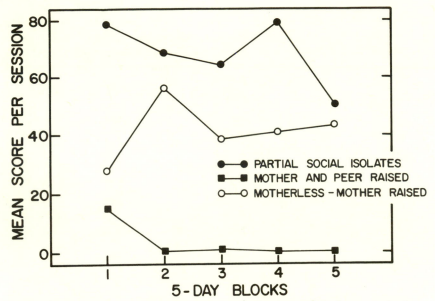

Figure 12-20   Playroom II disturbance scores for 6-month isolates, motherless-mother infants, and normal monkeys.

infants denied an opportunity to form affectional attachments to their age mates release aggression earlier than normal animals, and this aggression appears in a more violent and uncontrollable form. The aggression of the motherless-mother infants was qualitatively different from the social isolates in that it was less prolonged and vicious. Aggression in the motherless mother group usually occurred when the dominant male and his consort females attacked one of the two subordinate males. Often there was no apparent provocation for these attacks.

Social sex behavior throughout the test period was practically nonexistent in the semisocial isolate group, considerably higher in the normal infants, and relatively frequent in the motherless-mother animals. These sex behaviors in the latter group involved both mounting and presenting, peaked sharply in the third test block, and involved the double foot clasp pattern by the dominant male of the motherless-mother group....

The isolate infants exhibited a very low level of play throughout the test sessions, whereas the normal infants rapidly adjusted to the new test situation and played effectively and effusively. The only surprising data disclosed...relate to the delayed and depressed play levels of the motherless-mother infants, but this may relate to the release of aggression when they entered this strange situation. Observation on their previous social behaviors (Seay and Harlow, 1965) had suggested a somewhat heightened level of aggression which may have been reflected in a difference between the frequency of their noncontact play compared to the level of noncontact play of a normal control group. The most striking finding disclosed by these data is the extreme depression of play among the members of the isolate group relative to the high level of play by the two normal groups.

Limited social data on the 6-month semisocially isolated monkeys and the motherless-mother monkeys were obtained 6 months later, after a minimum of 45 days of continuous housing in groups of four in large living cages (Alexander and Harlow, 1965). These data were collected both when the monkeys were housed in homogeneous groups and in heterogeneous groups of four. The heterogeneous groups were composed of one semisocial isolate, one motherless-mother infant, one monkey from the previously described together-together group, and one from a fourth group composed of like-aged monkeys with extensive social experience.

When the isolate infants and the motherless-mother infants were tested as homogeneous groups in a relatively restricted situation, single playpen living cage and playpen unit, both groups showed low aggression and infrequent sex behaviors. Complete sexual patterns are defined as those in which one animal presents and allows itself to be mounted by another which mounts and thrusts appropriately. These were observed 10 times in the motherless-mother group, but never occurred in the semisocial isolate group. The frequency of components of sexual interaction in the motherless-mother group was also higher than in the semisocial isolate group. The level of play behavior was essentially the same, suggesting some degree of social rehabilitation on the part of the 6-month semisocial isolates. However, there was one striking difference between these two groups in this follow-up study: There was a persistent difference in the frequency of huddling behavior, a category including all types of hugging, nestling, and clinging behaviors; such behaviors may be regarded as an expression of infant-infant affection. The 6-month semisocial isolates engaged in these behaviors only rarely.

In the heterogeneous group there was again a considerable difference in frequency of components of sex behavior and in the number of complete sexual interactions. In each case the level of the motherless-mother animals greatly exceeded that of the 6-month semisocial isolate monkeys. Thirty-four complete sexual interactions occurred in which a motherless-mother infant took part, as opposed to seven in the isolate group. Another striking difference was found in the positions occupied by the two groups of juvenile monkeys in the dominance hierarchy. The isolate monkey occupied last place in the hierarchy in six of the eight heterogeneous groups. The motherless-mother infants never occupied the lowest position in the hierarchy and occupied the first three positions with an approximately equal frequency.

These findings suggest that 6 months of semisocial isolation produce a deficit in sex behavior and dominance competence which persists even after prolonged, continuous social contact. The deficit in play behavior, and the intragroup hyperaggressiveness which were evident at 6–9 months of age, however, were no longer present at 15–17 months of age. It would appear that these effects of partial social isolation are removed by prolonged "group therapy."

Effects of Total Social Deprivation

Infant monkeys subjected at birth to 3 months of total social isolation and then exposed to the wonders or horrors of the external world typically go into a state of emotional shock with regression, characterized by the autistic posture of self-clutching of head and body by the arms and legs while remaining in a prone position.... Indeed, this shock was so severe that one of these monkeys died within 6 days, apparently from complete emotional anorexia, and another probably would have perished had not the staff been alerted and resorted when necessary to forced feeding. Fortunately, this phenomenon did not recur in any of the other four infants released from 3 months of total social deprivation. When pairs of these surviving 3-month total social isolates were subsequently tested with equal-aged control infants, the autistic posture commonly recurred in the playroom, as seen in Figure 12-21. Nevertheless, the surviving total isolates made a remarkable adjustment to the strange playroom situation (Playroom II). As is shown in Figure 12-22, the 3-month isolate monkeys showed comparable frequency of threats and frequency of contact play to the controls during the first month of playroom testing. The absolute frequency of play in the second month of playroom testing was lower for the isolates than the controls, but the difference was not statistically significant (Griffin, 1965). The really surprising fact is the lack of social behavior differences during the first month of social testing since the total social isolates did exhibit considerable emotional disturbance during the first week after removal from isolation.

An independent study on the effects of 3 months of total social isolation had been previously conducted by Boelkins (1963) who used a different experimental design. In Boelkins' study the socially deprived animals were tested as two independent groups of four animals in playroom I for 6 months following social deprivation, and their behavior was compared with that of two independent groups of four monkeys that had been allowed to play together in playroom I from the first 13 days of age onward. As can be seen in Figure 12-23, Boelkins found similar trends in the development of rough-and-tumble play responses in his 3-month total isolates and the normal animals. The higher absolute frequency of contact

Figure 12-21 Autistic posture in playroom when tested with controls.

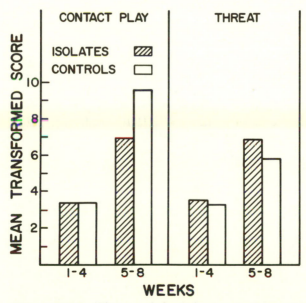

Figure 12-22 Threat and play behaviors by 3-month total socially isolated and controls tested in Playroom II.

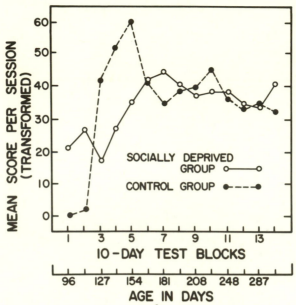

Figure 12-23 Development of contact play by 3-month total socially isolated and normal infants.

play responses in the socially deprived animals is doubtless a function of their greater physical maturity. Boelkins subsequently compared the frequency of rough-and-tumble play by the 3-month socially deprived group and the control group, holding opportunity for social interaction constant, and under these circumstances he found no significant between-groups differences. Thus, Boelkins' data are in essential agreement with those of Griffin in that they give no indication of any long-term socially debilitating effects following 3 months of social isolation if the monkeys subsequently have opportunity to socially interact with age mates.

These data obtained for the 3-month social isolates by Griffin (1965) contrast sharply with the data obtained on monkeys totally socially isolated during the first 6 months of life (see Rowland, 1964; Harlow *et al.*, 1964). Social threat data for the 6-month isolates and their controls are given in Figure 12-24; transformed scores were used for statistical reasons. The ratio to the actual frequencies of threat for the 6-month isolates and their controls is approximately 1 to 4 and the differences were significant far beyond the 5% level. The curves for the 6-month isolates and their controls for frequency of threat during the 32 weeks of observations which were subsequently conducted in the playroom are shown in Figure 12-25. From the 24th week on, frequency of social threat increased somewhat in the 6-month isolates but these social threats were consistently directed to other isolates....

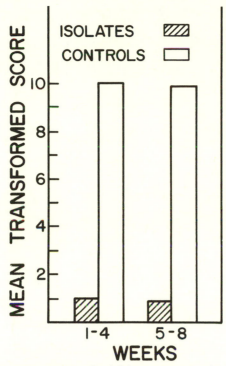

Figure 12-24   Social threat responses by 6-month total socially isolated monkeys and their controls.

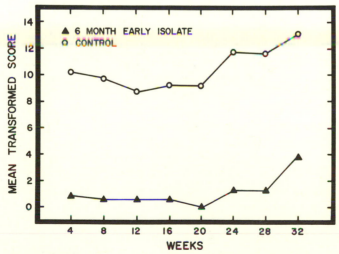

Figure 12-25   Social threat by isolates and control monkeys throughout 32 test weeks.

215

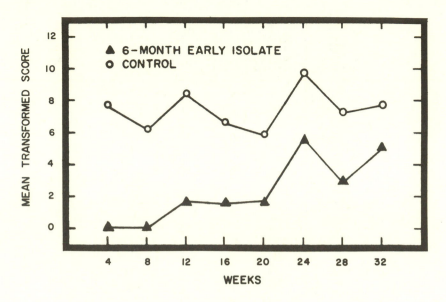

Figure 12-26 Rough-and-tumble play by 6-month isolates
and controls throughout 32 test weeks.

For all practical purposes, no contact play was observed in the 6-month isolated monkeys during either of these first two 4-week isolation periods, whereas a large amount of such play occurred between the controls. The level of contact play increased materially in the 6-month isolate group (Figure 12-26) during the course of the 32 weeks of testing, but again the contact play that was exhibited was play between isolates and not between isolates and controls. Actually, social interaction between the 6-month isolated monkeys and their controls was for all practical purposes nonexistent throughout the entire 32-week test period, except for bursts of aggression which the controls occasionally directed toward the isolate animals. Similar developmental curves were found on many measures taken for the 6-month early isolates and their control group, including measures of oral object play, social approach, play initiation, and approach-withdrawal play. Frequency of autoerotic behavior was much higher in the isolates than their controls, a difference that persisted throughout the entire 32 weeks of testing even though the differences between the groups decreased with time. A strikingly different developmental pattern between the two groups is that of rigidity.... The rigidity measure showed that when they contacted a control animal, the isolates exhibited a progressive tendency to turn away, avert the face, and maintain a fixed rigid posture of the body. By this measure, progressively increasing

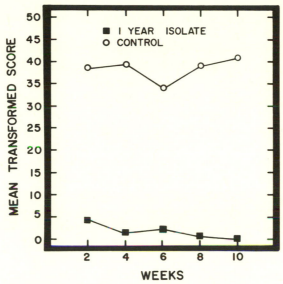

Figure 12-27 Activity play by 12-month social isolates and controls.

differences between the two groups no doubt reflect the avoidance responses by the isolates to the controls, as the latter exhibited increasing frequency and severity of aggressive responses toward the isolates.

The effects of 6 months of total social isolation were so devastating and debilitating that we assumed initially that 12 months of isolation might not produce any additional decrement. This assumption proved to be false; 12 months of isolation almost obliterated the animals socially, as is indicated by the playroom data for activity play, the simplest form of play, shown in Figure 12-27.

Activity play was chosen as a primary measure since it represents a primitive play level involving minimal interanimal contact. The 12-month isolates showed practically no activity play, and the trend was a decrease with time. The control monkeys, on the other hand, displayed a relatively constant, high level of activity play. Observation of the 12-month isolated animals and their controls had to be terminated after 10 experimental weeks because the controls became increasingly aggressive toward the helpless isolate animals and might have killed them had we continued social testing.

Very similar scores for the 12-month isolates and their controls were also obtained for frequency of object play and social approach. The incidence of biting responses ... showed an intriguing developmental trend since, for all practical purposes, no biting response ever appeared in any of the 12-month social isolates, whereas the frequency of biting responses increased progressively in the control group. Biting responses which are found in the play of normal monkeys during the second year of life were totally absent in isolates, who never bit any control animal and never even tried to bite another member of the isolate group. Contrariwise, the controls engaged in increasingly frequent biting responses, almost all of them directed toward the helpless 1-year isolates. Under these circumstances it is not at all surprising to find the enormous differences between the two groups in the incidence of general disturbance (see Figure 12-28). The control animals rapidly adjusted to the playroom situation and showed essentially no disturbance from the fourth week onward. Contrariwise, the 12-month isolates showed a high level of disturbance throughout, and this disturbance tended to increase. A rather interesting difference between the 6-month early and 12-month total social isolate animals is that the 6-month deprived did show a relatively high level of autoerotic behavior, whereas the 12-month total social isolate animals failed to develop any autoerotic behaviors; in other words, a year of total social isolation appeared to suppress all social and sexual behaviors.

The behavior of the 6-month late isolate group, the group of animals raised in partial social isolation for the first 6 months of life and in total social isolation for the next 6 months, differed sharply from the behavior of either the 6-month early or the 12-month social isolates and their controls. The 6-month late isolates were more aggressive than their control subjects and appeared to make a better, rather than a worse, social adjustment during the postisolation test period. The inability of the control subjects to cope with the aggression of the 6-month late isolates led, as is shown in Figure 12-29, to a decrease in general disturbance by the isolates and an increase in general disturbance by the controls. The 6-month late isolates showed more object play and a higher increase of approach than the control subjects. No sexual or autoerotic behavior was noted for either group during the course of the observations and no patterns of effective social play were established.

It should be noted that these control subjects had undergone 12 months of partial social isolation, a degree of social isolation that depresses or destroys effective play capabilities, so that apparently the only "social" behaviors that could result related to aggression. Either by chance or by some unanalyzed variable, these behaviors are more prominent in the late isolate group than in their controls. The data obtained for the 6-month late isolates and their controls seemed anomalous at the time, because the isolates appeared to make better social adjustments than their controls, although the only real measure of social adjustment was greater aggression. These apparently paradoxical data, however, ceased to be paradoxical in terms of the long-term follow-up social study recently completed by Mitchell (1965).

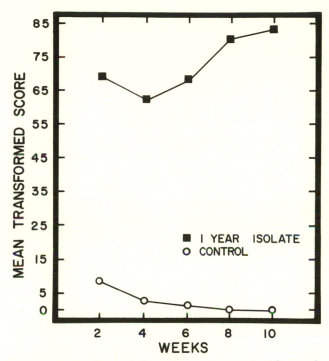

Figure 12-28 General disturbance responses by 12-month
social isolates and controls.

The Mitchell follow-up study obtained data on the total social isolates at 28–44 months of age. Two of the 12-month isolates and three each of the 6-month early and 6-month late isolates were paired with more normally raised macaque adults, age mates, and juveniles. Eight monkeys that had been raised with both a mother and peers served as a control group. The purpose of this investigation was to determine if the social deficiencies found when the isolates were juveniles either disappeared, persisted, or strengthened at puberty.

As is seen in Figure 12-30, the two 12-month isolates were very fearful and exhibited no physical aggression, although symbolic aggression or threats were quite high in these animals. The 12-month group was also clearly inferior to all other monkeys in play and sex (see Figure 12-31). The two 6-month isolate groups were pooled (in Figures 12-30 and 12-31) because there were no longer any obvious differences between the early and late groups. The combined 6-month isolate groups, as can be seen in Figure 12-30, were less fearful than the 12-month isolates but were still more afraid than the controls. They engaged in a little play, all of which was noncontact or approach-withdrawal play, and exhibited some

Figure 12-29   Inability of controls to cope with aggression of 6-month late isolates.

sexual behavior (see Figure 12-31), but remained inferior to the controls on both of these behaviors. Most of their positive social behaviors occurred concomitantly with signs of disturbance, fear, or aggression. They evinced a greater number of threats and significantly more physical aggression than the more socially sophisticated monkeys (Figure 12-30). The aggression was often an unnatural attack against a huge adult male or a needless beating of a juvenile. These behaviors were never seen in normal females and were essentially nonexistent in normal males at puberty.

Hence, the apparently paradoxical aggression obtained for the 6-month late isolates as juveniles persisted at puberty, and a similar hyperaggressiveness appeared in the 6-month early group. Prior to puberty, the agonistic behavior of the latter group had consisted almost entirely of fear. Moreover, while no signs of hostility had been found in the 12-month isolates when they were juveniles, the follow-up disclosed that this most severely deprived group made more threat responses than both the combined 6-month isolate groups and the controls.

A probable reason for this appearance of hostility is simply that full-blown aggression develops late in the rhesus monkey (Cross and

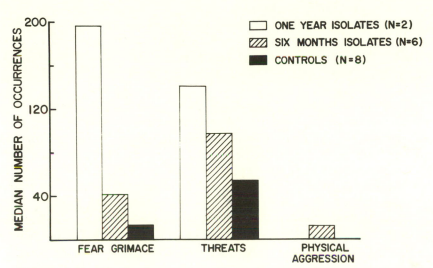

Figure 12-30 Median frequencies of fear grimace, symbolic aggression, and physical aggression in 12-month isolates, 6-month isolates (pooled), and controls.

Harlow, 1965). Externally directed threat responses appear early in the first year but increase progressively up to the sixth year. The strength of outward aggression increases most rapidly during the second year in males and later in females. Responses indicative of social fear, on the other hand, may appear at 90 days and are certainly well developed at 180 days

Figure 12-31 Median frequencies of social play and social sex in 12-month isolates, 6-month isolates, and controls.

of age. Hence, social fear had matured when the isolates were tested as juveniles while hostility had not yet fully developed. The misuse of both agonistic responses apparently resulted from the isolates having no opportunity to learn the use and meaning of the gestures in an early peer affectional system.

None of the eight total social isolates tested at puberty was a socially normal animal in any situation. Fear and hostility were ever-present responses and appeared in highly individual ways. A number of the isolates adjusted to specific situations but none adapted to all situations. For example, some of those who did not attack juveniles showed "suicidal" aggression toward adults, while some who were unafraid of adult males were terrified of a frightened juvenile.

Forms of disturbance other than fear and hostility were also highly individualistic. All isolates were cautious and rigid in their movements, engaged in little social exploration, and exhibited signs of severe disturbance. However, these behaviors were quite varied from animal to animal. Some remained in one corner of the playroom and rocked, others crouched but did not rock, and several showed a high-incidence of self-clasping and self-orality.

Peculiar "ritualistic movements" which differed markedly from animal to animal also occurred in the isolates. These movements were rigidly performed and out of context from the ongoing behavior of the monkey, sometimes to the point of absurdity. For example, one 6-month early isolate male (B93) slowly moved his right arm toward his head in a rigid pose and, upon seeing his own approaching hand, suddenly appeared startled by it. His eyes slowly widened and he would at times fear grimace, threaten or even bite the hand "sneaking up on him." If he did not respond, "it" would continue to move toward him, his eyes becoming wider and wider, until the hand was entirely clasping his face. There he would rigidly sit, with saucer-sized eyes staring in horror between clutching fingers.

Thus, many idiosyncratic aberrations occur in these animals as well as the more generally agonistic abnormalities. Indeed, all monkeys that have been deprived of the development of peer affection are affected by agonistic aberrations. These same monkeys, however, are deficient in positive affectional responses. On the other hand, monkeys reared continuously with peers and without mothers are neither hyperaggressive nor abnormally fearful toward their peers but show an abnormally high peer attachment, e.g., the together-together huddling syndrome. The role of the peer affectional system appears to be the crucial one of developing latent age-mate affection which subtly serves to control or to muffle the manifest emotions that later mature.

REFERENCES

Alexander, B. K., and Harlow, H. F. 1965. Social behavior of juvenile rhesus monkeys subjected to different rearing conditions during the first six months of life. *Zool. Jb. Physiol. 71*, 489–508.

Boelkins, R. C. 1963. The development of social behavior in the infant rhesus monkey following a period of social isolation. Unpublished M.S. thesis, University of Wisconsin, Madison, Wisconsin.

Crawford, M. P. 1937. The cooperative solving of problems by young chimpanzees. *Comp. Psychol. Monogr. 14*, 1–88.

Cross, H. A., and Harlow, H. F. 1965. Prolonged and progressive effects of partial isolation on the behavior of macaque monkeys. *J. exp. Res. Pers. 1*, 39–49.

Green, E. H. 1933. Friendships and quarrels among preschool children. *Child Develpm. 4*, 237–262.

Griffin, G. A. 1965. Effects of three months of total social deprivation on social adjustments and learning of rhesus monkeys. Unpublished M.S. thesis, University of Wisconsin, Madison, Wisconsin.

Halverson, H. M. 1931. An experimental study of prehension in infants by means of systematic cinema records. *Genet. Psychol. Monogr. 10*, 107–286.

Hansen, E. W. 1962. The development of infant and maternal behavior in rhesus monkeys. Unpublished doctoral dissertation, University of Wisconsin, Madison, Wisconsin.

Harlow, H. F. 1958. The nature of love. *Amer. Psychol. 13*, 673–685.

Harlow, H. F. 1962. Development of the second and third affectional systems in macaque monkeys. *In* "Research Approaches to Psychiatric Problems: A Symposium" (T. T. Tourlentes, S. L. Pollack, and H. E. Himwich, eds.), pp. 209–229. Grune & Stratton, New York.

Harlow, H. F., and Harlow, M. K. 1962. Social deprivation in monkeys. *Sci. Amer. 207*, 136–146.

Harlow, H. F., and Zimmermann, R. R. 1959. Affectional patterns in the infant monkey. *Science, 130*, 421–432.

Harlow, H. F., Harlow, M. K., and Hansen, E. W. 1963. The maternal affectional system of rhesus monkeys. *In* "Maternal Behavior in Mammals" (H. L. Rheingold, ed.), pp. 254–281. Wiley, New York.

Harlow, H. F., Rowland, G. L., and Griffin, G. A. 1964. The effect of total social deprivation on the development of monkey behavior. *Psychiat. Res. Rep. 19*, 116–135.

Harlow, H. F., Dodsworth, R. O., and Harlow, M. K. 1965. Total social isolation in monkeys. *Proc. Natl. Acad. Sci. U.S. 54*, 90–97.

Harlow, H. F., Harlow, M. K., Dodsworth, R. O., and Arling, G. L. 1966. Maternal behavior of rhesus monkeys deprived of mothering and peer association in infancy. *Proc. Amer. philos. Soc. 110*, 58–66.

Harlow, M. K., and Harlow, H. F. 1965. Romulus and rhesus. *Listener 75* (1872), 215–217.

Hines, M. O. 1942. The development and regression of reflexes, postures, and progression in the young macaque. *Contr. Embryol. Carnegie Inst. 30*, 153–209.

Imanishi, K. 1963. Social behavior in Japanese monkeys, *Macaca fuscata. In* "Primate Social Behavior" (C. H. Southwick, ed.), pp. 68–81. Van Nostrand, Princeton, New Jersey.

Itani, J. 1963. Paternal care in the wild Japanese monkey. *Macaca fuscata. In* "Primate Social Behavior" (C. H. Southwick, ed.), pp. 91–97. Van Nostrand, Princeton, New Jersey.

Jensen, G. D. 1961. The development of prehension in a macaque. *J. comp. physiol. Psychol. 54*, 11–12.

Magnus, R. 1924. "Körperstellung." Springer, Berlin.

Maslow, A. H. 1943. A theory of human motivation. *Psychol. Rev. 50*, 370–396.

Mason, W. A. 1963. The effects of environmental restriction on the social development of rhesus monkeys. *In* "Primate Social Behavior" (C. H. Southwick, ed.), pp. 161–173, Van Nostrand, Princeton, New Jersey.

Mason, W. A., and Hollis, J. H. 1962. Communication between young rhesus monkeys. *Animal Behav. 10*, 211–221.

Mason, W. A., and Sponholz, R. R. 1963. Behavior of rhesus monkeys raised in isolation. *J. psychiat. Res. 1*, 299–306.

Mitchell, G. D. 1965. Long term effects of total social isolation upon the behavior of rhesus monkeys. Unpublished M.S. thesis, University of Wisconsin, Madison, Wisconsin.

Montgomery, K. C. 1955. The relationship between fear induced by novel stimulation and exploratory behavior. *J. comp. physiol. Psychol. 48*, 254–260.

Mowbray, J. B., and Cadell, T. E. 1962. Early behavior patterns in rhesus monkeys. *J. comp. physiol. Psychol. 55*, 350–359.

Nissen, H. W., Chow, K. L., and Semmes, J. 1951. Effects of restricted opportunity for tactual, kinesthetic, and manipulative experience on the behavior of a chimpanzee. *Amer. J. Psychol. 64*, 485–507.

Pavlov, I. P. 1927. "Conditioned Reflexes" (Transl. by G. V. Anrep). Oxford Univ. Press, London and New York.

Riesen, A. H. 1961. Stimulation as a requirement for growth and function in behavioral development. *In* "Functions of Varied Experience" (D. W. Fiske and S. R. Madde, eds.), pp. 57–80. Dorsey Press, Homewood, Illinois.

Riesen, A. H., and Kinder, E. F. 1952. "Postural Development of Infant Chimpanzees." Yale Univ. Press, New Haven, Connecticut.

Rosenblum, L. A. 1961. The development of social behavior in the rhesus monkey. Unpublished doctoral dissertation, University of Wisconsin, Madison, Wisconsin.

Rowland, G. L. 1964. The effects of total social isolation upon learning and social behavior in rhesus monkeys. Unpublished doctoral dissertation, University of Wisconsin, Madison, Wisconsin.

Seay, B. M. 1964. Maternal behavior in primiparous and multiparous rhesus monkeys. Unpublished doctoral dissertation, University of Wisconsin, Madison, Wisconsin.

Seay, B., and Harlow, H. F. 1965. Maternal separation in the rhesus monkey. *J. nerv. ment. Dis. 140*, 434–441.

Seay, B., Alexander, B. K., and Harlow, H. F. 1964. The maternal behavior of socially deprived rhesus monkeys. *J. abnorm. soc. Psychol.* 69, 345–354.

van Wagenen, G. 1950. The monkey. *In* "The Care and Breeding of Laboratory Animals" (E. J. Farris, ed.), pp. 1–42. Wiley, New York.

Wolfle, D. L., and Wolfle, H. M. 1939. The development of cooperative behavior in monkeys and young children. *J. genet. Psychol.* 55, 137–175.

NOTE

This research was supported by USPHS grants MH-4528 and FR-00167 from the National Institutes of Health to the University of Wisconsin Primate Laboratory and Wisconsin Regional Primate Research Center, respectively.

13

Sex Differences in Passion and Play

Harry F. Harlow and Helen E. Lauersdorf

Had God created man or monkey each with one identical form and fashion, many problems of pride and passion would never have arisen. Indeed, if that unfortunate celestial decision had been made initially, more than pride and passion would presently fail to exist, for there would never have been more than one man or one monkey. But that was not the decision made, and both species, two sexes, and multiple differences do certainly exist.

Even if one merely looks at people, disregarding current clothes and coiffures, anatomical differences can be discerned, and if one merely looks at monkeys, anatomical differences between the sexes are inescapable. In the absence of garments or gossamer it becomes obvious that the sexes differ—even at the level of face validity for males and two-faced validity for females. This, of course, merely means that females are twice as valid and probably four times more reliable than males.

Therefore, it is not amazing that anatomical differences between males and females should go completely unquestioned. It is an indisputable biological fact that behavioral differences between the two sexes are many more times as characteristic, diverse, and different from the frigid, frozen, and fatuous differences of anatomy. Thus, it is surprising that sex differences in behavior are questioned and strongly argued by some to be a result of cultural influences only. There are always greater individual and

Harlow, H.F., and Lauersdorf, H.E. (1974) Sex differences in passion and play. *Perspectives in Biology and Medicine*, *17*, 348–360. ℗ 1974 by The University of Chicago. All rights reserved. Printed in U.S.A.

intersexual differences in behavior than in bodies, or in movements than in muscles. Every little movement has a meaning all its own.

We would like to discuss differences between the female and male sexes that we have found to hold true after and over many years of research. Our subjects have been rhesus monkeys, man's close relative on the phylogenetic ladder. These sex differences begin at birth and encompass all developmental stages, from early sex reflexes through early sex behavior personal characteristics, juvenile play, the subsequent maturation of aggression, and then into adulthood and the roles of parenthood.

INFANTILE SEXUAL REFLEXES

There is nothing either subtle or surreptitious about sexual behaviors whether they are studied and measured in babies, in youths, or in people old enough to know better. Let us start with infant sex, uncontaminated by lust or learning. All newborn primates—monkey, ape, and man—are capable of exercising at least two unlearned sexual responses, penile or clitoral erection and pelvic thrusting (1). The sexual significance of these responses is not completely apparent until maturation is combined with meaning at about 3 years of age in the monkey and about 12 years in man. Behaviorally, monkeys grow up or mature four or five times as fast as people, so that sexual interest and capability become apparent in human beings and monkeys at the same stage developmentally, but at a different age chronologically.

It can be argued that the aforementioned behaviors do not demonstrate differences between the sexes, since penile and clitoral erection have much in common—extremely common as far as the prudish are concerned. Furthermore, the form of pelvic thrusting in male and female monkeys is very similar. Indeed, in this particular case, the behavior may be more similar than its body basis, since pelvic anatomy was differentially designed to maintain female functions even more biologically important than intermittent intromission.

However, both erection and pelvic thrusting behaviors in the neonate differ enormously between sexes in frequency of occurrence, and this is true for both human beings and monkeys. Monkey mothers press naked baby monkeys against their motherly bodies, particularly during nursing, and the male babies thrust against the mother's body with greater frequency and faith than do the females.

SEX DIFFERENCES IN POSTURAL PROPENSITIES

Adequate sexuality does not develop in monkeys until the third or fourth year of life, but long before sex is very adequate it is very evident. For example, we have carefully studied groups of male and female monkeys that, in terms of developmental age, have been partway toward the benign bliss of connubial constructiveness or competence. In terms of age our female and male monkeys were almost halfway to heterosexual heaven, but in achievement they had not yet entered the gates of Eden. At 1 year of age their sexual patterns were poorly formed or fragmented, but even these fragmented forms could clearly be classified as male or female. Inept or inexperienced male monkey sex might involve the male grasping the female's body and using this polarized position as a base for full-fashioned pelvic thrusts. However, many male infants engage in planless postures such as those who grasp the frustrated female by the head and thrust at her neck (Figure 13-1). These misguided males have constituted our first head-start program—which has been less successful than other programs by the same name. There have also been males who grasped the back of the female at the midline and thrust across or underneath her body. This position and posture left them working at cross-purposes with reality. The infant postures have always been adult-like but never totally achieve adult results. Under these circumstances the male monkeys have been consistent underachievers. Double foot-clasp of the female's legs, for

Figure 13-1 "Head start" posture.

Figure 13-2   Only her heart was in the right place.

example, the acme of adult masculine monkey perfection, is not an infant male posture.

Female infants similarly have given their behavioral best, but like the males their best has consisted of inelegant and inadequate sex responding. The females commonly sit flush on the floor, staring either ardently or amorously at the male above them (Figure 13-2). Only their hearts are in the right place. Alternatively they might stand on all four legs in a loose and limp posture that would support or facilitate neither recreation nor procreation. The data presented in Figures 13-3a and b are a titanic tribute to very early sex-specific sexuality, sometimes theoretically described as instinct theory or species-specific theory. Almost 9 percent of the boy baby monkeys' sex responses have clearly been of masculine sex type, and 98 percent of the girl baby monkeys' sex responses are clearly of female

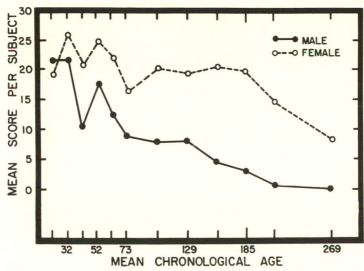

Figure 13-3a Sex differences in the development of passive responses during the playpen situation.

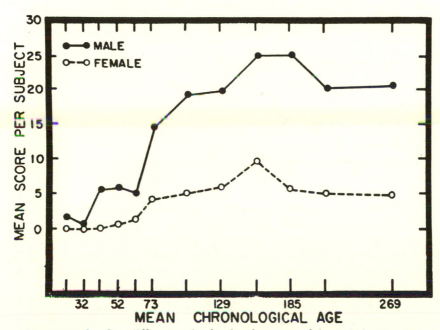

Figure 13-3b Sex differences in the development of threat behavior during the playpen situation.

sex type, even when fragmentary or inadequate. With infant male and female monkeys too young to have had a thought of guile worthwhile or too young to have ever been caught considering leavening living with lust, one can separate the males from the females on the basis of behaviors alone.

SEX DIFFERENCES IN PERSONAL RESPONSIVENESS

Even more striking data on early male-female sexual differentiation of specific behavior patterns in monkeys were obtained many years ago by measuring the developmental age and frequency of a number of behavior patterns. These are not sexual behaviors per se, but relate to aggression and dominance and other activities which are indirectly basic to passion and procreation. Threat is a masculine pattern, even though threat responses can be exhibited by both males and females. Threat responses tend to develop earlier and subsequently appear much more frequently in male monkeys. Indeed, the differences are highly significant at 80 days of age, and the deviation between sexes is subsequently accentuated (Figure 13-3b). In one or two out of 100 cases we have observed an unusually aggressive, threatening female rhesus monkey, and apparently the same phenomenon has been observed in human females.

Just as threat is a masculine tendency in man and monkey, so is passivity a feminine quality. Our monkey data show very early sex differentiations in this behavior category, and the frequency differences between males and females progressively deviate and become significantly different from 60 to 100 days of age onward.

Treading with reluctant feet
Where the brook and river meet,
I am the passive female type
Who waits until the time is ripe.

A second, more complex female pattern is that of rigidity. This pattern may manifest itself in the female as a result of facial or bodily confrontation with a male. Since facial staring is a threat, the female averts her head, walks a few steps away, and assumes the rigidity posture (Figure 13-4). It is as if she knows that they also serve who only stand and wait. Often the male follows, and if he does he positions himself toward the female in an elementary, inadequate sex posture. If, over a period of months, conditioned or learned responses become predominant and super-imposed over the unconditioned or instinctive responses, there is a high likelihood that a new generation of male and female monkeys will again appear. We emphasize that God created man in his own image, and

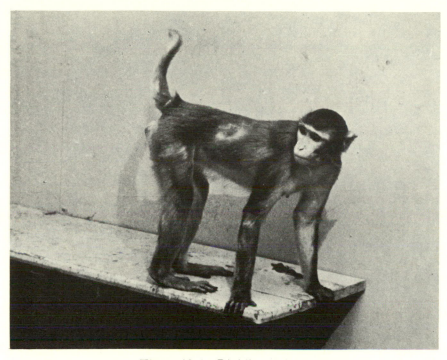

Figure 13-4   Rigidity position.

spurred on by this effort he next created Eve. Perhaps this could be termed Evelution. It certainly shaped the future of man. And with subhuman primates too, just as sex shapes monkeys, monkeys shape sex. It is sex of one and half a dozen of the other.

THE PRICELESS GIFT OF PLAY

Perhaps it is not surprising to find profound differences in the sex behavior of bisexual animals or even to find sex differences in early behavior patterns which relate in part to sexual behavior. However, forgetting and forgiving sex per se, we still find significant sex differences in behaviors which are far more social than sexual. Our researches on monkeys have disclosed the enormous importance of infantile play in the development of socialization and indirectly in the subsequent development of normal erogenous behaviors. For example, if adequate sexual positioning were obtained in men and monkeys either by instinct or by sheer trial and error, it would be a transparent miracle.

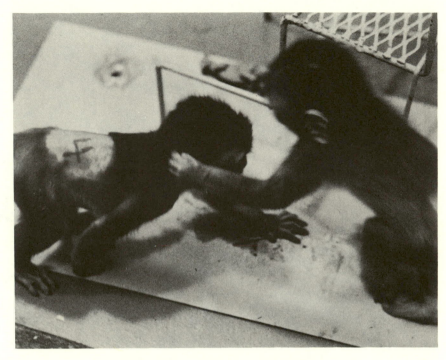

Figure 13-5   Rough-and-tumble play.

Actually, the trappings of social sexual sanctity are the product of multiple variables, some unlearned and instinctual and others learned. The interaction of the variables operates in a lawful manner if monkeys are raised in a normal environment. There is a destiny that shapes our ends, roughhew them though we may. Successful social sex is always a function of both yearning and learning, but the yearning must come first.

The social sexual gifts obtained from peer play transcend and supplement both the contact comfort and basic trust first imparted to the infant by the mother. Subtle, successful socialization is achieved by the purpose and patterns of play whose basic social functions have never been understood, in spite of a plethora of paper and limitless waste of words directed to the topic.

One of the functions of play is its role in the selection and separation of sex roles, achieved by both innate and acquired variables. Males are playful and females are playful, but both play out an appropriate role. The primary pattern of monkey play, engaged in by both sexes at an equally early age, has also been described as a basic human child play pattern (2), and we call it rough-and-tumble play (Figure 13-5). As monkeys and children become older, this play becomes more violent and vigorous, and the females progressively retreat and withdraw to engage predominantly in girlhood games, leaving the area of mild mayhem to the males.

Females always have been playful and always will be playful, but they want to play in their own fashion. Anyone who watches a fifth-grade school picnic will see that young children, male and female, play in exactly the same manner as monkey youngsters. The little boys are rough and rambunctious toward male and female playmates; they wrestle and roll, snatch, grab, and hit, but, in spite of the tempo and turmoil, nobody really gets hurt. Contrariwise, the little girls sometimes push and pull other little girls, but they do not challenge boys, and they do not wrestle, roll, snatch, grab, or hit.

One of Freud's greatest creative theoretical constructs was that of the sexual latency period, and Freud's theoretical construct would have been of even greater importance if he had been right. Freud was wrong. Freud believed that the period of time from 6 to 12 years of age when the two sexes are intrigued only by members of their own sex and disinterested in members of the opposite sex was a function of the Oedipus complex, father fear, repression, the castration complex, and possibly penis envy and the Electra complex. Seldom has a behavior so totally simple been endowed with such a wealth of sensuous and sexually seductive symbols.

Monkeys also have a sexual latency period in which boys will be boys and girls will be girls, and never the twain shall meet until much later. If one properly translates monkey age into human chronological age, the latency periods of monkeys and humans are comparable. The latency period is not a result of repressed sexual surges, but is patterned out of play.

As we have already emphasized, little boys and little girls have enormous and eager play preferences. Their play preferences are simple, direct, and sensible. Boys play with boys and girls play with girls, from 6 to 12 years of age if they are people and from 6 to 36 months if they are monkeys. This is not a result of father fears in monkeys, because most monkeys are quite unaware of their fathers. If it results from a castration complex, none of our monkeys has ever discerned or disclosed it.

Bluntly put, the latency period is entirely dependent upon the fact that play is a powerfully pervading motive in infant humans and monkeys. The two sexes play in different ways, and each sex is disenchanted with the way the other plays. The latency period begins when play definitely becomes sexually differentiated and ends when a passion for play—the opposite-sex kind—ends in playful passions. Play need not be sexual but sex should be playful.

Shortly after rough-and-tumble play surfaces, infant monkeys manifest another play pattern, which we call approach-avoidance play (Figure

Figure 13-6   Approach-avoidance play.

13-6). Approach-avoidance, or contact-noncontact, play is primarily a chasing game where one monkey chases after another, or even two or three others, with the role of chaser and chased frequently reversed. In spite of the pace and passion this play may develop, there is surprisingly little body contact. There is considerable evidence to support the premise that approach-avoidance play is a female type as contrasted with the masculine rough and tumble.

Play is the primary pathway to social success, and after that to masculine and feminine mastery. Play in the infant is not a premeditated activity with any intent toward long-term adult achievement. Playmates play for play itself, but the very acts of play prepare the infant for the more mature behavioral acts of social and sexual success, social life, social and maternal love, inhibition of fears and frailties, and infant indulgence. Infant play may appear to be pointless, but it is actually very purposeful.

Thus, play, or diverse play patterns, is the play or ploy that separates the sexes until the gonads bring their gifts. Through the bisexual behavior patterns we have already described, monkeys and humans attain full maturity, and the aging infants subsequently care to roll away their proper patterns of play and proceed to play out their proper role. Each monkey chooses one of two roles, the masculine or the feminine. These roles are parallel, if not separate and equal.

THE AWESOME AGE OF AGGRESSION

Threat responses and rough-and-tumble play are probably infantile precursors of aggressive responses, but true aggression full of fight and fury is a response which matures considerably later in life. In the male monkey vigorous aggression, in almost full-fledged form, is not present until about 3 years of age, as contrasted with the appearance of threat at 3 months and aggressive rough-and-tumble play as early as 9 months. The female, who engages in rough-and-tumble play at an equally early age, holds back and does not evince vigorous aggression until more than a year later than the male.

We have data on the age of the gradual appearance of aggression in monkeys measured in a number of different test situations. If monkeys are allowed to play daily in small groups, transient and tempered aggression will be seen at 9–15 months. If monkeys are housed in individual cages and subsequently tested for aggression 5 days a week, violent aggression against an experimenter who sits passively and observes will be exhibited beginning at 2 years of age in the male and at 4 years of age in the female at 2.

We have already alluded to sex differences in aggression, and the nature of these developing sex differences is illustrated in Figure 13-7. Aggression is one of the few behavioral traits that develops earlier in the male than the female monkey, and the same maturational principle doubtless holds for man. Since the male monkeys are the primary social guardians of feral monkey groups, the relatively early expression of aggression, which can be turned against external predators, has significant social value. The female has no great need to be aggressive until she has an infant to protect.

SEX DIFFERENCES IN PARENTHOOD

No one will be surprised to learn that there are sex differences in parenthood, since almost all mothers are females and almost all fathers are males. What is more surprising is the fact that long before any monkey or man engaged in any planned or unplanned parenthood, the priority of plans had already been provided by God. We tested a group of preadolescent female monkeys and a group of preadolescent male monkeys at a developmental age prior to any consideration of passion or progeny to see how they would

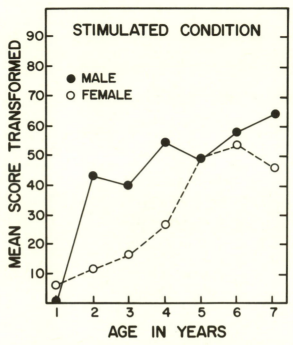

Figure 13-7   Externally directed aggression.

respond to newborn monkey infants. We discovered the obvious—the only discovery that most people ever make. The females exhibited strong affectional maternal responses to the neonates. The males showed no affectional responses of any type whatsoever. The females had never seen any infants previously. The males never wanted to see any infant again.

Even after the appearance of progeny it is still easy to tell the female from the male, since the female is the animal that is cuddling and nursing the infant. The male does not play these roles because he lacks the females' mammary magnificence and he is more devoted to canine capabilities.

Monkey maternal love begins at birth, and infant love for the mother develops almost immediately afterward. Some analysts have expressed the idea that infant love for the mother develops *in utero*, but we believe that this theory has room for improvement.

All females go through two developmental stages with every infant, a totally loving stage and, at a later appropriate age, a separative stage where they gently but firmly push the infant out of the nest and insure that he or she will adapt to his age mates.

In some manner, mysterious but momentous, the adult male becomes an appropriate father, but he can still be distinguished from the female by behavior alone. He protects his monkey group from external enemies and

Figure 13-8   Protective father.

maintains internal group order (Figure 13-8). Mothers are not allowed to abuse infants and there is no battered-child problem. Larger infants are not permitted to hurt or harass smaller monkeys. Both mothers and fathers have their functions—succulence in the mother and social security in the father.

Differently phrased, love by the mother is specific to the baby or infant that she has borne. Love by the father is a diffuse infant love designed to achieve social coordination, protection, and well-being. Thus, to the very end the father loves no infant—he loves all infants, though not with maternal passion and pride.

When the Creator, operating through the mechanisms of evolution, achieved the two separate entities, man and woman, he did so out of need and nicety. Man cannot live without woman, any more than he can live by bread alone. Successful primate societies are obviously aided and abetted by meaningful divisions of labor that are best achieved through biological fact rather than sociological friction. Sex differences in primates appear both in anatomical form and in behavioral patterns, and they appear early in life and then differentiate further. The fact of sex differences does not discriminate between one sex or the other. Actually, the complementary functions of each are enhanced. There is nothing demeaning in being either a female or a male. Sex differences are essential because of the complicated and complementary functions required to meet the needs of all successful higher-order social animals—particularly the primates.

REFERENCES

1. W.C. Lewis. *Int. J. Psychoanal.*, *46*: 372, 1965.
2. N.G.B. Jones. *In*: D. Morris (ed.). *Primate ethology*, p. 347. Chicago: Aldine, 1967.

14

The Heterosexual Affectional System in Monkeys

Harry F. Harlow

The inspiration for this address came from observational data obtained from seven guinea pigs—two males and three females in a colony and two females brought in temporarily. Observations were provided by my ten-year-old daughter Pamela. These observations were made with love and endearment, and the behavior observed was endearment and love. Furthermore, these observations were made at a level of objectivity difficult for an adult to attain in this field.

Male and female guinea pigs are very fond of each other. They stare blissfully into the limpid pink or ruby or midnight-blue pools of each other's eyes. They nuzzle and they cuddle and the end production is not characterized by rush or rape. After all, one does not have to hurry if there is no hurry to be had. This, Pamela has witnessed several times. A caged, virgin adult female was brought by a friend for mating. Twirp, Pamela's large, black, gentle male, was put into the cage with the new female. He purred, nuzzled her, brushed up against her, smelled and licked her, and gradually conquered the frightened animal. A half-hour later they were snuggled up next to each other, peaceful and content, and they lived in bliss for several weeks until another friend brought in her female and Twirp repeated his patient, gentle approach. Twirp has convinced me that some male guinea pigs, at least, are endowed with an innate sense of decency, and I am happy to say that this is the way most male monkeys behave. I presume that there are some men who have as deep a depth of dignity as guinea pigs.

The guest stands, unfortunately, ended peaceful coexistence in the colony. For many months the five adult guinea pigs had lived amiably in one large cage, with Twirp in command and the second male playing second fiddle. While Twirp was host to the visiting females, White Patch commanded the permanent harem. When Twirp was reintroduced to the colony cage, it took but ten seconds to discover that he would not be tolerated. White Patch bared his teeth and lunged at Twirp, and to save the males, a new cage was acquired.

This led to various divisions of the females and led Pamela to discover particular male guinea pigs like particular female guinea pigs, and they squeal piteously when separated, even when the female is so bulging with babies that she can offer the male nothing in terms of drive reduction. Particular female guinea pigs like particular male guinea pigs. Tastes seem fairly stable, for even after weeks of peaceful residence with the unfavored male, the female will still attempt to get to her favorite male, and after weeks of quiet residence with unfavored females, the male will still try to get to his favorite female.

The females, like the males, defend their rights. In the happy one-cage days two females were separated from the group to care for their litters. White Thrush, in an advanced state of pregnancy, lived alone with the males. When Chirp was returned to the colony cage after three weeks of maternal chores, both males approached enthusiastically, making friendly gestures. But Hell hat no fury like a female guinea pig spurned, and White Thrush would not tolerate infidelity. She hissed at Chirp, and lunged, and as Chirp fled from the cage, White Thrush pursued, teeth bared. The males also pursued, clucking and purring in anticipation. The males won, and White Thrush sulked the rest of the day. Guinea pigs apparently have a well-developed heterosexual affectional system.

Sex behavior in the guinea pig has been intensively investigated, and there are exhaustive studies on what has been called the sex drive, but I know of no previous mention of or allusion to the guinea pig's heterosexual affectional system. No doubt this stems from the paradigm which has been established for research in this area.

In a typical experiment a male guinea pig and a female guinea pig in estrus are taken from their individual cages, dropped into a barren chamber, and observed for 15 minutes. In such a situation there is a high probability that something is going to happen and that it will happen rapidly and repeatedly. The thing that happens will be reliable and valid, and all that one needs to do to score it is to count. It is my suggestion that from this time onward it be known as the "flesh count." Sometimes I wonder how men and women would behave if they were dropped naked into a barren chamber with full realization that they had only fifteen minutes to take advantage of the opportunities offered them. No doubt there would be individual differences, but we would obtain little information on the human heterosexual affectional system from such an experiment.

Sex is not an adventitious act. It is not here today and gone tomorrow. It starts with the cradle, and as a part of the human tragedy it wanes before the grave. We have traced and are tracing the development of the heterosexual affectional system in monkeys.

We believe that the heterosexual affectional system in the rhesus monkey, like all the other affectional systems, goes through a series of developmental stages—an infantile heterosexual stage, a preadolescent stage, and an adolescent and mature heterosexual stage. Although these stages are in considerable part overlapping and cannot be sharply differentiated in time, we would think of the infantile stage as lasting throughout the first year and being characterized by inadequate and often inappropriate sexual play and posturing. The preadolescent stage, beginning in the second year and ending in the third year in the female and the fourth year in the male, is characterized by adequate and appropriate sexual play and posturing, but incompleteness. The adolescent and adult stage is characterized by behaviors which are similar in form but give rise to productive outcomes which are also reproductive.

Since in this paper sex is an unavoidable issue, we present illustrations of normal adult macaque monkey sex behavior. Sexual invitation may be initiated by the female, as in Figure 13-4, by a present pattern with buttocks oriented toward the male, tail elevated, and the female looking backward with a fear-grimace (not threat) pattern involving flattened ears and lip smacking. As you can see, this pattern need not involve rape nor even rush on the part of the male. The male may also solicit....and assumes a posture. These patterns seldom elicit violent, uncontrolled, reflex behaviors. Normal male and female overt sex behavior involves the male having assumed the complex sex posture involving ankle clasp, dorsoventral mounting, and clasp of the female's buttocks. The partner demonstrates the complete female sexual pattern of elevating the buttocks, lowering the head, and looking backward. There have been millions of rhesus monkeys for millions of years, and there will be more in the future.

We have traced the development of the infantile heterosexual stage during the first year of life in two test situations using observational techniques. One is our playroom, illustrated in Figure 12-3, which consists of a room 8 ft. high with 36 sq. ft. of floor space. In this room are a platform, ladder, revolving wheel, and flying rings to encourage the infants' adaptation to a three-dimensional world, and there is an assortment of puzzles and toys for quieter activities. Two groups of four infants each, half of each group male and half female, have been observed in the playroom daily over may months. The second apparatus is shown in Figure 11-1. This is the playpen situation, and it consist of four large living cages and adjoining pens. Each living cage houses a mother and infant, and a three-inch by five-inch opening in the wall between cage and playpen units enables the infants to leave the home cage at any time but restrains the mothers. The playpen units are separated by wire-mesh panels which are removed one or two hours a day to allow the infants to interact in pairs during the first 180 days and both in pairs and in groups of four during the next half-year of life. Again, we are referring to data gathered from two playpen setups, each housing four infants and their real or surrogate mothers. Insofar as the infantile heterosexual stage is concerned, it makes little or no difference from which situation we take our data.

The outstanding finding in both the playroom and playpen is that male and female infants show differences in sex behavior from the second month of life onward. The males show earlier and more frequent sex behavior than do females, and there are differences in the patterns displayed by the sexes. The males almost never assume the female sex-posture patterns, even in the earliest months. The females, on the other hand, sometimes display the male patterns of sex posturing, but this is infrequent after ten months of age. Predominantly, females show the female pattern and exceptional instances are to other females, not males. Frequency of sex behavior for both males and females increases progressively with age. There is no latency period—except when the monkeys are very tired.

The early infantile sexual behaviors are fragmentary, transient, and involve little more than passivity by the female and disoriented grasping and thrusting by the male. Thus, the male may thrust at the companion's head in a completely disoriented manner or laterally across the midline of the body, as in Figure 14-1. However, it is our opinion that these behaviors are more polymorphous than perverse.

Thus, as soon as the sexual responses can be observed and measured, male and female sexual behaviors differ in form. Furthermore, there are many other behaviors which differ between males and females as soon as they can be observed and measured. Figure 14-2 shows the development of threat responses by males and females in the playroom, and these differences are not only statistically significant, but they also have face validity. Analysis of this behavior shows that males threaten other males and females but that females are innately blessed with better manners; in particular, little girl monkeys do not threaten little boy monkeys.

The withdrawal pattern—retreat when confronted by another monkey—is graphed for the playroom in Figure 14-3, and the significance is obvious. Females evince a much higher incidence of passive responses,

Figure 14-1 Immature male and female sexual posturing.

which are characterized by immobility with buttocks oriented toward the male and head averted, and a similar pattern, rigidity, in which the body is stiffened and fixed.

In all probability the withdrawal and passivity behavior of the female and the forceful behavior of the male gradually lead to the development of normal sex behaviors. The tendency for the female to orient away from the male and for the male to clasp and tussle at the female's buttocks predisposes the consorts to assume the proper positions. The development of the dorsally oriented male sex-behavior pattern as observed in the playroom situation is shown in Figure 14-4 and may be described as a composite yearning and learning curve.

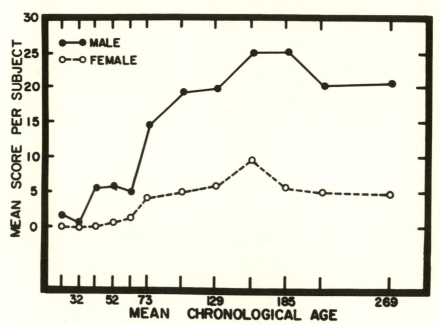

Figure 14-2 Frequency of threat responses by males and females in the playroom.

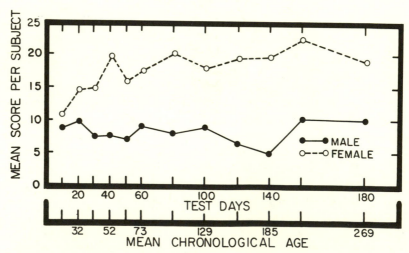

Figure 14-3 Frequency of withdrawal responses by males and females in the playroom.

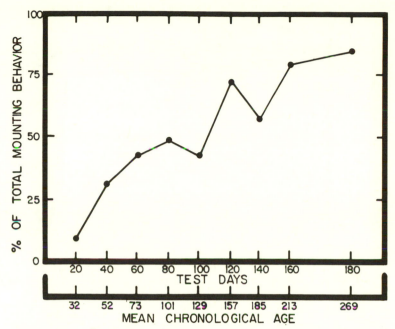

Figure 14-4 Percentage of male mounts (immature and mature) in the playroom.

Infant male and female monkeys show clear-cut differences in behavior of far greater social significance than neonatal and infantile sex responses. Grooming patterns, which are basic to macaque socialization, show late maturation, but...when they appear, they sharply differentiate the two sexes. Caressing is both a property and prerogative of the females. Basic to normal macaque socialization is the infant-infant or peer-peer affectional system, and this rises out of and is dependent upon the play patterns which we have described elsewhere and only mention here....Play behavior in the playroom is typically initiated by males, seldom by females. However, let us not belittle the female, for they also serve who only stand and wait. Contact play is far more frequent among the males than the females and is almost invariably initiated by the males. Playpen data graphed in Figure 14-5 show that real rough-and-tumble play is strictly for the boys.

I am convinced that these data have almost total generality to man. Several months ago I was present at a school picnic attended by 25 second-graders and their parents. While the parents sat and the girls stood around or skipped about hand in hand, 13 boys tackled and wrestled, chased and retreated. No little girl chased any little boy, but some little boys chased some little girls. Human beings have been here for two million years, and they'll probably be here two million more.

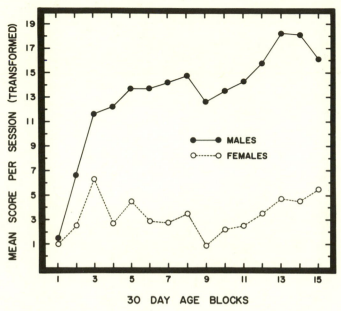

Figure 14-5 Frequency of rough-and-tumble play for two males and two females in the playroom.

These secondary sex-behavior differences probably exist throughout the primate order, and, moreover, they are innately determined biological differences regardless of any cultural overlap. Because of their nature they tend automatically to produce sexual segregation during middle and later childhood, but fortunately this separation is neither complete nor permanent. Behavioral differences may very well make it easy through cultural means to impose a sexual latency period in the human being from childhood to puberty. We emphasize the fact that the latency period is not a biological stage in which primary sex behavior is suppressed, but a cultural stage built upon secondary behavioral differences.

We believe that our data offer convincing evidence that sex behaviors differ in large part because of genetic factors. However, we claim no originality for the discovery of intersex behavioral differences. In 1759 Laurence Sterne in his book *Tristram Shandy* described male and female differences at the most critical period in Tristram Shandy's development; indeed, it would not be possible to conceive of a more critical period.

"*Pray, my dear,* quoth my mother, *have you not forgot to wind up the clock?*——*Good G*——*!* cried my father, making an exclamation, but taking care to moderate his voice at the same time——*-Did ever woman, since the creation of the world, interrupt a man with such a silly question?*"[1]

Men and women have differed in the past and they will differ in the future.

It is possible that the listener has been dismayed by the frequent reference to sex and the relatively infrequent references to affection. Out of these infantile behavior patterns, both sexual and nonsexual, develop the affectional bonds and the social ordering that appear to be important or even essential to the full development of the heterosexual affectional system of macaques. Traumatic affectional errors, both transient and prolonged, may have devastating effects upon subsequent social and sexual behaviors.

For some years we have been attempting to establish experimental neuroses in infant monkeys by having them live on unfriendly and inconsistent mother surrogates. One preparation was a rejecting mother that on schedule or demand separated her baby when a wire frame embedded in her spun-nylon covering was displaced violently upward and backward. The baby was disturbed, but as soon as the frame was returned to its resting position, the baby returned to cling to its surrogate mother as tightly as ever. Next we developed an air-blast mother with a series of nozzles down the entire center of her body which released compressed air under high pressure—an extremely noxious stimulus to monkeys. The blasted baby never even left the mother, but in its moments of agony and duress, clung more and more tightly to the unworthy mother. Where else can a baby get protection? Apparently our infant had never read Neal Miller's theory that avoidance gradients are precipitous and approach gradients gradual and tenous, for love conquered all.

We next devised a shaking mother, which on schedule or demand shook her infant with unconscionable violence until its teeth chattered. The infant endured its tribulations by clinging more and more tightly. At the present time we believe we may be on the threshold of success through Jay Mowbray's creation of the porcupine mother, which extrudes brass spikes all over its ventral surface. Preliminary studies on two infants suggest that they are emotionally disturbed. Whether or not we eventually succeed, the fact remains that babies are reluctant to develop experimental neuroses, and at one time we even wondered if this were possible.

During the time that we were producing these evil mothers, we observed the monkeys which we had separated from their mothers at birth and raised under various mothered and nonmothered conditions. The first 47 baby monkeys were raised during the first year of life in wire cages so arranged that the infants could see and hear and call to other infants but not contact them. Now they are five to seven years old and sexually mature. As month after month and year after year have passed, these monkeys have appeared to be less and less normal. We have seen them sitting in their cages strangely mute, staring fixedly into space, relatively indifferent to people and other monkeys. Some clutch their heads in both hands and rock back and forth— the autistic behavior pattern that we have seen in babies raised on wire surrogates. Others, when approached or even left alone, go into violent frenzies of rage, grasping and tearing at their legs with such fury that they sometimes require medical care.

Eventually we realized that we had a laboratory full of neurotic monkeys. We had failed to produce neurotic monkeys by thoughtful planning and creative research, but we had succeeded in producing neurotic monkeys through misadventure. To err is human.

Because of housing pressures some of these monkeys and many of our surrogate-raised monkeys lived in pairs for several years while growing to sexual maturity, but we have seldom seen normal sex behavior, and we certainly have not had the validating criterion of newborn baby monkeys. Instead, these monkeys treat each other like brother and sister, proving that two can live in complete propinquity with perfect propriety as long as no one cares.

Their reason for being, as we saw it, was to produce babies for our researches, and so at this point we deliberately initiated a breeding program which was frighteningly unsuccessful. When the older, wire-cage-raised males were paired with the females at the peak of estrus, the introduction led only to fighting, so violent and vicious that separation was essential to survival. In no case was there any indication of normal sex behavior. Frequently the females were the aggressors; even the normal praying mantis waits until the sex act is completed.

Pairing such cloth-surrogate-raised monkeys as were sexually mature gave little better end results. Violent aggression was not the rule, and there was attempted sex behavior, but it was unreproductive since both the male and female behaviors were of the infantile type we have already described.

At this point we took the 17 oldest of our cage-raised animals, females showing consistent estrous cycles and males obviously mature, and engaged in an intensive education program, pairing the females with our most experienced, patient, and gentle males, and the males with our most eager, amiable, and successful breeding females. When the laboratory-bred females were smaller than the sophisticated males, the girls would back away and sit down facing the males, looking appealingly at these would-be consorts. Their hearts were in the right place, but nothing else was. When the females were larger than the males, we can only hope that they misunderstood the males' intentions, for after a brief period of courtship, they would attack and maul the ill-fated males. Females show no respect for a male they can dominate.

The training program for the males was equally unsatisfactory. They approached the females with a blind enthusiasm, but it was a misdirected enthusiasm. Frequently the males would grasp the females by the side of the body and thrust laterally, leaving them working at cross purposes with reality. Even the most persistent attempts by these females to set the boys straight came to naught. Finally, these females either stared at the males with complete contempt or attacked them in utter frustration. It became obvious that they, like their human counterpart, prefer maturer men. We realized then that we had established, not a program of breeding, but a program of brooding.

We had in fact been warned. Our first seven laboratory-born babies were raised in individual cages while being trained on a learning test battery. William Mason planned to test their social behaviors subsequently, and great care had been taken to keep the babies socially isolated and to prevent any physical contacts. Neonatal baby monkeys require 24-hour-a-day care, and infant monkeys need ministrations beyond a 40-hour week. We had assigned the evening care to Kathy, a maternal bit of fluff who had worked for several years as a monkey tester while studying to become an elementary school teacher.

Checking on his wards one night near 10 p.m., Mason found Kathy sitting on the floor surrounded by seven baby monkeys, all eight of the primates playing happily together. Before the horrified scientist could express his outrage, Kathy had risen to her full height of five feet two. Already anticipating the carping criticisms which he was formulating, she shook her finger in his face and spoke with conviction: "Dr. Mason, I'm an education student and I know that it is improper and immoral to blight the social development of little children. I am right and you are wrong!"

Although we were angry with Kathy, we did think there was a certain humor in the situation and we did not worry about our monkeys. We simply transferred Kathy to an office job. Alas, she could not have been more right and we could not have been more wrong! We have already described the social-sexual life of these 7 monkeys and the next 40 to come.

Two years later we had more than theoretical reasons to be disturbed because Mason tested a group of these isolation-raised monkeys, then between 2.5 and 3.5 years of age, and found evidence of severe social abnormalities, which might be described as a sociopathic syndrome. He matched the laboratory-raised monkeys on the basis of weight and dentition patterns with monkeys that had been born and raised in the wild for the first 12 to 18 months, then captured and subjected to various kinds of housing and caging treatments for the next year or two. In the test situations the laboratory-raised monkeys, as compared with feral monkeys, showed infantile sexual behavior, absence of grooming, exaggerated aggression, and absence of affectional interaction as measured by cooperation.

We are now quite certain that this sociopathic syndrome does not stem from the fact that the baby monkeys were raised in the laboratory but from *how* they were raised in the laboratory. Our infants raised in the laboratory by real monkey mothers and permitted opportunity for the development of normal infant-infant affection demonstrate normal male and female sexual behavior when they enter the second year of life. Furthermore, our playroom and playpen studies show that infant monkeys raised on cloth mothers but given the opportunity to form normal infant-infant affectional patterns also develop normal sexual responses.

In a desperate attempt to assist a group of 18 three- to four-year-old cloth-surrogate-raised monkeys, half of them males and half females, we engaged in a group-psychotherapy program, placing these animals for two months on the monkey island in the Madison Zoo.... Their summer vacation on the enchanted island was not without avail, and social grooming responses rapidly developed and were frequent in occurrence. After a few days of misunderstanding, patterns of social ordering developed, and a number of males and females developed friendship patterns. Unfortunately, sexual behavior was infrequent, and the behavior that was observed was completely inadequate—at least from our point of view. In desperation we finally introduced our most experienced, most patient, and most kindly breeding male, Smiley (the male in Figure 14-1), and he rapidly established himself as king of the island and prepared to take full advantage of the wealth of opportunity which surrounded him. Fortunately, the traumatic experiences he encountered with unreceptive females have left no apparent permanent emotional scars, and now that he has been returned to our laboratory breeding colony, he is again making an important contribution to our research program. If normal sexual behavior occurred, no member of our observational team ever saw it, and had a female become pregnant, we would have believed in parthenogenesis.

But let us return to the monkeys that we left on the island and the older ones that we left in their cages. A year has passed, and the frustrations that both we and our monkeys experienced are in some small part nothing but a memory. We constructed larger and more comfortable breeding cages, and we designed a very large experimental breeding room 8 feet by 8 feet by 8 feet in size with appropriate platforms and a six-foot tree. Apparently we designed successful seraglios for I can report that not all love's labors have been lost. It does appear that the males are completely expendable unless they can be used in a program of artificial insemination. Certainly we can find no evidence that there is a destiny that shapes their ends unless some Skinnerite can help us with the shaping process. We have, however, had better success with some of the females, particularly the females raised on cloth surrogates.

Even so, one of the wire-cage-raised females is a mother and another is pregnant. Three cloth-surrogate females are mothers and four or five are expectant. We give all the credit to three breeding males. One, Smiley, does not take "no" for an answer. Smiley has a way with females. Patient, gentle, and persuasive, he has overcome more than one planned program of passive resistance. One female did not become pregnant until the fifth successive month of training. Month after month she has changed, and now she is mad about the boy. Male No. 342 behaves very much like Smiley. Even when females threaten him, he does not harm them. Given time, he has been able to overcome more than one reluctant dragon, and he is a master of the power of positive suggestion.

Breeding male No. 496 has helped us greatly, particularly with the younger, cloth-surrogate-raised females. His approach differs from that of Smiley and No. 342. His technique transcends seduction, and in contract bridge terms it may be described as an approach-forcing system.

Combining our human and male-monkey talents, we are winning the good fight and imparting to naive and even resistant female monkeys the priceless gift of motherhood. Possibly it is a Pyrrhic victory. As every scientist knows, the solution of one scientific problem inevitably leads to another, and this is our fate.... Month after month female monkeys that never knew a real mother, themselves become mothers—helpless, hopeless, heartless mothers devoid, or almost devoid, of any maternal feeling.

NOTE

[1] Sterne, Laurence. *The life and opinions of Tristram Shandy, Gentleman.* J.A. Work (Ed.), New York: The Odyssey Press, 1940, p.5.

PART FIVE
PSYCHOPATHOLOGY

15

Induction and Alleviation of Depressive States in Monkeys

Harry F. Harlow

During the last two years we have initiated a research programme designed to induce or simulate various forms of human depression in rhesus monkeys. If monkeys can be made depressed for a prolonged period of time a variety of biological and social studies becomes possible. Prior to this particular programme, we had already conducted two studies on infantile or anaclitic depression produced by separating infant monkeys from their mothers at six months of age (Seay, Hansen and Harlow, 1962). This research had served as a model for other investigators testing the effects of infant separation from the mother and mother separation from the infant on rhesus, bonnet, and pigtail macaques.

SEPARATION: MOTHER IN SIGHT

In our original researches we separated pairs of infant friends from their respective mothers while the infant friends were playing together in a spacious play compartment (Figure 15-1). The mothers, meanwhile, were continuously confined to two living cages contiguous to the play area, the entrance to which was too small for the mothers to use. Mother/ infant separation was achieved by inserting plexiglass slides between each of the two living cages and the play compartment when the infants had left

Harlow, H.G. (1974) Induction and alleviation of depressive states in monkeys. In N.F. White (Ed.), *Ethology and psychiatry*. Toronto: University of Toronto Press, pp. 197–208. Reprinted by permission of University of Toronto Press.

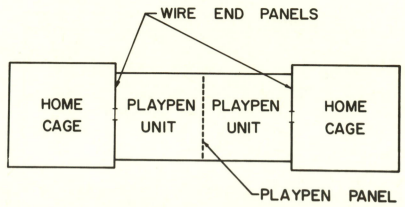

Figure 15-1   Deprivation apparatus.

their homes to play together. Thus, in this situation the mothers and infants were physically but not visually separated.

Both the separated infants and mothers were disturbed by these procedures, even though the intensity and duration of the disturbance was greater for the infants than for the mothers. Indeed, the infants' successive behaviours were startlingly reminiscent of the separation stages of protest and despair, as described by Bowlby (1969), following human mother/infant separation. Protest by the monkeys consisted of violent crying vocalizations, compulsive random locomotion, and assault directed against the offending plexiglas slide. After a day or so the frequency of the protest behaviours declined and behaviour patterns obviously portraying despair developed. These included a general decrease in activity and an increase in self-clasp and huddling behaviours.

Objective time-sampling records were continued for three-week periods before, during, and after separation. These data revealed that play activities were almost obliterated during the entire separation interval, even though they had been high before separation was begun, and again became frequent and intense shortly after separation ended (Figure 15-2). We believe that the inhibition of play was our most valid and meaningful measure of depression, and the differences in amount of play during separation contrasted to the amount of play both before and after separation were highly significant statistically.

SEPARATION: MOTHER OUT OF SIGHT

We conducted a second experiment which was essentially a replication of the first except for the fact that opaque fibreboard screens were substituted

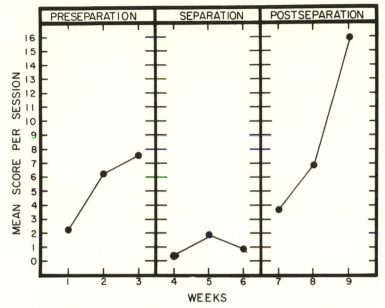

Figure 15-2   Infant approach-withdrawal play responses.

for the transparent plexiglas dividers placed between the two home cages and the play area. Here again the infants passed through Bowlby's stages of protest and despair, and play behaviour was significantly depressed during the separation period. However, much to our surprise, the intensity and probably the duration of the depression, as measured by the objective tests, was lower when sight of the mothers was entirely shut off from the infants' view, than when the plexiglass screens were used. It was as if the monkeys had heard of the notion "out of sight, out of mind."

SEPARATION: BETWEEN INFANTS

The breaking of any affectional bond should cause a strong separation reaction, and we had previously demonstrated that affection between mother and child was probably no stronger than affection among infant playmates. Working on this assumption, a Wisconsin graduate student, Mr. Stephen Suomi, separated groups of four infants from each other, not once but for twelve consecutive sessions. The infants were together for three days per week and separated for four. Each separation of each infant group elicited violent protest responses of vocalization and increased movement, which were followed in about twenty-four hours by responses

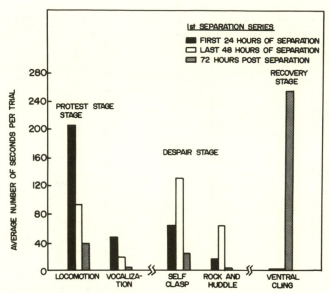

Figure 15-3   Effect of 12 separation sessions on behavior
of monkeys.

of despair, as indicated by self-clasp and huddle. Upon reunion the infants
clasped each other tightly (Figure 15-3). Furthermore, there was no
indication of adaptation to any of these stages of protest, despair, and
reunion throughout the twelve sessions. The reaction to the twelfth
separation was no more or no less severe than to the first separation.

The behaviour of the separated infants when together was measured
at three months of age, when separation began, and also at six and nine
months of age, when the repetitive sessions were being conducted. Ventral
clinging and self-mouthing, which are normal infantile behaviours at three
months of age, showed no decrease in frequency at six months or nine
months of age, when they should have been essentially non-existent.
Contrary results were obtained for play, which is a behaviour that is just
developing in normal monkeys at three months of age, but which attains
high levels at six months and very high levels at nine months of age. In the
repetitively separated monkeys the fragmentary play observed at three
months failed to increase materially at six or nine months, an unheard-of-
event for normal monkeys. These measures and other related measures
show that twelve repetitive separations had stopped normal behavioural
maturation and left the six- and nine-month-old monkeys in a state of
infantilization or maturational arrest (Figure 15-4).

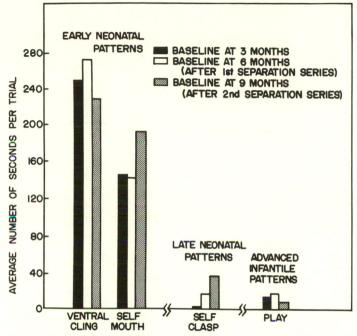

Figure 15-4 Arrest of behavioral maturation by repetitive separation.

THE VERTICAL CHAMBER

In an effort to produce depression or depressive-like states by means other than repetitive separation, which is a relatively slow and time-consuming process, we created a special apparatus called the vertical chamber, a sloping vertical cage with a fine mesh bottom and a hardware cloth top.... A group of monkeys, ranging from six to thirteen months of age, were individually confined in these chambers for a month, and their behaviours were measured for two subsequent months. Infantile behaviours of huddling and self-clasp remained high throughout this period, whereas more complex behaviours of locomotion and environmental exploration were greatly depressed (Figure 15-5). Thus depression was achieved with startling speed and was maintained for a significant time.

In the next study we compared the behaviour of monkeys that were confined to the vertical chamber for six weeks antecedent to ninety days of age with the behaviour of monkeys from two control groups, one raised in bare wire cages, and one raised with normal infant playmates. Again, the monkeys placed in the vertical chambers subsequently exhibited a high

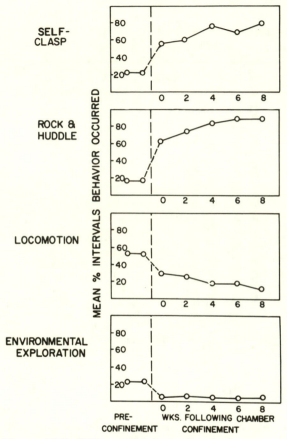

Figure 15-5 Effect of 30 days pit experience on selected behaviors of four wire-cage-reared monkeys (age 6–13 mo.).

incidence of infantile behaviours of cling and huddle, behaviours which were almost non-existent in the other two groups (Figure 15-6). Contrariwise, complex behaviours of exploration, social contact, and play did not develop in the monkeys after release from the vertical chambers but developed normally in the members of the other two groups. The behaviour of these three groups of monkeys has now been traced for a year after release from the vertical chambers, and the long-term effects are clear. The monkeys placed in the vertical chambers show a high incidence of self-mouth, self-huddle, and self-clasp behaviours, whereas social contacts and play are almost non-existent. Contrariwise, the members of both the control groups show little or no self-mouthing, self-huddling, and self-clasping, and exhibit a high level of social contacts and play behaviour.

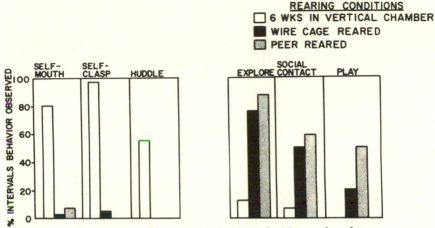

Figure 15-6 Playroom behaviors, 9–11 months of age.

DEPRESSION

These behaviours of the chambered infants as they approached behavioural maturity might be described as either depressed or infantilized. Depression, of course, often involves regression or an exaggeration of infantile needs and behaviour, therefore, the two terms need not involve much controversy. By simply assuming that depression is a state of regression we might avoid controversy over terminology. Aside from terminology, it is obvious that a relatively brief state of semi-isolation in the vertical chamber produced abnormal behaviours that were remarkably stable in young monkeys (Figure 15-7).

THERAPY

Having demonstrated that depression or depressive-like abnormal states could be induced in monkeys by a number of means, we attempted to rehabilitate abnormal monkeys by the ministrations of other monkeys serving as "therapists."

Previous studies had demonstrated that monkeys raised from birth until six months of age in total isolation and then placed with age-mates were totally destroyed socially. The isolated monkeys avoided social contacts, they did not play, and they were fearful and disturbed. Furthermore, these abnormal social behaviours persisted over periods of years and tended to become exaggerated rather than improved with time. Sexual

Figure 15-7   Depressed monkey infant.

behaviour was abnormal or non-existent and some reluctant females that were deviously impregnated were inadequate or brutal mothers. The only vigorous trait that developed was brief episodes of mixed fear with uncontrolled aggression often directed toward infants. Aggression against infants is almost never seen in normal adults. In this study we are assuming that six months' total isolation produced depression or a depressive state in monkeys.

When the social isolates were six months of age they were placed in quad cages, which are large cages subdivided into four chambers and used for either housing or social testing. The therapist monkeys had been raised in quad-cage quadrants with a surrogate mother and had been allowed interaction with age-mates during the first three months of life, a time at which play was beginning to develop.

Therapy sessions involved placing an isolated monkey with a younger therapist monkey twice a week in a quad cage, and twice a week in a large, unfamiliar playroom (Figure 15-8). Once a week two isolates and two therapists were placed in the playpen as a group of four.

Figure 15-8   Isolate on left, therapist gently approaching from right, behavior typical of early therapy.

RESULTS

The isolate monkeys rapidly overcame any fear that they originally had of the therapist monkeys and began to accept and even reciprocate body contact instead of withdrawing and huddling (Figure 15-9). Within a few weeks they made little or no attempt to flee and began to reciprocate physical interaction. After six months of interaction, reciprocal play between isolates and therapists was not uncommon. Even after this time isolate animals occasionally showed abnormal posturing at the beginning or sometime throughout a test session.

By unavoidable accident both of the isolated monkeys were males and both of the therapist monkeys were females. Many years of testing monkeys in playrooms had taught us that the play patterns of male and female monkeys are fundamentally different. Male monkey play, in a pattern called rough-and-tumble play, involves a maximal amount of bodily contact, whereas female monkey play is characterized by chasing back and forth with bodily contact minimal or non-existent—a non-contact

Figure 15-9 Therapy proceeds, with more involvement.

form of play. After the socially isolated monkeys and the therapists had
come to live on equal terms as a group of four, we were astounded to
realize that the isolate males played together and engaged in rough-and-
tumble play (Figure 15-10), whereas the therapist females formed their
own play group and engaged in non-contact play. The males could not
have learned rough-and-tumble play from the females, who never played
this way. By rehabilitating the males, the females had enabled the males to
develop their own masculine heritage, which was above and beyond any
simple act of female social imitation. These results, showing sex-char-
acteristic differences in rhesus infant play behaviour, suggest that our
interpretations follow the injunction: Render unto males the things that
are males', and to females their foibles and fancies.

REFERENCES

Bowlby, J. 1969. *Attachment*. New York: Basic Books
Harlow, H.F. 1958. The nature of love. *American Psychologist. 13*, 673–85

Figure 15-10 Isolate males engaging in rough-and-tumble play (a typical male monkey play pattern).

Harlow, H.F. and Harlow, M.K. 1962. Social deprivation in monkeys. *Sci.Am.* 207, 136–46.

Harlow, H.F., Suomi, S.J., and McKinney, W.T. 1970. Experimental production of depression in monkeys. *Mainly Monkeys, 1,* 6–12

Seay, B., Hansen, E. and Harlow, H.F. 1962. Mother-infant separation in monkeys. *J. Child Psychol. Psychiat.* 3,123–32

Suomi, S.J., Harlow, H.F., and Domek, C.J. 1970. Effect of repetitive infant-infant separation of young monkeys. *J. Abnormal Psychol.* 76, 161–72

16

Total Social Isolation in Monkeys

Harry F. Harlow, Robert O. Dodsworth, and Margaret K. Harlow

Human social isolation is recognized as a problem of vast importance. Its effects are deleterious to personal adjustment, normal heterosexual development, and control of aggressive and delinquent behaviors. Isolation generally arises from breakdowns in family structures resulting in orphaned or semiorphaned children or in illegitimate children who, for one reason or another, are raised in institutions, inadequate foster homes, or, occasionally, in abnormal homes with relatives.

It is difficult or impossible to study scientifically the impacts of culturally produced social isolation at the human level. The variables are multitudinous and recalcitrant to experimental manipulation and control. Our research has consequently been concerned with the effects of social deprivation in rhesus monkeys. Previously published research has established parallels in the normal social development of human and monkey young.(1–3) There is every reason to believe that the same basic laws operate for these two closely related species and that social conditions which produce abnormality in one species will have comparable effects on the other. Although human behavior is more complex, more variable, and subtler than that of subhuman primates, one should, nevertheless, find insights into the problems created by human social isolation from study of social isolation in monkeys.

For the past ten years we have studied the effects of partial social isolation by raising monkeys from birth onward in bare wire cages such as those shown in Figure 12-19. These monkeys suffer total maternal depri-

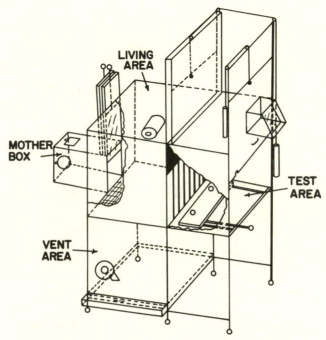

Figure 16-1   Total social isolation chamber.

vation and, even more important, have no opportunity to form affectional ties with their peers. We have already reported the resulting progressively deepening syndrome of compulsive nonnutritional sucking, repetitive stereotyped movements, detachment from the environment, hostility directed outwardly toward others and inwardly toward the animal's own body, and inability to form adequate social or heterosexual attachments to others when such opportunities are provided in preadolescence, adolescence, or adulthood.(4)

More recently, we have initiated a series of studies on the effects of *total* social isolation(5) by housing monkeys from a few hours after birth until 3, 6, or 12 months of age in the stainless-steel chamber illustrated in Figure 16-1. During the prescribed sentence in this apparatus, the monkey has no contact with any animal, human or subhuman. Although social isolation is total, no attempt is made to maximize *sensory* deprivation. The chamber is constantly illuminated, transmits sounds, and affords relatively adequate opportunities for cutaneous-proprioceptive expression and exploration. The room outside the living cage was sound-masked by a 70-db white noise source, but loud sounds from the corridor produced attentive and even freezing responses.

Three groups of newborn monkeys were isolated in individual chambers for 3, 6, and 12 months, respectively. In addition, one group was kept in partial isolation in individual cages in the laboratory nursery for the first 6 months, then placed in the isolation chamber for 6 months. There were six monkeys in the 3-month group and four monkeys in each of the other groups. Isolation effects were measured by comparing the social behavior of pairs of isolated monkeys after release from the chambers with that pairs of equal-aged monkeys raised in partial isolation. Each experimental pair and its control pair were tested together as a stable group of four in the playroom situation illustated in Figure 12-3. The four subjects were released in the room for 30 min a day, 5 days a week, for 32 weeks. Long-term effects were subsequently assessed in the playroom from 1 to 2 years after termination of isolation. Two observers recorded the occurrence of selected individual behaviors and social interactions.(6,7) In addition, the effect of isolation on intellectual development has been assessed by means of a comprehensive battery of learning tests, including discrimination, delayed response, and learning-set formation.(8)

No monkey has died during isolation. When initially removed from total social isolation, however, they usually go into a state of emotional shock, characterized by the autistic self-clutching and rocking.... One of six monkeys isolated for 3 months refused to eat after release and died 5 days later. The autopsy report attributed death to emotional anorexia. A second animal in the same group also refused to eat and would probably have died had we not been prepared to resort to forced feeding. This phenomenon of extreme emotional anorexia has not appeared in the 6- or 12-month groups.

Our data indicate that the debilitating effects of 3 months of social isolation are dramatic but reversible. If there is long-term social or intellectual damage, it eludes our measurements. Given the opportunity soon after release to associate with controls of the same age, these short-term isolates start slowly during the first week and then adapt and show the normal sequence of social behaviors. In human terms they are the children salvaged from the orphanage or inadequate home within the first year of life.... Progress in learning-set formation is the most reliable measure we have of relatively complex learning in the rhesus monkey. The performance of both the 3-month isolate group and their controls is indistinguishable from that of equal-aged monkeys tested in other experiments utilizing learning-set problems.

Isolation extending through the first 6 months of life, on the other hand, severely impairs the potentiality for socialization as indicated by playroom data comparing 6-month isolates with their controls and with 3-month isolates and their controls. Of the many social measures obtained, only two are shown here for illustrative purposes. Frequency of threat,

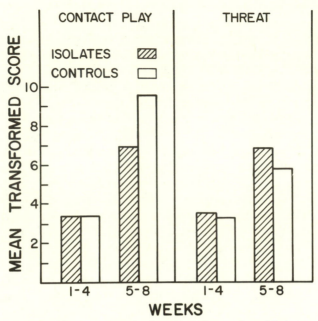

Figure 16-2   Incidence of contact play and social threat
in 3-month social isolates.

one of the most reliable social measures, is graphically presented in Figure
16-2 for both the 3- and 6-month isolates and their appropriate controls
during the first 4 weeks and the second 4 weeks after total social isolation.
There are no significant differences in frequency of threat between the
3-month isolates and their controls during either test period; there is no
reason to believe that the slightly higher frequency of threat by the isolates
is other than a chance difference. These data contrast strongly with the
differential frequency of threat behavior by the 6-month isolates and their
controls during both observational test periods. Transformed scores were
used for statistical reasons. The ratio of the actual frequencies of threat for
the 6-month isolates and their controls was approximately 1–4. The
differences were significant far beyond the 0.05 level. During the next 6
months the 3-month isolates and their controls showed no differential
trends in frequency of social threat. The curves for the 6-month isolates
and their controls over the 8 months of observation in the playroom are
shown in Figure 16-3. From the 24th week on, frequency of social threat
increased somewhat in the 6-month isolates, but these social threats were
consistently directed to other isolates.

    A comparison of the frequency of contact ("rough-and-tumble")
play (Figure 16-4) for the 3-month isolates and their controls showed no
difference during the first 4-week period and no subsequent differential

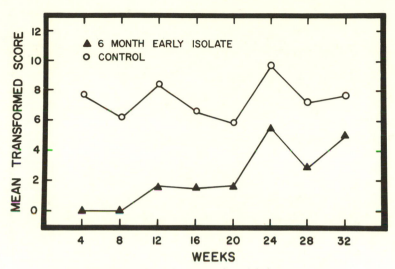

Figure 16-3   Developmental social threat trends.

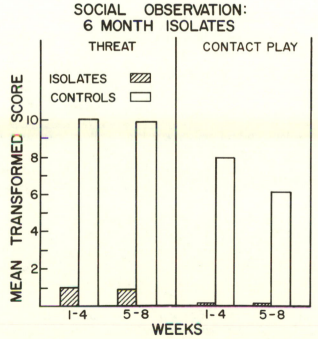

Figure 16-4   Incidence of contact play and social threat
in 6-month social isolates.

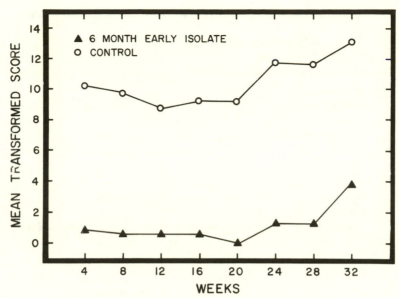

Figure 16-5   Developmental trends in contact play.

developmental trend. These data differ sharply from those for the 6-month isolates and their controls. Essentially no contact play was observed in the 6-month isolate monkeys during either of the first two 4-week postisolation periods, whereas a large amount of such play occurred for the controls. The level of contact play increased materially in the 6-month isolate group (Figure 16-5) during the course of the 32 weeks of testing, but again the contact play that was exhibited was play between isolates and not between isolates and controls. Actually, social interaction throughout the entire 32-week test period between the 6-month isolate monkeys and their controls was for all practical purposes nonexistent except for bursts of aggression which the controls occasionally directed toward the isolate animals.

The effects of 6 months of total social isolation were so devastating and debilitating that we had assumed initially that 12 months of isolation would not produce any additional decrement. This assumption proved to be false; 12 months of isolation almost obliterated the animals socially, as is suggested by the playroom data for activity play, the simplest form of play, shown in Figure 16-6.

Activity play was chosen as a prime measure since it represents a primitive play level involving minimal interanimal contact. The 12-month isolates showed practically no activity play, and the trend was a decrease with time. The control monkeys, on the other hand, displayed a relatively

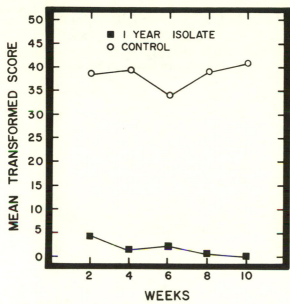

Figure 16-6 Activity play of 12-month isolates.

constant, high level of activity play. Observation of the 12-month isolated animals and their controls had to be terminated after 10 experimental weeks because the controls became increasingly aggressive toward the helpless isolate animals and might have killed them had we continued social testing.

A striking difference between the 6-month and the 12-month socially isolated monkeys occurred in the frequency of autoreotic behaviors. Such behaviors occurred, although with low frequency, in the 6-month isolate group; they were virtually nonexistent in the 12-month socially isolated subjects. Control monkeys, on the other hand, displayed a high level of such behaviors.

Total social isolation during the second half year of life produced a radically different syndrome from that for the first half year. Within a relatively short period of time after release from isolation, the 6-month late isolates adjusted adequately to equal-aged playmates. This finding is indicated . . . by the frequency of social approach exhibited by these subjects as compared with their controls. Although the differences are not statistically significant, the 6-month late isolates made more approaches than the controls, no doubt reflecting the somewhat greater aggressiveness of the isolates and the consequent caution of the controls. Observational data show that the 6-month late-isolate group was hyperaggressive compared with its control group whereas both the 6- and 12-month socially isolated

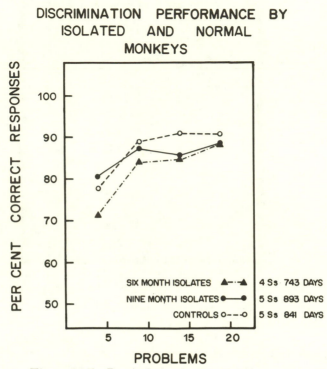

Figure 16-7 Postisolation learning-set formation.

subjects were characterized by a marked lack of aggression compared with their controls.

The effects of 6 and 12 months of total social isolation on learning are confounded in our studies since we attempted, with success in some cases, to measure by remote-control test methods the isolated monkeys' ability to solve learning problems during their periods of confinement. Thus, even when the infants failed to progress during isolation, they were being given intellectual stimulation which could have played a significant role in their apparent intellectual normality after release. The learning data obtained on delayed-response and learning-set tasks after removal from total social isolation disclosed no significant differences between 6- and 12-month isolated monkeys and their equal-aged controls, but the consistency of the small differences that did occur suggests the possibility that larger samples might support a difference. The learning-set data are presented in Figure 16-7. The performance of the control monkeys tends to be higher than that of the 6-month isolates, and the performance of the 6-month isolates tends to be higher than that of the 12-month isolates. The striking fact, however, is that all the socially isolated monkeys learned effectively after being removed from the social isolation cages. We cannot, at the present time, adequately assess the effect of prolonged total social isolation on the intellectual capabilities of rhesus monkeys. The ultimate appraisal must await experiments in which no training is given during isolation. We can, however, state with confidence that the "intellectual mind" is far less crippled than the "social mind" by prolonged total social deprivation if adequate experience is provided subsequently. Inasmuch as this intellectual sparing is contrary to the current theory of the effects of social deprivation on the intellectual development of human children, a review of the human data may be in order. The so-called intellectual deficits reported for deprived children may well be social deficits in large part rather than intellectual ones.

An experiment presently being prepared for publication by G.D. Mitchell(9) provides data on the social behavior of members of our total-isolation groups toward more normally raised macaque monkeys over long time periods. Eight isolated subjects were assembled, two from the 12-month isolated group, and three each from the 6-month early- and 6-month late-isolation groups. They ranged in age from 2 years and 4 months to 3 years and 5 months. The other members of our totally socially isolated groups were not available because of various research commitments. Studies investigating the long-term social behavior of all members of all the groups subjected to total social isolation are presently in progress.

Mitchell tested the social behaviors of individual isolates and normal monkeys toward age mates, adults, and 1-year-old infants. The 12-month isolates showed no play, no aggression, almost no sex behavior, but a high level of fear to adults, to age mates, and even to the infants. Two of the 6-month early isolates showed no play, but one—a female—showed adequate play with adults, age mates, and infants. One of the three showed aggression toward adults, age mates and infants. One showed aggression only toward adults. The third—the female—showed aggression only toward age mates and infants. Sex behavior was almost nonexistent except for scattered, diffuse sex responses directed toward infants. Two of the three showed extreme fear toward adults but not toward age mates or infants, while the third showed no fear at all.

The 6-month late isolates differed from the 6-month early isolates primarily in only one aspect of behavior: two of the three showed uncoordinated sexual responses toward age mates and one of these showed the same kind of responses to adults. In play, one of the 6-month late group showed essentially normal responsiveness with age mates and also with infants and adults. One showed virtually no play at all, and the third played only with infants. Two of the three showed the same suicidal aggression toward adults as did two of the 6-month early isolates, a behavior rarely seen in normal monkeys. All three showed hostility toward infants, even though two of them were females. This behavior is essentially nonexistent among normal monkeys. Perhaps most surprising was the finding that none showed much hostility toward age mates even though they had been hostile to age mates in the initial observations following isolation. One showed almost no fear to any age range of subjects, while the third showed moderate fear to adults but not to age mates or infants.

In summary, on the follow-up tests, the 12-month isolates were highly fearful and showed almost no positive social behavior and no aggression. Except in sexual behavior, the 6-month early and late isolates were highly similar, as groups, in their social responses. One member of each group showed essentially normal play behavior, and two of each group showed little or no play. Two members of each group showed suicidal aggression toward adults, and five of the six members of the combined groups showed the abnormal phenomenon of aggressing against infants. None of the six was a socially normal animal, for even the two that played with the test animals were hostile to infants and none of the six showed adequate sex behavior. The adjustments of the members of these two groups were highly individual in that a number adapted adequately to specific situations, but none adapted adequately to all or even most types of situations. The effects of isolation in the first year thus were clearly evident 12–24 months (mean, 18 months) after removal from isolation in spite of the prolonged social experience provided the subjects following isolation.

The findings of the various total-isolation and semi-isolation studies of the monkeys suggest that sufficiently severe and enduring early isolation reduces these animals to a social-emotional level in which the primary social responsiveness is fear. Twelve months of total social isolation is apparently sufficient to achieve this result consistently in rhesus monkeys. In contrast, short periods of total social isolation leave no permanent deficits in potentialities or social adjustment. For the rhesus monkey, this period of sparing is at least 3 months. Periods of total isolation somewhere between 3 months and 12 months or prolonged periods of semi-isolation result in different degrees of social damage and permit variable behavioral adaptations, perhaps as a function both of basic individual differences and of social learning experiences. Individuals subjected to the same deprivation conditions can thus emerge as generally fearful or fearless, generally hostile or without aggression, or selectively fearful or selectively hostile. Placed in a free-living situation, most of these animals would be driven off or eliminated before they could have an opportunity to learn to adapt to the group.

REFERENCES

1. Harlow, H.F., M.K. Harlow, and E.W. Hansen in *Maternal Behavior in Mammals*, ed. H.L. Rheingold (New York: John Wiley & Sons, Inc., 1963).
2. Harlow, H.F. *Sci. Psychoanalysis*, 7, 93–113 (1964).
3. Seay, B., B.K. Alexander, and H.F. Harlow *J. Abnorm. Soc. Psychol.*, *69*, 345–354 (1964).
4. Cross, H.A. and H.F. Harlow *J. Exptl. Res. Pers.*, *1*, 39–49 (1965).
5. Harlow, H.F., G.L. Rowland, and G.A. Griffin *Psychiatric Research Report 19* (American Psychiatric Association, 1964).
6. Rowland, G.L. doctoral dissertation, University of Wisconsin, 1964.
7. Griffin, G.A. M.S. thesis, University of Wisconsin, in preparation.
8. Harlow, H.F. *Am. Scientist*, *47*, 459–479 (1959).
9. Mitchell, G.D. M.S. thesis, University of Wisconsin, in preparation.

NOTE

This research was supported by a grant from the University of Wisconsin Graduate School, and by USPHS grants MH-04528 and FR-0167 from the National Institutes of Health to the University of Wisconsin Department of Psychology Primate Laboratory and Regional Primate Research Center, respectively.

17

Maternal Behavior of Rhesus Monkeys Deprived of Mothering and Peer Associations in Infancy

*H. F. Harlow, M. K. Harlow,
R. O. Dodsworth, and G. L. Arling*

We have known for over five years that female rhesus monkeys raised from birth onward in our laboratory without recourse to real monkey mothers and with no or little opportunity to form affectional associations with age mates early in life are either impossible or difficult to breed, even with sexually experienced males from our breeding colony. The problem is by no means confined to rhesus monkeys or to the laboratory, however, for it occurs with high frequency among various mammals in zoos where lone specimens are acquired as infants or are born in captivity and raised individually.

Originally we believed that none of 56 laboratory-born females raised under conditions of social deprivation could be sexually rehabilitated, but over a period of years and after many mating sessions scheduled when the females were in estrus, 18 have been voluntarily inseminated by our breeding stock males and 18 that failed under voluntary conditions have been inseminated with the aid of a rack that restrains, positions, and supports the female during copulation. Of these 36 females, 20 have thus

Harlow, H. F., Harlow, M. K., Dodsworth, R. O., & Arling, G. L. Maternal behavior of rhesus monkeys deprived of mothering and peer association in infancy. *Proceedings of the American Philosophical Society*, 1966, *110*, 58–66. Reprinted by permission of University of Toronto Press.

TABLE 17.1   Rearing Conditions, Impregnation, and Maternal Behavior of Twenty Socially Deprived Females Toward Their First Infants

Mother	Mothering Condition	Age When Placed With Cagemate	Island Placement	Nature of Impregnation	Fate of Infant
		I. Abusive Mothers			
68	Cloth Surrogate	—	—	Rack	Killed
59	Cloth Surrogate	—	—	Voluntary	Survived
75	Wire Surrogate	—	—	Voluntary	Separated after injury
63	Wire Cage	—	—	Voluntary	Survived
70	Wire Cage	—	—	Rack	Killed
81	Wire Cage	—	—	Voluntary	Killed
27	Wire Cage	—	—	Rack	Survived
38	Wire Cage	—	yes	Voluntary	Killed
		II. Indifferent Mothers			
94*	Cloth Surrogate	—	—	Rack	Survived
16	Wire Cage	—	—	Rack	Survived
58	Cloth Surrogate	—	—	Voluntary	Survived
A6**	Cloth Surrogate	7 Mo.	—	Voluntary	Died of starvation
22	Wire Cage	—	yes	Voluntary	Survived
21	Wire Cage	—	—	Voluntary	Survived
35	Wire Cage	—	—	Voluntary	Survived
		III. Adequate Mothers			
91	Cloth Surrogate	10 Mo.	—	Voluntary	Survived
A1	Cloth Surrogate	10. Mo.	—	Voluntary	Survived
49	Wire Cage	12 mo.	—	Voluntary	Survived
32	Wire Cage	—	yes	Rack	Survived
54	Wire Cage	—	yes	Voluntary	Survived

*Early indifferent. See text.

**Infant sucked at nipples but apparently milk was insufficient. Removed from mother at 32 days, but did not respond to treatment. Autopsy attributed death to starvation.

far produced one or more viable infants, and their behavior toward these infants has been observed using a check list.[1] Subsequently we have analyzed their histories in terms of five variables, one relating to the nature of their impregnation as described above, two relating to their own "mothering" in infancy, and two relating to their earlier peer experience. Table 17.1 presents relevant data about the 20 mothers and their behavior toward their first infants.

The first mothering condition is "no mothering," the females being raised alone from the first hours after birth in bare wire cages in which they could see and hear other infants but make no physical contact with them, as illustrated in Figure 12-19. The infants were bottle-fed by hand in the first weeks, then from a bottle clamped to the cage, and they were weaned to a cup at 45 days or later. Laboratory practices have changed over the years, but in general the earlier animals were hand-fed longer and weaned at older ages than the later ones. One female was raised on a lactating wire surrogate mother during the first six months of life, then in a standard cage subsequently. All the data we have collected on single wire surrogates indicate that this condition does not differ from that of the bare wire cage in its behavioral effects,[2] and so the lone wire-surrogate-raised female is treated as a member of the wire-cage group. The second mothering condition is that of the cloth surrogate. This situation usually involved the presence during the first six months of both a cloth and wire surrogate mother, either of which might nurse, but the presence or nursing status of the wire surrogate has been demonstrated to be a variable of little or no importance, and consequently only experience with the cloth mother is considered here (see Figure 17-1).

There are two conditions relating to association with peers. It was originally planned that no infant would have contact with other infants during the first year of life, but we suffered from a surplus of infants and a shortage of wire cages with the result that a limited number of infants did have delayed living experience with age mates, starting at 7 months to 12 months of age, providing the first condition (see Table 17.1). Subsequently, 20 semi-isolation-raised monkeys between 3 years 1 month and 4 years 4 months of age were placed for 2 months as a group on a monkey island in Madison's zoo. This social experience had therapeutic value during the period of residence on the island as indicated by the initiation of grooming, gradual reduction of aggression, and formation of some friendship and play groups. However, in no case did we observe any normal heterosexual behavior although there were many instances of autoerotic behavior in both sexes and sexual posturing by females (see Figure 17-2).

The behavior of the 20 "motherless" monkey mothers toward their infants were observed closely after delivery, and the mothers were classified as abusive, indifferent, or adequate on the basis of their treatment of the infant in the first month. Table 17.1 groups the subjects by maternal rating. To be rated abusive, a mother's interaction with her offspring had to be one of extreme physical cruelty. She sometimes sought out the baby to strike or bit it without provocation. When the infant contacted her, she often pushed or kicked it from her body. In four cases the baby was killed. In one instance (No. 75) the infant was separated within an hour of birth after the mother had bitten off or mangled six fingers. Two weeks later, after the infant had recovered, it was placed with the mother, but she immediately started to bite the infant's toes and the infant was then permanently removed.

Figure 17-1 Wire and cloth surrogate mothers. This infant has a nursing wire mother and a non-nursing cloth mother.

The principal criterion for separating the remaining, nonabusive mothers into indifferent and adequate categories was nursing behavior. If the mother failed to nurse the baby so that it had to be removed from her periodically for hand-feeding until it could drink from a cup in the cage, she was classified as indifferent. Mothers 16 and 94 did eventually establish adequate nursing relationships after 30 and 5 days, respectively, and are consequently classified as "early indifferent." Indifferent mothers showed frequent punishing behavior toward their infants, but it was much less severe and less pervasive than that of the abusive mothers. An adequate mother was one that nursed her infant consistently from the start so that it never needed to be removed for handfeeding. There was a considerable range of maternal proficiency among the five mothers rated as adequate,

Figure 17-2 Autoerotic behavior in male monkey and sexual posturing in female monkey during residence on island in Vilas Park.

with some showing poor positioning of the infant in ventral contacts and a large amount of infant punishing. There is, however, considerable variability in these maternal behaviors among laboratory females raised and captured in the wild, and the behavior of the five "adequate" motherless mothers was at the low extreme, but not clearly outside the range, of the feral-raised mothers.

Maternal behavior is first considered in relation to the mothering conditions of the subjects during infancy. Two of the 7 mothers raised on cloth surrogates were abusive, 3 were indifferent, and 2 were adequate as compared with 6 abusive, 4 indifferent, and 3 adequate mothers among the 13 no-mothering subjects (wire cage or wire surrogate). The small numbers preclude any definitive conclusion about a possible ameliorating effect of cloth surrogates on later maternal behavior, but the data are suggestive.

The social experience variables provide somewhat more provocative data. Of the 4 mothers caged with peers by 12 months of age, 1 was indifferent and 3 were adequate in maternal behavior. Grouping abusive and indifferent mothers together to make an inadequate mother category

TABLE 17.2   Behavior of Motherless Mothers to Second and Third Infants

		Maternal Rating			
Mother	Infant 1	Infant 2	Infant 3	Mothering Condition	Social Experience
35	Indifferent	Indifferent		Wire Cage	—
59	Abusive	Adequate	Adequate	Cloth Surrogate	—
38	Abusive	Adequate		Wire Cage	—
63	Abusive	Adequate		Wire Cage	—
58	Indifferent	Adequate	Adequate	Cloth Surrogate	—
A6	Indifferent	Adequate		Cloth Surrogate	Peer
91	Adequate	Adequate		Cloth Surrogate	Peer

and testing it against the adequate category for effects of limited early peer experience yield a difference significant at the 0.03 level by Fisher's exact probability test. The second social experience variable, group living on the monkey island for two months as preadolescents or adolescents, provided less dramatic results. Two of the 4 mothers with this background were adequate and 2 were inadequate, a difference significant only at the 0.20 level by Fisher's exact probability test. No mother had had both social experiences. If the two kinds of social experience are combined and tested against maternal adequacy vs. inadequacy, it is found that all 5 adequate mothers had had social experience contrasted with only 3 of the 15 inadequate mothers. This difference is significant at the 0.08 level.

The breeding rack has been in use for a relatively short time, and thus far 6 females impregnated on the rack have delivered viable babies. All 6 had failed to be inseminated after repeated trials under voluntary conditions, and thus they represent a group selected for failure to adjust sexually, one criterion of social adjustment. None of these 6 had had cage mates by 12 months of age, and only 1 had had island experience. Of the 14 voluntarily impregnated mothers, half had had limited social experience. The data are too few, as yet, to be conclusive, but they suggest a correlation between sexual inadequacy and maternal inadequacy. Three of the rack-bred mothers were abusive, 2 of them killing their babies, 2 were early indifferent, and 1 was adequate. Corresponding numbers for the voluntarily impregnated mothers are 5 abusive, including 2 killings and 1 separation, 5 indifferent, and 4 adequate mothers.

The most surprising finding about the motherless mothers is not their behavior toward their first infants but their treatment of subsequent offspring. Thus far, 7 have had second infants and 2 have delivered third babies. Table 17.2 presents the relevant data. With one exception the maternal behavior of the motherless mothers to these second and third infants was rated as adequate—a finding predicted by no member of the

Primate Laboratory staff. The case of mother 38 was particularly astounding since she crushed and mangled her first infant during its first two weeks. The infant was then separated and given all possible medical aid but survived for only 42 days.

The developmental course of one representative maternal response of the first two multiparous motherless mothers (No. 58 and 59) to their second babies was surprising. We were completely unprepared to discover that the frequency of permitted ventral contact was higher for these two multiparous motherless mothers than for two comparable multiparous feral mothers. This phenomenon has not been observed through the developmental course of the mother-infant relations of the next five motherless mothers toward their second babies although four of them could not be differentiated from normal mothers in ventral contacts. Unpublished data by Arling[3] reveal another phenomenon equally unexpected in the maternal treatment of the second and third babies. In the home cage these motherless mothers engage in more interactive play with their offspring than do normal monkey mothers. Indeed, feral-raised rhesus mothers show only transient and ephemeral mother-infant play.

Four motherless mothers (Nos. 21, 58, 59, and 63) have been subjected to intensive study for a period of six months following the birth of their first babies. By good fortune they delivered infants within a 26-day span, and it was possible to place the mothers and their infants in the standardized playpen situation illustrated in Figure 11-1. This apparatus consists of four large living cages, each housing a mother and infant, and adjoining play compartments. A small opening in each living cage restrains the mother but gives the infant continuous access to its playpen. During two daily one-hour test sessions, the screens between the playpen compartments of opposing cages were raised, permitting the infants to interact as pairs. Cage assignments were changed every two weeks so that each infant could associate with every other infant an equal amount of time. Two experimenters independently observed and recorded the behavior exhibited during test sessions.

All four infants survived the experimental period even though we frequently feared that the infants of mothers 59 and 63 would be killed, and the infants of mothers 21 and 58 were maintained by rescuing them regularly for hand-feeding during the first three weeks. Unlike normal mothers, these motherless monkeys ignored the removal of their infants.

The developmental course of maternal rejection during the first 30 days was plotted... for the 4 motherless mothers, 2 of which were rated as abusive and 2 as indifferent, and for 4 feral-raised mothers in the same living situation. During the first 10 to 15 days of life, when the infant is relatively helpless and locomotion is minimal, the incidence of brutality by the motherless mothers was relatively low. However, as the locomotor

Figure 17-3a   Motherless mother pushing infant from her body.

capabilities of the infants matured, the motherless mothers became increasingly punitive. We attribute this to the almost unbelievable persistence on the part of the infants in attempting to make maternal bodily contact. If denied ventral contact, they would seek dorsal contact of any type and worm their way around the mother's body to the ventral surface. The mothers would persistently scrape the infant off their body, as illustrated in Figure 17-3a, sometimes kicking it or brushing its face against the cage floor. Another response was ignoring the infant entirely, as shown in Figure 17-3b. In spite of rejection or brutality the infants never gave up.

The course of maternal responsiveness is presented in Figure 17-4 in terms of frequency of maternal rejection by the motherless mothers compared with a group of equal-aged primiparous monkey mothers captured in the wild and presumably normal. During the first 90 days normal mothers seldom rejected their infants whereas the frequency of infant rejection by motherless mothers was extremely high. After 90 days the

Figure 17-3b   Motherless mother staring blankly above her baby, not recognizing the baby as such.

frequency of rejection by feral mothers increased sharply, reflecting the start of the normal, second stage of maternal behavior which has been described and interpreted by Hansen[4] and by Harlow, Harlow, and Hansen.[5] During this period the frequency of infant rejection was lower for the motherless mothers than for the normal monkey mothers, although the motherless mothers never displayed the degree of infant interest, supervision, and protection observed in the normal mothers. The difference in frequency of rejection of infants by the two mother groups is significant in the first 90 days ($p = 0.05$) but not during the next 90 days.

A somewhat similar developmental course was found for frequency of mother-infant ventral contact..., although the infants of motherless monkey mothers never achieved as high a level of ventral contacts as did the infants of normal monkey mothers. Moreover, these data involve an artifact since the infants of the motherless monkeys made many maternal contacts which were immediately or soon terminated by their mothers,

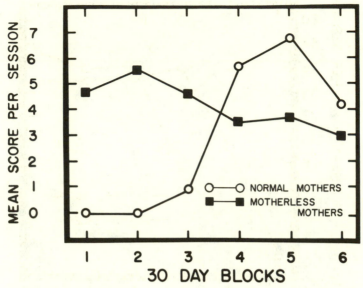

Figure 17-4   Rejection responses of feral mothers and motherless mothers to their infants during the first six months of life.

leading the infants to try again and again. The more frequently the monkey mother disengaged herself from her infant, the more frequently could the infant attempt to reinstate maternal contact and enhance the contact score. Duration of mother-infant ventral contacts would doubtless differentiate the groups more definitively. Nevertheless, all four infants did make frequent ventral contact with the motherless mothers during the first six months of life. This contact, we believe, is a powerful stimulus to the elicitation of maternal behavior, and we hypothesize that ventral contacts with their first babies were a factor leading to maternal acceptance by motherless mothers of their second and third infants even though this is an inadequate explanation for monkey mother 38's acceptance of her second infant.

A normative study by Seay[6] showed no differences in ventral contact between babies of normal primiparous and multiparous mothers during the first six months of life.... In only one respect did the two groups differ, and that is in frequency of rejection after the first month.... Multiparous mothers began to discourage some attempted contacts after the first month, while primiparous mothers were more tolerant, if not overprotective, and did not show an increment until the fourth month. Thus, multiparous females seem to begin the normal separation process earlier than primiparous females by firm, but not abusive, rejection of infant contact. It should be stressed, however, that in both groups during the first six months, positive,

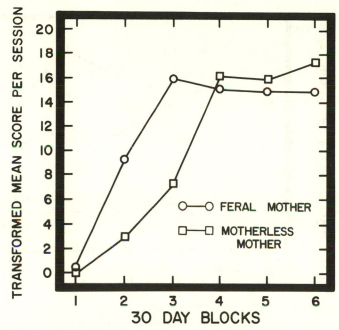

Figure 17-5 Mutual contact play between infants of feral mothers and between infants of motherless mothers in the playpen situation during the first six months.

accepting maternal responses far outnumbered the rejecting responses, and that even in the second year, normal females show more positive than negative responses to their infants.[7] This contrasts sharply with the behavior of the motherless mothers in their primiparous and multiparous phases, for they showed more and earlier rejection toward their first infants than toward their subsequent infants.

We were able to trace the course of infant-infant or peer affection in the four infants of the motherless mothers in the playpen situation. Infant-infant or peer affection as measured by contact play responses was delayed in the motherless-mother infants compared with the four infants of normal mothers (Figure 17-5), but essentially no differences were found from the fourth month onward. The developmental course of the more complex play pattern of noncontact play for infants of motherless mothers and normal mothers is similar (Figure 17-6), and although differences in frequency persisted throughout the six-month test period, they are not statistically significant. The motherless-mother offspring are now approaching four years of age and appear to be socially normal animals in all respects.

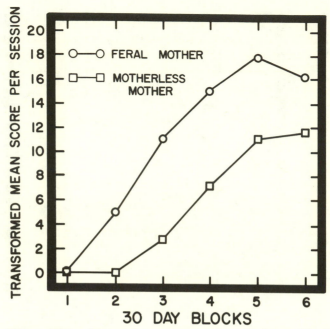

Figure 17-6 Approach, noncontact play of infants of feral mothers and infants of motherless mothers during the first six months of life.

The sex behavior of the originally unresponsive and frigid motherless mothers throughout the test years is of interest and has been observed intensively by Senko.[8] Some of these 20 motherless mothers have come to accept sexual approaches by the breeding stock males and to maintain upright posture during copulation. A few have even come to approach the males and to initiate sexual relationships. Yet in no case has the sexual behavior of these females been normal, and their responses to the males during copulation are not as interactive and reciprocal, as efficiently timed, or as enthusiastic as those of feral-born females.

The various observations of motherless mothers and normal mothers lead to the impression that motherless mothers are socially infantile creatures differing from their offspring primarily in aggression. In mammals aggression is a late-maturing behavior, developing after the young have normally established friendly relationships with mothers and peers. Rhesus monkeys show true aggression toward the end of the first year, and they become increasingly aggressive thereafter. In their early months they have normally had strong affectional ties to mothers and to age mates, and when aggression matures, they show restraints in venting it against their mothers and their friends. Indeed, monkeys raised in play groups tend to cooperate with each other in interactions against other play groups and against mothers not their own. When the young of a playpen group jointly aggress against a mother, the mother's own infant does not participate. Moreover, monkeys rapidly learn in group living to restrain aggression toward older and stronger monkeys and against younger monkeys, whose mothers will protect them, or, in the absence of mothers, they will be protected by the dominant males in the group. Monkey infants are privileged members of the group, and all individuals accept their status or are eliminated. Thus, feral-raised monkeys do not attack infants, and feral-raised females, when they produce babies of their own, accept them, care for them, and fight viciously to protect them.

The motherless mothers, on the other hand, were raised in semi-isolation without mothers or peer relationships in early life, with the few limited exceptions treated in the data. When aggression matured, they had no affectional ties to restrain them or experience in a group to enable them to learn to respect and accept infants and peers. Those placed on the island initially fought, but those that survived the first days did learn to restrain some of their hostility and even to form friendships. The animals kept in the laboratory came to vent aggression on other monkeys on the rare occasions they were placed with them, and in the absence of monkeys, they threatened attendants or even chewed on their own bodies.[9] When the females had babies, they tended either to attack them or to ignore them. Those mothers with limited social experience tended to be less hostile or indifferent to their infants than the mothers without any social experience except for mating sessions. The first babies of the motherless mothers must in many instances have initiated or greatly accelerated the socialization process, enabling them to accept subsequent babies for the most part. Indeed, the mothers even played with second and third babies, in contrast with normal rhesus mothers, which ordinarily have ceased to play with any monkey after they reach adulthood. The repeated mating sessions with breeding stock males have perhaps also played a part in socializing some of these females in another aspect of personal relationships. In this respect, the rack-bred females differed from the voluntarily-bred females, for they failed to be socialized by the males. The outstanding feature in the history of all 20 motherless mothers, however, is that none of them has had the continuing and multiple social experiences that come to all monkeys born in the wild and raised in a troop for the first year or more of life. The early deprivation of these mothers led to difficulties in mating and, in most, abnormal relationships with their babies even when they adjusted sufficiently to males to achieve impregnation unaided. The data do suggest that social experience, however meager or delayed, has some ameliorating effect on maternal behavior even when the experience is primarily with an infant the mother initially rejects.

The present data reveal the usefulness of retrospective analysis as contrasted with the more precise and esteemed anterospective analysis of the conventional scientific approach. As long as the variables under consideration are important and the observations accurate, retrospective, clinical-type analysis may reveal relationships of major importance that are either statistically significant or at a sufficiently high level of confidence to identify the need and nature of subsequent anterospective research.

NOTES

This research was supported in part by grant FR-00167 and grant MH-04528 from the National Institutes of Health, United States Public Health Service, to the Wisconsin Regional Primate Research Center and the University of Wisconsin Primate Laboratory, respectively, and by funds received from the Graduate School of the University of Wisconsin.

[1] B. Seay, B. K. Alexander, and H. F. Harlow, "Maternal Behavior of Socially Deprived Rhesus Monkeys," *Journ. Abnorm. Soc. Psychol.* 69, 4 (1964): pp. 345–354.

[2] H. F. Harlow, and R. R. Zimmermann, "Affectional Responses in the Infant Monkey," *Science* 130, 3373 (1959): pp. 421–432.

[3] G. L. Arling, "Effects of Social Deprivation on Maternal Behavior of Rhesus Monkeys." M.A. thesis, Univ. of Wisconsin, in preparation.

[4] E. W. Hansen, "The Development of Maternal and Infant Behavior in the Rhesus Monkey." Unpublished doctoral dissertation, Univ. of Wisconsin, 1962.

[5] H. F. Harlow, M. K. Harlow, and E. W. Hansen, "The Maternal Affectional System of Rhesus Monkeys." In H. L. Rheingold (ed.), *Maternal Behavior in Mammals* (New York, Wiley, 1963), pp. 254–281.

[6] B. M. Seay, "Maternal Behavior in Primiparous and Multiparous Rhesus Monkeys." Unpublished doctoral dissertation, Univ. of Wisconsin, 1964.

[7] Hansen, *op. cit.*

[8] M. G. Senko, "Effects of Partial and Total Social Isolation on Adult Heterosexual Behavior." M.A. thesis, Univ. of Wisconsin, in preparation.

[9] H. A. Cross, and H. F. Harlow, "Prolonged and Progressive Effects of Partial Isolation on the Behavior of Macaque Monkeys." *Jour. Exp. Res. Pers. 1,* 1 (1965): pp. 39–49.

18

Social Recovery by Isolation-Reared Monkeys

Harry F. Harlow and Stephen J. Suomi

Social isolation has long been identified as a powerful precipitating agent in disruption of normal social development in human beings. While ethical considerations and practical constraints have obviously restricted controlled scientific study of isolation with human subjects, it has been possible to systematically investigate the effects of total social deprivation upon closely related, nonhuman, primate species. The unequivocal finding of numerous researches on macaque monkeys has been that total social isolation for at least the first 6 months of life enormously damages or destroys subsequent social and sexual behavioral capabilities (1–3). Monkeys so reared were grossly incompetent in interactions with socially normal age mates. As infants and adolescents, they failed to initiate or reciprocate the play and grooming behaviors characteristic of their peers. As adults, these monkeys consistently exhibited abnormal sexual, aggressive, and maternal behaviors.

It is clear that early social deprivation is an enormously effective procedure for the production of psychopathological behavior patterns. Less well known is the degree to which social behaviors can be recovered after early social isolation. The data that follow indicate that social deprivation early in life does not necessarily produce irreversible behavioral deficits, and that rehabilitation of varying extent can be effected via judiciously chosen experimental procedures.

Several pairs of rhesus monkeys reared for the first 6 months of life in total social isolation chambers (4) were tested on a daily basis in a social playroom (4) with pairs of socially competent age mates. In comparison

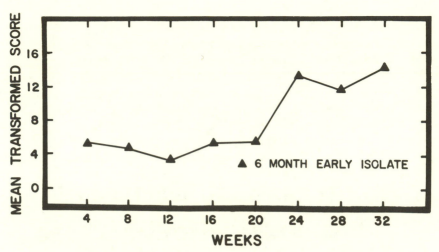

Figure 18-1   Inanimate object manipulation by 6-month isolates.

to the normal stimulus animals, the isolates were clearly inferior on virtually every behavioral measure throughout the 8-month testing period. They showed less object exploration, social approach, social contact initiation, social threatening, and play, while exhibiting high levels of disturbance activity and rigid and passive posturing (G.L. Rowland, unpublished doctoral dissertation, University of Wisconsin, 1964). Frequently, the isolates were targets of unprovoked aggression by the control peers. However, in terms of responses directed toward each other and not toward the control monkeys, the isolates showed limited recovery over the testing period.

From the fifth to the eighth month of testing, the frequency of play behavior between the isolate pairs usually increased from a zero-baseline to fairly respectable levels. Although this was clearly delayed and unsophisticated play by monkey standards, a little late-play is better than none. Inanimate object manipulation, which may be taken as a rough index of curiosity and exploratory tendencies, showed an even higher level of restitution (Figure 18-1). Threat was another social response that developed between pairs of isolate monkeys, even though its exhibition was extremely delayed and limited. The threat response, which is a communicatory mechanism, was judiciously expressed toward other isolates but was not directed toward the normal controls. These data suggested that monkeys subjected to total social isolation for a half-year period possessed latent potential for limited social recovery immediately after incarceration, even in the presence of aggressive normal peers. Monkeys reared in total social isolation for the first year of life showed no such recovery when tested under similar conditions (G.L. Rowland, unpublished experiments).

Social recovery of a different form was exhibited by another group of monkeys subjected to early social isolation. These were females who had reached sexual maturity but were apathetic or adamantly uncooperative when confronted with breeding-stock males that were sexually eager and adroit. By methods dark, dismal, and devious we impregnated several of these reluctant females over a period of years. We have called them "motherless mothers," since they never experienced mother love, nor any other kind of monkey affection, themselves. Most of the motherless mothers either completely ignored or abused their initial offspring.... However, unless the mothers actually killed their infants—and several did—the babies struggled for maternal contact day after day, week after week, month after month. The infants would cling to the mothers' backs, continually attempting to achieve ventral and breast contact despite efforts by the mothers to displace them. To our surprise, maternal brutality and indifference gradually decreased. From the fourth month onward, the persistent babies that were finally able to attain intimate physical contact with their mother were actually punished less and permitted nipple contact more than offspring of normal mothers.

Many of the motherless mothers have had second and even third babies. Those whose maternal feelings were eventually released by the persistent and determined body contact and nursing efforts of their first infants proved to be adequate or good mothers to their subsequent babies. Most of the motherless mothers that had abused or ignored their first infants throughout a predetermined 6-month postpartum period continued to be inadequate, brutal, or lethal mothers to subsequent progeny.

It seems that in the case of the adequate mothers, the babies inadvertently served as psychotherapists to their indifferent mothers and that these mothers spontaneously transferred maternal feelings induced by their first babies to their feelings for subsequent babies. The data on the rehabilitated mothers suggested that infants possess some specific abilities as behavioral therapists for abnormal adult females. However, rehabilitation was limited to maternal behavior and, in particular, those mothers continued to exhibit inappropriate and ineffective sexual behavior.

The rehabilitative potential of social contact was further illustrated in a third study. Four 6-month isolate monkeys were individually housed for 2 weeks after removal from the isolation chambers. Heated cloth surrogates were then introduced into their home cages. Within a few days the isolates began to contact the surrogates with increasing frequency and duration. Correspondingly, the incidence of disturbance behavior exhibited by the isolates showed a significant decrease from presurrogate levels.

After 2 weeks of individual surrogate exposure, the isolates were housed in pairs. In this situation they almost spontaneously exhibited social play, infantile sex, locomotion, and exploratory behavior..., but the social behavior was clumsy and the isolates continued to display sporadic disturbance activity. After 6 months they had shown no marked improvement.

We have long emphasized that the mother figure is a basic socializing agent, since it gives to its own infant social contact acceptability, essential to any subsequent social interaction—and basic security and trust. In this case surrogate mothers appeared to provide a certain degree of contact acceptability and security and trust sufficient for the isolates to suppress existing self-directed disturbance activity and to initiate crude social interactions with other isolates. However, since the inanimate surrogates could provide no further social stimulation, recovery failed to progress beyond the stage noted above.

The above researches all used social agents as a means for rehabilitation, and to a limited extent recovery of some form was achieved. Experiments designed to rehabilitate isolates via nonsocial means, e.g., exposure to slides during isolation (C.L. Pratt, unpublished doctoral dissertation, University of Wisconsin, 1969), gradual introduction into the postisolation test environment (5), or aversive conditioning procedures (6) have been less successful. It is intuitively compelling to argue that the strategy most likely to succeed in rehabilitation of monkeys exhibiting social deficits should occur after stimulation of a social, rather than nonsocial, form. It may also be argued that the social stimulation utilized in the above studies was far less than optimal.

In the first experiments, normal age mates may well have provided the isolate subjects with complex social stimulation, but they certainly did not provide social contact acceptability. Rather, they aggressed against the isolates and, not surprisingly, isolate recovery in this context was limited at best. In the case of the motherless mothers and their persistent infants, the babies provided their mothers with contact acceptability but little else. Here, although relatively normal maternal behavior was recovered, other aspects of monkey social activity were not. Likewise, surrogates provided isolates with contact acceptability, but for further social stimulation the isolates had only each other. They exhibited recovery of only the most unsophisticated social responses.

A better monkey "therapist" would be one that could provide contact acceptability without aggression, as well as more sophisticated social capabilities. Years of research in which we investigated the normal social development of rhesus monkeys has indicated that a normally developing infant of 3–4 months of age fits these requirements almost perfectly. Therefore, we designed a study employing this type of monkey therapist.

Figure 18-2 Monkey clinging to simplified surrogate.

Our therapists were four female rhesus infants that had been separated from their mothers at birth, but were raised in our nursery for 30 days and then housed with simplified surrogates (Figure 18-2) in quad cage quadrants (Figure 18-3). Furthermore, the therapist monkeys interacted 2 hr a day in groups of two and four, in either a double quad cage quadrant or in the standard playroom. Such rearing permitted relatively normal social development (7) (L.A. Rosenblum, unpublished doctoral dissertation, University of Wisconsin, 1961).

When four subjects raised from birth in total social isolation were 6 months of age and the therapists were 3 months of age, all eight monkeys were housed in individual quadrants of two quad cages. After a 2-week baseline period, each isolate was allowed to interact with its neighboring

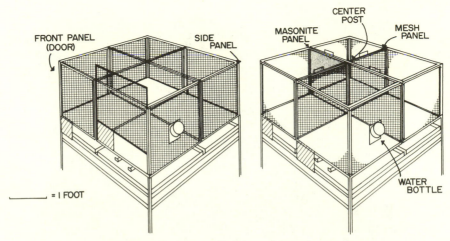

Figure 18-3   Combined living and experimental cage.

therapist in the quad cage 2 hr a day, 3 days per week, for a period of 1 month. The therapist monkeys also continued playroom interaction as a group of four. Subsequently, pairs of isolates were allowed to interact with pairs of therapists in the playroom. During the next 20 weeks, the number of quad cage social sessions was decreased and the number of playroom sessions involving two therapists and two isolates was progressively increased.

The isolates' initial responses to the therapy sessions were to huddle in a corner, and the therapists' first responses were to approach and cling to the isolates (Figure 18-4). Within a week in the quad cages and a month in the playroom, the isolates were reciprocating the clinging. Concurrently, the therapists were developing play patterns of increasing sophistication among themselves and attempting to initiate such patterns with the isolates. Within 2 weeks in the quad cages and a month in the playroom, the isolates were reciprocating these behaviors.

By 1 year of age, the isolates were scarcely distinguishable from the normal therapists in terms of frequencies of exploratory, locomotive, and play behaviors, an unprecedented reversal of the isolation syndrome. The decline of self-clasping and huddling, illustrated in Figure 18-5, demonstrated a dramatic cumulative recovery from these infantile or depressed behaviors throughout the therapy period and a return to normal or near-normal levels by the end of 6 months. An interesting fact is that the therapists showed a modest increase in the self-clasp response, possibly learned from the isolates, even though their basic social behaviors did not deteriorate.

Figure 18-4 Therapist clinging to huddling isolate.

Even more dramatic was the precipitous decline in the more mature abnormal responses of rock and stereotypy (Figure 18-6). By the fourth month of therapy, rock and stereotypy were at near-normal levels, and by the sixth month there were no differences—at least no differences between the deprived and therapist monkeys in absolute frequencies of these responses.

No doubt the most critical and valid measures of social recovery were those of social contact and play. Essentially complete recovery of both of these behavior patterns was attained by the isolates when they were tested with the therapist monkeys in the quad cage. In the larger and stranger playroom area there was eventually complete recovery of social contact and very satisfactory recovery of social play, as shown in Figure 18-7. Mutual interactive play by isolate and therapist monkeys is illustrated in Figure 15-10.

Because of limited animal availability, it was not possible to sex-balance both groups. All of the isolate monkeys were male and all of the therapist monkeys were female. We have long known that male and female monkeys

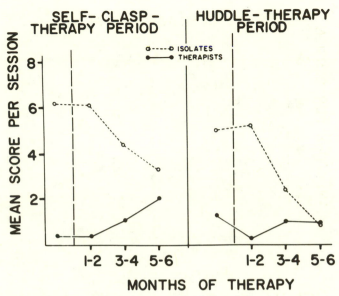

Figure 18-5   Self-clasping and huddling behaviors: therapy period.

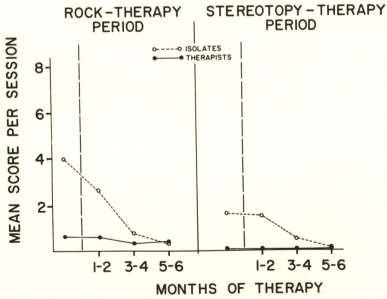

Figure 18-6   Rock and stereotypy behaviors: therapy period.

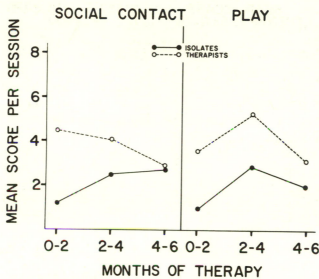

Figure 18-7 Social contact and play behaviors: therapy period.

play in fundamentally different patterns (8). Male play is typically rough-and-tumble in form, where the monkeys wrestle, roll, and sham-bite but seldom injure one another. Females are much more likely to engage in noncontact, approach-withdrawal play, which involves chasing back and forth with frequent role reversal and a minimum of bodily contact. Since our female therapist monkeys played only female games, they could not have trained the socially deprived males in the ecstasies and elegancies of masculine play. However, in the final playroom sessions, the males clearly exhibited a predominance of age-appropriate masculine play. Thus, the isolate males could not have developed their play patterns on the basis of imitation of the female therapist monkeys alone. Rather, it appears that the psychiatric sessions gradually imparted to the males the full grandiose gifts of masculinity, which the males in turn expressed in their play bouts.

The earlier data presented in this paper made it obvious that monkeys socially damaged by isolation early in life may attain very limited recovery of behavioral functions if they are allowed to interact for long periods of times with a group of equally socially blighted monkey subjects. The data also strongly indicate that the most elementary social behaviors are the easiest to elicit in the recovery process, while exhibition of more complex behaviors by social isolates requires longer and more delicate procedures.

The present data suggest that therapist monkeys must be selected in such a manner as to present no threat to abnormal monkeys and that socialization is probably achieved in large part, but not entirely, through imitative learning as the younger animals enter and pass through subsequent socialization stages. Obviously many problems are left unresolved by the present study, such as the maximal age at which the isolates can be rehabilitated and the depths of depression that are minimal to socialization. Likewise, the maximal effectiveness of different therapeutic conditions is left unspecified. For example, should therapy begin with the formation or re-formation of maternal bonds antecedent to peer associations, or should this be preceded by environmental adaptation? The present research has indicated that social rehabilitation of isolate-reared monkeys *can* be attained. It is the task of further research to disclose better means to achieve this end.

REFERENCES

1. Harlow, H.F., G.L. Rowland, and G.A. Griffin, *Psychiat. Res. Rep., 19*, 116 (1964).
2. Harlow, H.F., R.O. Dodsworth, and M.K. Harlow, *Proc. Nat. Acad. Sci. USA, 54*, 90 (1966).
3. Mitchell, G.D., E.J. Raymond, G.C. Ruppenthal, and H.F. Harlow, *Psychol. Rep, 18*, 567 (1966).
4. Harlow, H.F., and M.K. Harlow, *Bull. Menninger Clin., 26*, 213 (1962).
5. Mitchell, G.D., and D.L. Clark, *J. Genet. Psychol., 113*, 117 (1968).
6. Sackett, G.P., in *The Role of Learning in Psychotherapy*, ed. R. Porter (J.A. Churchill, Ltd., London, 1968), pp. 3–25.
7. Hansen, E.W., *Behaviour, 27*, 107 (1966).
8. Harlow, H.G., and M.K. Harlow, in *Behavior of Nonhuman Primates*, ed. A.M. Schrier, H.F. Harlow, and F. Stollnitz (Academic Press, New York, 1965), Vol. 2, pp. 287–334.

NOTE

This research was supported by USPHS grants MH-11894 and RR-00167 from the National Institutes of Health to the University of Wisconsin Primate Laboratory and Regional Primate Research Center, respectively.

PART SIX
OVERVIEW

19

Love and Aggression

Harry F. Harlow

The topics on which I speak from time to time and from place to place have a capricious custom of undergoing change between the choice of the topic and the time of the speech. For this very special occasion I originally decided on the subject of aggression, its cause and control, but, somewhere along the line I heard that I was scheduled to talk on the nature of love. As a compromise which does not at all change the subject matter of this presentation I shall use an alternate title, Aggression and Love.

Anger and aggression are designed through evolution to save and to salvage the individual without regard for the fate or future of any other living being. Aggression is a ruthless, savage, asocial behavior pattern, and a problem of primate importance is how does aggression become socially controlled.

Aggression is in a very real sense an innate emotion. In an equally real sense it is a learned emotion. For this reason, all aggression theorists have always been right whether, like Lorenz, they espoused aggression as innate or, like Montagu and other social behaviorists, they believed that all aggressions were learned.

The subtle secrets to these seeming contradictions lie in the developmental sequences of the love systems as contrasted with the developmental sequences of aggressive behavior. All of the primate data, be it loris or lemur, monkey or man, show that aggression, particularly violent aggression, matures relatively late while three of the basic loves mature very early or relatively early. These basic facts are obvious to monkeys whether or not they are obvious to men.

Kittay Lecture, October 31, 1976.

In a detailed, longitudinal study of the maturation of aggression in macaque monkeys over a period of seven years, Cross and Harlow gave annual tests to a group of eight to twelve monkeys. Full-blown aggression toward others, external aggression, develops relatively late in the male monkey and did not reach full strength until the fourth year of age. This is equivalent to the mid-teenagers in human life. In the female, external aggression develops even later. Aggression is one of the few behavioral traits which develops earlier in the male than in the female. The maturation of self-aggression, or aggression directed toward oneself, is delayed another year, until the fifth year of male monkey age, which would compare with human late adolescence. Again the same relationship holds between the male and the female. No matter what form the agonistic behavior assumes, the maturation is later in the female.

All, or almost all, primates have prolonged, ample amorous opportunities to love before any head start of hate develops. It is fortunate that aggression is a late maturing mechanism. Were it otherwise there would never have been even one primate society. At an early age all the infants would have destroyed each other, and societies without infants become societies without adults.

Of the five love systems, the first three—maternal, infant, and peer love—mature very early in both monkey and man.

Stressing the early maturation of most of the basic love systems, it should be emphasized that maternal love is present before and upon the infant's birth. Some analysts have believed that baby love emerged and was trained in the womb. This theory, however, is wont to have womb for improvement, but that does not matter. At least mother love is extant and essentially fully formed a long time, even a very long time, before any heritage of hate happened to emerge.

Maternal love has three primary functions. The first is to provide the infant with contact comfort. This is the all-encompassing mechanism of the mother-infant love systems. Although contact comfort replaced the bounties of the breast as the variable of most importance, nursing is still important and a fortunate function for mothers to have. The third primary function is protection. If you are a female, it is only a matter of time until you may have babies, maybe even a boy baby. When your little boy is about seven or eight years old, you will look out the kitchen window and see your boy and the neighbor boy engaged in a knock-down, drag-out fight and you will rush out to clobber the neighbor boy, knowing full well he was to blame for initiating the fight. This is called feminine instinct.

Through the maternal mechanisms the infant develops love for the mother. Out of these infant-mother interactions, augmented by the other variables of warmth and rocking motion, there is built up love for the mother and also basic security and trust. This is the mechanism properly described by Erickson, and it is a fundamental fact which helps to lead to the discovery of new worlds as the young infant develops. With the baby-maternal love bonds now well established, the maternal body and breast becomes less charming and less demanding. Beyond the maternal body beckons an ever-ever land of enchantment with new forms of fascination.

At the proper time, mother monkey gives her infant the greatest gift of all, permission to sally forth in sorties which are at first very brief. The early sorties are followed by desperate dashes back to mother where baby rubs in a new supply of social security from the contact comfort of mother's body. As the infant explores further and further away from mother, the world of peer and age mate is duly discovered. The infant's affectional bonds steadily increase in fact and in form and generalize to many familiar faces.

The basic mechanism of age mate affection is play. In the course of regular social play the monkeys learn to accept and become accustomed to physical contact with their playmates during the rough-and-tumble play. Social rules and regulations as well as sexual attitudes are initiated during the chase, for both the chaser and the chased. To coin a phrase, little girls who are never chased will remain chaste forever. As you can readily surmise, if you are going to develop a taste for thrust you must first develop a taste for touch. During play, social roles of deference and dominance, compliance and camaraderie are learned in an atmosphere of pleasant if not passionate affection, which prevents their misuse and amortizes aggression when it does appear.

The three basic affectional systems, then, have not only made their appearance but have become well established by the second year of monkey life. Affection develops long before aggression and in many guises. The maternal and infant reciprocal loves are from birth on, and age mate attachments grow ever stronger from the onset of play, at about three months.

The role played by the affectional behaviors in ameliorating aggressive acts and preventing violent aggression is dramatically illustrated when infants are deprived of the experiences of mother-infant love, infant-mother love, and age mate affection. Loss of these loves produces significantly more hostile and aggressive rhesus monkeys.

In the experiment on deprivation of the three basic loves, infants were raised in total isolation for six months of the first year and for six months in partial isolation, where they could see and hear other monkeys but could not be with them.

The infants raised in isolation were compared with normal, feral mother- and peer-raised infants in their reactions to total strangers. Some of these strangers were adult, older monkeys, some were age mates, and some younger than the isolates. As can be seen, the normal animals were far less aggressive than the isolate monkeys. This was true whether the strangers whom they aggressed were older, adult monkeys, were age mates, or were younger infants. The aggressions of the isolate animals even included suicidal assaults against much larger adult males or brutal beatings of babies, behaviors never seen in normal females and essentially nonexistent in four-year-old males. The isolate monkeys bit and tore violently at the hair and flesh of the strangers to a significantly greater degree than did the equal-aged mother-raised animals. The luckless victims would often assume the helpless, hopeless passive posture in an attempt to avert aggression. In these isolates no affectional ties had had a chance to be formed prior to the opportunity for these agonistic behaviors to emerge, and normal, positive age mate play had not been present to soften the sadistic sorties.

These deprivation experiments also gave strong support to the findings on late maturation of aggression. These same six-month total and six-month partial isolates were first tested at the end of their first year. There were no significant findings on aggression because there was not sufficient aggression to measure. These isolates were then held for two long years, until the average age of three years, the age at which aggression begins to burgeon. They were held in partial isolation and then tested again. It was at this testing that they were found to be significantly more hostile than the normal, socially raised monkeys.

The natural and normal responses to affectionate stimuli are the antithesis of those to aggressive stimuli. The world within us and the world without guarantee that, given a choice, we will love before we can hate. Anger is often improperly thought to be an emotion prepotent over love, but this is a result of the fact that psychologists have published many papers on aggression and few on love. If early, antecedent affectional responses occurred, they would establish strong ties which limit and preclude the possibility of incipient, intense aggression. To paraphrase Oscar Wilde:

> The love or loves that we felt first
> Will bind our hearts together
> And afterwards for best or worst
> These loves will last forever.
>
> We cannot kill the ones we love
> Or those loved by our mother.
> A hatred cannot come above
> Our loves for one another.

Primates either love early or they are apt to hate forever. The God-given maturational processes form the guarantees that aggression of all assortments shall not flourish if love in all or most of its varieties is antecedent.

Aggression does not spring full-blown out of primate brawn any more than sex blooms full-blown out of primate loins. Gradual growth provides a proving ground on which the outcome is determined during the maturation process. In play encounters, varied partial components of parasexual behaviors appear throughout early development and are socially assimilated. Peer play and peer love may be platonic, but they prepare the young peer for future loves full of nonplatonic passion. Likewise, long before maturity, aggressive behaviors are tested in fragmented form, most frequently during play. To the novice a playful challenge to chase or to be chased might well resemble an incipient aggressive attack. Sham biting plays its part in playful monkey antics, but play biting does not injure. Being subject to age mate and maternal censure and control, it loses its bite before the fangs are fierce. If affection has preceded the fact or act of toothy terror, the behavior might be described as toothy tenderness. The investigations of both Rosenblum and Hansen support the amelioration of aggression through social play behaviors. Rosenblum, on the basis of his study, believed that playful aggression appeared before the end of the first year, and Hansen found it early in the second. As aggression matures, socially restrained aggression develops out of normal childhood play.

Sociologists, with pious propriety, commonly differentiate between in-group and out-group aggression. In-group aggression is angry behavior, usually in ameliorated form, between the members of families and friends. It is aggression between members of one's social or cultural group, and it is altered by love ties that are formed well before anger, aggression, and outrage ever mature.

Out-group aggression carries the agonistic behavior beyond the confines of one's family, friends, or social group. Both in-group and out-group aggression may be either normal or abnormally violent, depending upon the previously nurtured positive affectional behaviors.

When loving lads and boy-scout escorts of little old ladies subsequently join the army, how are they converted into soldiers of war, capable of hatred and hostility and girded for blood battles? It isn't simple. One of the most common techniques is to dehumanize the enemy soldiers. Recruits are trained, retrained, and then retrained again that the enemies are not people but rather are monsters. Your allies are men; your enemies are monsters. The nationals of the enemy country are not human beings but are disturbed, distorted deviants supporting their armies.

During one of our major experiments we had an interesting illustration of social aggression combining both in-group and out-group elements. We had four mother-infant families, and the mothers could not leave the living cage because of the size of the exit door, but all of the babies could freely navigate between all four mother-infant living cages The mothers engaged in punitive but playful aggression toward the infants not their own. Since the infants did not appreciate playful punishment, they frequently employed group aggression as a countermeasure against a mother *not their own*. The infants would line up in a row, and when the mother would come to the edge of the cage and try to strike at them, the infants would seize the mother's outstretched hand and arm, pull the arm against the face of the cage, and snatch-grab at the hairy female body. It is of note that the mother's own infant never engaged in this charade.

Out-group aggression, directed toward individuals outside one's family or cultural group, shows to a greater extent the influence of learning and early emotional experiences than does normal in-group combativeness, but it still depends upon what happens to one's emotions prior to the opportunity for aggression and also antecedent to the full maturation of aggression. Under the munificent, maternal aegis, subhuman primate infants, as well as human children, ideally are given preparation on when and how to best respond in both in-group and out-group situations which might elicit agonistic responses. Modeling the maternal manner, the monkey makes threatening faces in rage, with make-believe threats. The matriarch fosters familiarity with selected strange but safe situations and offers alternative behaviors incompatible with antisocial aggressiveness. The toddler, for instance, is taught gentle gestures of affection toward a pitiful puppy instead of and before evoking anguished cries by agonistic, choking squeezes.

The monkey-crocodile dilemma illustrates the development of antisocial aggression. A dozen infant monkeys were placed on a monkey island containing a classical castle and surrounded by a moat. As the baby monkeys grew, they lived in a veritable paradise. They swam in the moat, dived into the waters, and returned to revel and frolic on the rocks. They never had it so good and, unfortunately, they never had it so good again.

At this point the zoo director placed a half dozen crocodiles six to ten feet long in the moat. The infant monkeys would swim, only to suddenly find that they faced a yard-long crocodile yawn, and this discouraged their swimming. Gradually they retreated, to spend twenty-four hours a day on the bank expressing to each other their opinion of crocodiles.

Since the crocodile-monkey conflict had no overt outlet, one might presume an absence of frustration and therefore of aggression. However, the monkeys tired of their banishment from paradise, and they developed aggressive activity within the limits of safety and sanctity imparted by earlier maternal ministrations. A careful coterie of the infants would form a line on the extreme edge of the moat and await the advent of a concrete-minded crocodile. As a crocodile neared the edge, one or two monkeys would seize the forelimbs of the creature and immobilize him, then drag the animal's body against the ragged, rough surface of the moat's wall. Other members of the monkey ménage would then approach the scene, immobilize another arm or leg, and chew on the crocodile's soft inner belly. This monkey aggression was not mellowed by affection and shows the transition from normal to violent aggression.

Opportunities for the generalization of affectional bonds to groups other than one's family, troop, or social in-group are far more limited with the subhuman primates than with man. Of far greater significance, however, is the devastating data that in man's everyday environment there exist countless creatures without adequate affectional ties. When love is lacking, hate steps in and creates such prevailing phenomena as adolescent gang violence, kidnappings, the Ku Klux Klan, or the battered child syndrome. Adolescent gangs born to a background of hate and early exposure to aggression can easily undo the influence of a new member's early parental affection, so strong are the attractions of age mates for each other. This could be especially possible if the new member lacked positive, early peer play. The behaviors of such hostile groups and individuals are characterized by aggression of form and violence such as to prove lethal. Violence in man can be at least as strong as violence in subhuman animals.

Aggression is commonly directed against others, but aggression can also be directed against oneself and in spite of the torment and torture involved can be just as drastically devastating. Freud was the first man to construct a major, theoretical contribution from these facts, the so-called death instinct. Freud was so impressed by man's inhumanity to man, even to the selfsame man, that he named it the death instinct in contrast to the libido. More recently, a large amount of data has been collected by Menninger on this phenomenon which he described under the literary rubric of "Man Against Himself." Other variants of this theme exist. Man has no monopoly on self-inflicted terror and tribulation, and all of the phenomena, excluding language, can be demonstrated in the monkey. As we have already shown, aggression against others follows an orderly course. Of prime importance is the fact that, ideally, aggression involves maturationally delayed behaviors already preceded by established love attachments. Self-directed aggression is also late in maturing and seldom appears before five years of age in the monkey male. Some self-destructive monkeys had been raised in partial social isolation, in individual cages within sight and sound of their equally asocial neighbors. They had had no opportunity for pleasant, loving interchange with either mothers or peers. The sight and sound of primates in untouchable proximity could not replace the feel and the frolic. Typically, monkey self-aggression is characterized by oral grasping and biting of the hands and legs, but it is not limited to those anatomical acts.

The most dramatic expression of agonistic behavior in both monkey and man is aggression against their own children, dramatic partially because to most people violence against their own begotten babies is inconceivable. Mother love presumably is the strongest of all emotions, at least toward infants, and a mother aggressing against her own child, even to the point of lethal aggression, is a potent, patent paradox. Yet mother love can be almost perpetually prevented by withholding mother love from the mother-to-be, even if she isn't going to be a mother for many years. We illustrated the battered child syndrome by the creation of our motherless mothers. Our motherless mothers were animals who had never known mother love themselves and had never had the chance to express love to a mother nor to exchange affection in play with age mate monkeys. Our unloved motherless monkey mothers showed two different basic behaviors. One was to totally ignore the babies. The experimenter could actually reach into the cage and remove the infant without the mother paying any attention at all to the proceedings. Being stepped on would probably be less of an insult than being walked over as if you didn't exist, but for some motherless mothers, the baby as such just does not exist. This response of ignoring an infant offspring is completely foreign to the behavior of both human and monkey mothers who, at the dimmest detection of distress, rush to the babies and clasp them to their breasts with tender love and care. The other maternal pattern of the motherless mothers was grim and ghastly. When the mother's infant made actual contact with the mother's body, the mother would disattach the infant. She would literally scrape it from her body and abuse the baby by various sadistic devices. The mother would push the baby's face against the floor and rub it back and forth. This is not good maternal love; this is love defaced. In most instances our experimenters were able to stop sadism at this point, but some mothers were so violent and vicious that the baby was barely saved or even lost. Not infrequently the mother would encircle the infant's head with her jaws, and in one case the skull of the neonate was crushed before the mother and child could be separated, so little had we anticipated the severity of the events in the reproduction of the battered child syndrome. Again we emphasize the fact that these motherless mothers had never known affection of any kind, in spite of being raised in a faultless, physically hygienic environment with bodily needs satisfied—their baby love needs, however, were left locked in limbo.

The motherless mothers gave more to science than to their own offspring. Not only did they open doors of understanding of the battered child syndrome, but there was the confirmation of our conviction of the power and persistence of infant love for the mother. If the infants were among those favored and fortunate enough to be just ignored by their mothers, or if they had survived the battering, they persisted in their intense efforts to make and maintain contact with the maternal body whether or not the mother scraped them away or engaged in maternal mayhem. The amount of punishment the infants would accept was a measure of their motivation.

The second bonus from the babies was that after they had continuously conned mother into accepting protracted contact, some of the contact comfort, softness, and warmth seemed to rub off on the hard heart and head of the unnatural mother. Furthermore, after the maternal contact had been achieved over a period of time, there tended to be gradual but progressive maternal rehabilitation with partial or total submission to the infantile affection. The few mothers who succumbed were impressively more normal in the treatment of subsequent infants of their own. The monkey infants who succeeded in promoting maternal rehabilitation were the most junior of our junior therapists and the youngest psychiatrists in our experimental laboratory history.

It has long been an accepted fact that emotions are conditioned much more readily than they may be unconditioned or reconditioned. This is true, but the rehabilitation of rhesus monkeys suffering from abnormal, antisocial pathological behaviors has recently injected insight into the problem and contributed two innovative therapeutic techniques.

We were not smart enough to fully appreciate the underlying principle when the motherless mothers were rehabilitated by the persistent and patient persuasions of the baby monkeys. Our recent series of rehabilitation experiments of isolate monkeys has revealed the paramount power of "junior therapists." We had earlier tried introducing six-month isolate animals to same-aged monkeys who had been socially raised with mothers and peers. This attempt almost annihilated our already prostrate primates. They were petrified with fear and behaved in such strange fashions that the normal age mates bestook them for outlanders who made perfect, passive targets for outrageous group aggression.

The new technique combined six-month isolate rhesus monkeys with even younger psychiatrist monkeys. We have always believed that psychiatrists should be of the same species as the patients. We named these psychiatrists "junior therapists." The junior therapists were just half as old as the psychopathic isolate monkeys, three months of age to the isolates' six months. Being younger, smaller, and more gentle, these monkey therapists posed no threat to the fearful isolates. The age of three months is also the age at which play is just beginning to appear and is enticing to baby monkeys. Initially, two isolates and two junior therapists were housed in separate units of a four-unit cage whose inner barriers could be raised to allow two hours of interaction each day between the four infants. When the barriers were raised, the first reaction of the isolates was to retreat to a corner to cower and clasp themselves. The tiny therapists, unafraid and undaunted, followed and clung closely to them. Gradually, the contact comforted the isolates, and it was not long before they were clinging back. The next step was to be able to face other monkeys as well as to cling to them. The presence of others became tolerated, and then interaction between the therapists and the isolates occurred. The reality of others began to be realized. Little by little and literally step by step the junior therapists modeled and led the isolate monkeys into play and finally, play held sway. Perchance, in this first series of rehabilitation experiments, all of the junior therapists were female and all of the pathological infants were male. Subsequent studies indicate, however, that it is not essential to be a female to be a successful psychiatrist.

Twelve-month-old totally isolated rhesus infants had long been considered completely callous to any social rehabilitation. Novak, however, devised an ingenious experiment using very gradual stepwise procedures in adapting the isolates to each new situation, both solitary and social. For two weeks after being removed from the isolation cages, the monkeys lived in separate units of a quad cage masked with Masonite on all sides. The isolates could see each other but could not see the junior therapists in another cage in the same room.

After two weeks, the overall Masonite was removed and nineteen-inch high panels were substituted. Above these panels was see-through mesh. At this point, Novak introduced what she terms "self-paced" therapy. The water bottle spout was attached above the Masonite barrier. The monkeys had to climb to it to get water and, unavoidably, caught glimpses of the therapists in the other cage. They began to watch them. It is very difficult to maintain pathological postures such as huddle, rock, and self-clasp when climbing a wire wall. The therapist monkeys were allowed to interact socially part of the day, and the isolates began to watch them more often when they were playing together. The isolates had their first peek at play.

Through the combination of stepwise procedures, self-paced therapy, and junior therapists, Novak was successful in rehabilitating the twelve-month isolates. The two final measures of successful rehabilitation which have been consistently used in our experiments are normal play and normal sex. The rehabilitation of the twelve-month isolates required patience and was prolonged, but normal play was achieved without disruptive delay. Sex, unfortunately, could not be anticipated prior to the maturity of certain physiological functions, but when that time arrived, copulation confirmed our firm conclusions.

The achievement of aggression control through early establishment of adequate affectional bonds is widespread in our culture but to varying degrees of success, no matter what segment of society is concerned. A fundamental law, perhaps the most fundamental of psychological laws, is the fact that all important behaviors operate through multiple variables and not unitary factors. Aggression is no exception. A packet of factors is usually potent in affecting the hostile behavior of any one individual or group, and there is no monopoly on aggression among the economically impoverished and deprived. The lavish neglect of the affluent may fill a child's free time with T.V. prime time instead of positive peer playtime. In the same social stratum, social prerogatives may preclude the close maternal-infant interaction which forms a firm foundation. A child may be fortunate and favored with happy mother and infant loves and yet, so strong are the ties of age mates, be drawn into an adolescent drug group or gang already on its well-to-do but wanton way.

The principles propounded in this presentation are an extension of the underlying principles found to govern the development of the affectional systems. Just as each successive affectional system sinks or succeeds depending upon the fulfillment of the antecedent love system, so also can the socialization and amelioration of antisocial behaviors depend upon the adequacy of the antecedent love systems. The relationship between love and aggression is of all pervading importance in monkeys and in man. Research has shown that developmental timing and sequencing of the loves and of aggression are of vast significance in preventing or altering aggression. When the development is out of normal sequence, aggression is uncontrolled and extremely difficult to alter or eliminate. New therapeutic techniques are making rehabilitation more of a reality, but the ideal solution is to prevent antisocial aggression through anticipation. How many loves were included in the old-fashioned axiom "Love conquers all?"

20

Psychopathological Perspectives

Harry F. Harlow and Melinda N. Novak

Within the short temporal span of only 2,500 years significant gains have been made in the diagnosis, classification, and treatment of varied mental disorders. No longer is hysteria a wandering of the wanton womb, as described by Aesculapius, but instead it is a conversion neurosis. What has transpired over the last 2,500 years is that the interpretation has changed. It is not the physical disorder which has produced the psychic suffering; it is the psychic suffering that has been converted into the physical disorder.

The Greeks also recognized depression, and from time to time they had good reason to be depressed. However, the Greeks had no patented pills to alleviate their suffering. Today we have a wealth of patented pills, and some of the best abbreviate the period of suffering, whether or not they alleviate the pangs of suffering. We also have electroconvulsive shock, but no physician would engage in a treatment so shocking. However, it is medically acceptable if the treatment is called "electroconvulsive therapy." Shock is sadistic, but therapy is therapeutic. Quoting Shakespeare, "A rose by any other name would smell as sweet." We also have various verbal therapies which are as powerful curative agents for the alleviation of depression as is spontaneous remission.

Retrospectively, the brief and bewildered pictures which we have just painted are the perspectives of the past. The time-honored techniques of research and rescue will with good reason be used throughout the foreseeable future, but there is also reason to believe that they will be sup-

Harlow, H. F., & Novak, M. A. (1973) Psychopathological perspectives. *Perspectives in Biology and Medicine, 16*, 461–478.

plemented—and to a considerable extent superseded—by perspectives apparent at the present but only faintly fathomed for the future.

Research in psychopathology has gone far, and it will continue to go farther. The major psychoses are so disparate and dour, so bedeviled and destructive, that research on any kind of subject is justified, and mortal men of anguish and agony have often been the subjects of choice.

However, since it is for the most part ethically impossible to perform the manipulations necessary to delineate the factors involved in the etiology of human psychopathology, many researchers have turned with perfect propriety to the study of the development of psychopathology in non-human primates. The study of simian psychopathology involves the manipulation of possible etiological factors, the characterization of the psychopathology that is induced by these factors, and comparison of the behavioral changes in the monkey with behavioral aberrations in the human. Even though there are limitations to the use of nonhuman subjects in psychopathological research, the limitations are not as loathsome as indicated by Kubie (1) who did not believe that subhuman primates were suitable subjects for psychopathological research. This is Kubie's absolute right, but we hope that he is absolutely wrong.

SUBHUMAN ANIMALS AS PSYCHOPATHOLOGICAL RESEARCH SUBJECTS

In most medical fields, exploratory and even definitive research is conducted on subhuman animals. This is accepted and acceptable if proper care, caution, and control are conducted to prevent animal abuse and affliction beyond the discomfiture which the disease entails.

Platitudes rather than prudence have restricted the use of subhuman animals as subjects for psychopathological research. One of the problems in the use of nonhuman animals for psychopathological research results from the common assumption that there cannot be madness without mentality, and certainly not human madness without human mentality. Diagnosis of human madness in terms of the classifications convenient for humans is difficult to make for human morons, idiots, and imbeciles. This does not mean that human imbeciles and idiots do not have human psychoses. They suffer from communication problems similar to subhuman animals. Perhaps behavioral studies of subhuman animals will reveal what the psychopathologies of humans really are, and this alone would be progress beyond the programs of Aesculapius. Similarly, it should be stressed that nonhuman primates are not mindless mammals, and there are few, if any, basic human mental abilities, including basic language (2,3), which are not found in somewhat simplified form in nonhuman primates. The limits of subhuman animals as subjects for human-oriented psychopathological research will be determined by time and tests and not by wands or witless wonderers.

A limitation of subhuman subjects for human psychopathologic investigation is the fact that men are more sentient than other animals and probably have greater range and subtlety of affectional feelings. However, dementias are often far from subtle disorders. Another limitation of subhuman subjects for psychopathological studies lies in the fact that man is born and bred into a far greater range of cultural factors than the subhuman simians, but human cultural complexities are not an unmixed blessing in psychiatric description and diagnosis.

The great advantage of research with subhuman simians and other subhuman forms lies in the precision of control that can be exerted over psychotic-determining variables, including heredity; life history; deliberate induction of trauma or sequences of trauma; adequacy and inadequacy of individual or sequential environments; alteration of physiological states (homeostatic and hormonal); and alteration of anatomical structures, particularly neural and glandular. Finally, at the treatment level the initial use of drastic or even dangerous treatment regimes is acceptable for subhuman subjects and not acceptable for man.

There are many advantages in using human subjects in psychopathological researches and many advantages in using simian or other nonhuman subjects. These subject pools were not given by God to confuse and confound psychiatric investigations. The animals and the data they provide are not contradictory but complementary to the human data and should be treated as such.

As pointed out by McKinney and Bunney (4), three primary criteria must always be met in judging whether or not a human psychiatric syndrome has been produced in subhuman animals, either tenuously or in totality. The external behavioral expression, and hopefully the internal expression also, must resemble or mirror the form of the deviant human behaviors. Second, the causative agents producing the neurotic or psychotic state in the subhuman animal must be equivalent to or identical with those producing the human psychiatric condition. Finally, therapeutic agents or events capable of cure or containment of the disorder in man should be similarly effective on the treated subhuman forms.

If research demonstrates that these criteria can be met on any major human psychoses or neuroses, research should be conducted on any and all human disorders that meet the first two of our three stated criteria, comparability of form and cause in human and subhuman animals. It is important to know all of the psychic states with major communality in human and nonhuman animals, and it is also important to know the mental aberrations in which high communality does not exist. If there are some derelict diseases that are forever exclusively monkey and others that are hopelessly and haplessly human, this basic information would assist in classification and clarification of causative agents and appropriate therapies for diverse forms of dementia.

WISCONSIN PLANS AND PERSPECTIVES

The major goal in the study of psychopathology in nonhuman primates is to device methodologies and procedures producing reliable and valid behavioral anomalies. At the University of Wisconsin Primate Laboratory we have developed and are developing a family of behavioral techniques designed to produce psychopathology in monkeys, with the goal of gaining understanding and insight into human psychopathology, both its cause and cure.

One major technique which we have used for the production of pathological syndromes is that of isolation. We have investigated the effects of partial isolation, where a monkey can see and hear but not touch other monkeys, as well as the effects of total social isolation initiated at birth or after a period of social experience. We have tested the effects of brief isolation periods and prolonged periods. We have differentiated between sensory privation and behavioral privation. We are presently struggling to elucidate the effects of terrifying or fearful situations on the development of psychopathological behaviors, and the results appear to be positive, even if not yet definitive. Fear or terror states are effectively produced, but situational generalization of fears remains limited. Finally, we are continuing a long-term program on the induction of various forms of depression in monkeys of varying ages. The technique for inducing infantile anaclitic depression by separation of infants from loved objects has been extremely rewarding, and the monkey-human analogues are precise. Recently we have discovered that profound and prolonged depressive states can be induced by relatively brief confinement of monkeys in specially designed vertical chambers, and this technique of depression production opens up new domains of monkey psychopathology, including the investigation of underlying biochemical variables.

We have divided our discussion of monkey pathology, then, into three areas—privation and deprivation syndromes (5), fear or phobia, and depression. In the first area our data are more precise and perfect than those achieved in any human study to date. In the second group of studies we have probably added nothing to the human literature, and these nonhuman investigations are incomplete. In the third area our studies of anaclitic depression are models for human studies that might be undertaken. Our preliminary studies of postanaclitic depression suggest that we need additional information concerning case-history variables and possibly other variables.

PRIVATION AND DEPRIVATION SYNDROMES

A simple and sure way of endangering or even eradicating the primate personality lies in the technique of total social isolation. The ultimate effect of social isolation on the primate personality is clearly a function of the interaction of the length of the isolation interval and the stage of development at which isolation commences. It appears, however, that these variables may operate in different ways to affect the organism. For example, if the stage of development at the onset of isolation is kept constant, but the length of the isolation interval is varied, the resulting difference can be classified as one of degree. Monkeys totally socially isolated for 12 months from birth exhibit a greater frequency of withdrawal, behavioral bizarreness, and social incompetence than do monkeys totally socially isolated throughout the first 6 months of life (6). However, if the length of the isolation interval is kept constant but the stage of development at the onset of isolation is varied, the behaviors of the differentially deprived animals differ qualitatively from one another. The behavior of monkeys isolated during the first 6 months differs quantitatively as well as qualitatively from the behavior of monkeys isolated during the second 6 months of life, and these differences are apparent whether or not the antecedent social environments of the monkeys isolated during the second half-year of life were normal or involved only limited amounts of social interaction. Thus, time of onset of isolation for the late isolates appears to be more important than the nature of antecedent social experience as long as some social experience is allowed.

In an elaboration of the qualitative differences between monkeys as a function of the age of onset of isolation, two basic forms of isolation and their resulting syndromes can be delineated (5). Privation refers to the form of isolation in which the organism is incarcerated at or shortly after birth so that no social bonds have been formed. Here, maturational forces become the sole, actually socially soulless, factor creating the personality. The resulting syndrome produced by this form of isolation is characterized by the overwhelming presence of strange stereotypic behaviors, such as self-clasping, rocking, and huddling, that persist under subsequent social test conditions. Commonly these stereotypic behavior patterns prevent positive environmental or social interaction because of their persistent nature. Furthermore, the monkey is captured and confined within his own selfish existence by his initial failure to comprehend the form and function of other members of his species. This initial failure is undoubtedly caused by his complete lack of experience with other monkeys. Nevertheless, consideration, comprehension, and appropriate responsiveness to other monkeys can be learned under certain favorable conditions of rehabilitation therapy which will be described later.

Deprivation, the second form of isolation, refers to the conditions under which the monkey enjoys normal or at least fragmentary social experiences with species members until some arbitrary or predestined time, when the gates of mercy and social meaning are closed and the animal is left to grow up in a confine devoid of the companionship of lingering loving forms. In these cases, separation from social partners and peers becomes the primary factor altering the emerging personality. Unlike privation, the behaviors resulting from deprivation are not characterized particularly by the presence of strange stereotypic responses and a profound inability to respond to objects social or otherwise, but rather by a disorder of affect comprising violent vocalization, cringing fear, and heightened aggression. These behavioral characteristics are either absent or fragmentary in animals subjected to privation.

The main difference in the effect of privation as opposed to deprivation in monkeys is clearly related to the development of social bonds. The absence of social bonds before privation results in the production of later individual, self-oriented repetitive behaviors, while the presence of social bonds before deprivation leads to the development of social affectional disorders. This fact is not at all surprising, since an animal isolated from birth has no social role models for development and comparison of emotional states but rather has an existence centered around his own anatomy. It is likely that monkeys experiencing privation have very limited emotional states because of the constancy and simplicity of their environment. Similarly, it is not surprising to discover that deprivation produces a heightening of emotional states involved with fear, aggression, and depression. The deprived animal, already familiar with the joyous bonds of social servitude and love, is thrust into a situation where all lingering love is lost and environmental stimulation is minimal compared to what the animal has known—indeed a true incarceration of both body and spirit. Surprisingly enough, the deprivation syndrome has been found in similar form in monkeys with much normal antecedent experience and animals with limited antecedent social experience.

The meaningfulness of the dichotomy of privation versus deprivation has been stressed by Gewirtz (5) on the basis of extant human pathology. The information that we have obtained on simian forms from similar isolation procedures differs from the human data only in the fact that the precise controls which we could exercise over our monkey subjects make the differential concepts plausible and precise.

We already have an ample array of studies making it possible to compare the behavioral devastations produced by varying intervals of privation. Total social isolation during the first 3 months of life produces no permanent social loss; indeed, shortly after the monkey recovers from the shock of exposure to a new and profoundly more complex world, he successfully interacts with normal age mates and becomes an accepted member of a normal social group within a month (7).

In contrast, the effects of total social isolation throughout the first 6 months of monkey life are drastic and direfully damaging. Monkeys exposed to this experience develop strange stereotypic behavior patterns, no two of which are ever exactly alike. Social interaction with normal monkeys is either nonexistent or tediously and tenuously attained, although there is some spontaneous recovery in exploratory and play behaviors with other isolates if they are allowed to interact after the total social isolation period.

Even when, in the second or third year, the 6-month isolates have become endocrinologically adequate sexually, as indicated by normal female estrus cycles and the presence of sperm in the testes of the males, their gymnastic qualifications are only quaint and cursory as compared with sexual achievement customary at these ages. Isolates may grasp other monkeys of either sex by the head and thrust aimlessly, a semierotic exercise without amorous achievement. Another erotic genuflection is that of grasping at another monkey, male or female, at the midline and thrusting across their bodies. This exercise leaves the early totally isolated monkey working at cross-purposes with reality.

Finally, social apathy does not prevent the 6-month isolate monkeys from developing vigorous and violent aggression at the appropriate monkey age of 2–3 years. However, the aggression of these isolates differs from that of normal animals in its completely asocial qualities. The mature total isolates aggress against infant monkeys, an act commonly beneath the dignity of normal monkeys. Or the isolates may make a single, sacrificial, suicidal sortie against a large adult, an act never attempted by socially experienced adolescents.

It came as no surprise that 12 months of total social isolation produced even more dramatic social obliteration. A year of total social isolation erased any and all propensities for social play or social interchange and destroyed nearly all monkey social communication. Even misguided attempts at sexual dalliance were dissipated; and, even worse, the right to honest and honorable onanism appeared to be lost. Furthermore, there was no spontaneous improvement or recovery of any positive behavior during a 4- to 5-month interval. It appeared that all was lost for the 12-month total social isolate.

We had previously concluded that 6 months of privation produced permanent devastating results. However, recent therapy techniques that were initiated in our laboratory by Suomi and Harlow (8) indicated that this was wrong. In our early studies of the effects of 6 months of isolation, the isolated animals were always paired with equal-aged socially normal monkeys. A 6-month normal monkey is a complex organism for the isolate to behold. At this age he is a skillful playmate already possessing the rudiments of rough-and-tumble play and playful aggressiveness, and he is an extremely curious animal not to be easily scared or discouraged. Suomi, assuming that the 6-month normal monkey was much too socially complex for the unsocialized isolate, decided to pair 6-month total social isolate monkeys with 3-month socially normal female monkeys. The 3-month normal female is a cuddler and a clinger who is just beginning to explore the environment and develop play behavior. The long-term results of such a pairing changed the strange and troubled isolates into enthusiastic participants in social interactions, both with individuals or in group situations. The ultimate complete socialization of the 6-month isolate monkeys was totally unexpected but warmly welcome.

It had long been Wisconsin dogma that 12 months of social isolation socially eradicated and erased the victims; indeed, we believed on perfectly reasonable grounds that the social life and all social proclivities of our 12-month socially isolated animals were virtually destroyed. However, undaunted by fate or facts, Novak (9) embarked upon a program to rehabilitate a group of four 12-month isolate monkeys. Six months of progressive therapy involving gentle adaptation to strange animate and inanimate objects, reinforcement of social responses of increasing complexity, pairwise and group interactions with male and female 4-month-old therapist monkeys, and at a later time with age mate therapist monkeys resulted in the development of socially rehabilitated animals. All of Novak's 12-month isolates subsequently made a very adequate social adjustment to the younger therapists and then a somewhat adequate or nearly adequate social adjustment to the equal-aged normal monkeys. Indeed, the adjustment was so good that experienced primatologists seldom differentiate between the normal and isolate monkeys during sessions involving social contacts and interchanges including vigorous play.

Our amazing success with rehabilitating both 6- and 12-month isolate monkeys indicated that Novak's interpretation of the effects of privation, as already described in this paper, is correct. She assumed that privation produced monkeys that responded bizarrely not because of affect instability, but rather because these were the responses the monkeys had developed in their isolation chambers. The bizarre behaviors of self-clasping and rocking are clearly functional in the isolation chamber. Infant monkeys, isolated or not, possess a strong clasping reflex, which in the case of the early isolated monkey is utilized to clasp himself, since no other warm and dimensionally distinct object is available. Similarly, rocking behaviors produce rhythm and stimulation in the less-than-stimulating environment.

Researchers studying chimpanzees have also suggested that these stereotypic behaviors are evoked under conditions of extreme isolation (10). Thus, the early isolated monkeys learned behaviors that were functional but bizarre in social contexts. Barring the presence of any major critical period during the first year of life, it should have been possible to teach the isolated monkeys the appropriate social behaviors by using the processes of imitation and reinforcement, and this is precisely what our therapy procedures did with such resounding success.

In contrast to privation, deprivation, which is the incarceration of a previously socialized animal, appears to produce problems in affect. In a study by Joslyn (11), six socially sophisticated juvenile monkeys and six monkeys raised with their mothers were deprived of all social contacts between the ages of 18 and 26 months. The effects of this deprivation involved the development of subtle changes in fear and hostility such that the late-isolated monkeys displayed both more dominance-oriented behaviors and more social fear or withdrawal than controls. This alteration in effect waned in 4 months' time. These late isolates did not develop the strange stereotypic behaviors that characterized the early isolates but rather displayed changes in the relative amounts of affective behaviors. Other deprivation studies of Rowland (6) and Clark (12) found that deprived monkeys that had enjoyed only minimal social experiences (e.g., partially isolated monkeys) prior to isolation were affected only minimally by 6 months of subsequent isolation. Both groups of deprived monkeys rapidly interacted with control monkeys that had received the same kind of rearing experiences as the isolated monkeys except for the isolation itself. Nonetheless, the interaction was marked with changes in affect. The isolated monkeys were mildly hyperaggressive. The Rowland and Clark monkeys similarly showed no behavioral bizarreness as compared with their respective control groups. Furthermore, when the socially deprived monkeys glided gracefully into puberty, their sexual responses were exercised, not exorcised.

The evidence indicates that privation and deprivation produce qualitatively different syndromes—privation producing intense behavioral anomalies and deprivation producing disorders in affect associated with increases in aggression and fear. Most of the effects of privation can be successfully ameliorated through patient adaptation procedures and social imitation, while the effects of deprivation appear to eventually disappear with renewed social contact.

An interesting psychopathological interpretation has been offered by Beavers and Lewis (13) who have suggested that the delayed total social isolation had produced a new form of psychotic monkey, the sociopathic monkey. These monkeys had no difficulty in interacting with equal-aged peers, but the interactions were characterized by spontaneous, unprovoked acts of aggression and avoidance of social contact. By and large social contact is avoided, and when forced upon them it provokes animosity and assault. As subsequently shown, depression can be produced in monkeys with relative ease.

FEAR

In an attempt to reveal some further insight into the cause and cure of psychopathological disturbances, we set out to examine the effects of intense fear-producing situations on monkey behavior. We developed a diabolical device to produce turmoil and terror. This apparatus, euphemistically called the terror trap, consisted of a small upper chamber and a large lower chamber. The lower chamber contained three sections of which the two outer sections contained toy monsters of varying types— robots with flashing, protruding guns; spaceships; or other toys with flashing lights and flapping arms. The middle section was devoid of toy monsters. The upper chamber rested directly above the middle section of the lower chamber and could be manually lowered into the lower chamber, and as such resembled an elevator shaft. Thus, a subject was initially placed in the upper chamber and after a 1-minute delay was lowered into the fear apparatus to face the assault of arm-flapping, light-flashing, buzzing, or shrieking monsters—one on each side of him.

The apparatus was extremely successful in producing terror in monkeys, as evidenced by their bizarre behaviors. Several monkeys clung to the mesh ceiling of the elevator, remaining in this position for as long as 15 minutes. Other monkeys that chose to remain on the floor typically withdrew from the situation by huddling, self-clasping, and sleeping. Many screamed and screeched throughout the entire interval of containment and internment or until they became hoarse from the violence of their vocalization. All subjects developed intense fears or phobias, although the generalization from the test situation to the home cage was surprisingly slight.

Initially Novak subjected four partial isolates 6 months of age to the so-called terror trap individually for 15 minutes a day for 6 weeks. These partial isolates had never had any physical contact with other monkeys and consequently displayed exaggerated home-cage behavior involving extensive rocking, huddling, and self-clasping. While in the fear apparatus, these behaviors were exaggerated and other positive behaviors were completely eliminated. Although some distress was associated with the apparatus itself, the distress disappeared with time when the monsters were not present. The distress associated with the monsters was severe and persisted throughout the 6-week interval. Nonetheless, the home-cage behaviors of these monkeys during terror-trap testing showed a paradoxical improvement. Negative behaviors such as self-clasping, rocking, and huddling decreased in frequency, while positive behaviors such as visual exploration and locomotion increased in frequency.

Novak also tested four surrogate and peer-reared monkeys 2 years of age and two surrogate and peer-reared monkeys 1 year of age in the terror trap. The monkeys were exposed to the fearful situation for one 15-minute period per week for 8 weeks. Plasma cortisol as well as behavioral measures—such as screeching and huddling—indicated that none of these animals adapted to the test situation even after 8 weeks of time. Again, there were only minimal effects on the home-cage behavior of these monkeys, such as a slight rise in fear grimacing and clasping.

Unfortunately, the terror trap has not produced the plethora of generalized behavioral anomalies that have been associated with other psychopathological procedures, and the variables for producing widely generalized phobic responses are open for investigation. It seems likely that longer exposure to fearful situations at earlier ages might produce more dramatic results. We have already seen from the privation and deprivation studies that insufficient stimulation, particularly social stimulation, produces drastic generalized deficits in monkeys. It seems reasonable to assume that excessive stimulation, be it nonsocial or social, can also produce widespread behavioral disabilities.

DEPRESSION

Choosing a psychopathological syndrome of power, persistence, and generality, we initiated our comprehensive program on the production and, hopefully, the cure of depressions. There were multiple reasons for this approach. We had already inadvertently produced depression in the rhesus infant while directing our efforts to variables influencing maternal love. This is atypical. Love often ends in depression, but seldom does depression end in love.

An early simple form of human depression is induced in infants by separating them for more than momentary periods from their mothers. This form of human depression was described by Spitz (14) and termed "anaclitic depression." Extensive human data on anaclitic depression have also been presented by Bowlby (15), who called the first two stages of the syndrome "protest" and "despair." During the protest stage the child and the baby monkey seek maternal succor by vocalizations and by movement directed toward the mother. The stage of despair begins when attempts to reestablish maternal contact and comfort have ceased. During the despair period, vocalization and movement are drastically reduced or cease, and the monkey often assumes a prone posture with head and body wrapped in its arms and legs. Although the face is often unseen, the postural picture has enormous face validity.

When some human children are reunited with the mother, their responses toward the maternal figure are those of rejection, and Bowlby actually called this reunion stage "disattachment." However, many human children and almost all baby monkeys eagerly and avidly reattach to the mother, and we prefer to describe the third stage as that of reunion or reattachment.

In our studies of monkey mother-child separation we simultaneously separated two infant friends, a half-year of age, from their mothers. This procedure enabled us to measure the effect of maternal separation on the highly social responses of play, since the infants remained together. Play was nonexistent throughout the stage of despair, and there was no sign of recovery until the despair period ended. Unfortunately, the measured despair period lasted only 3 weeks, whereas there is reason to believe that the socially depressive effects lasted 3 months or more.

Thus, anaclitic depression produced by personal social loss—the loss of the mother love—is strong, abiding, apparently universal, and at least moderately persisting. The form of the infant's response throughout the course of depression is highly similar to that of the human child. Both cause (the loss of the mother) and cure of depression (the return of the mother) are also highly similar or identical in monkey and man.

Anaclitic depression had always been studied in terms of mother-child separation until Suomi, Harlow, and Domek (16) measured the effects of separating infant friends. Starting at 3 months of age, Suomi separated the infant friends for 4 days and reunited them for 3-day periods until a total of 20 separations had been completed over a 6-month period. At each and every separation the infants went through stages of protest and despair, followed by reattachment when they were conjoined. Thus, separation anxiety showed no signs of adapting with either time or trials. Separation always led to distress which was persistent and pervasive and was followed by reattachment which was benign and beatific. Disattachment never appeared.

A decade ago the Harlows (17) analyzed the multiple love systems and concluded that age mate or peer love is as strong a motive as maternal love. The systems are, of course, radically different and are produced and excited by different social functions, but both love systems are very intense and very persisting.

However, the 20 successive age-mate separations between pairs of monkeys raised with peers gave rise to an unexpected phenomenon of great theoretical interest, a phenomenon of complete or almost complete behavioral maturational arrest. Normal 90-day-old animals show relatively high levels of orality and self-cling. These responses fairly rapidly disappear and are essentially nonexistent in normal monkeys at 9 months of age. Conversely, social exploration and play are responses which are just developing at 90 days of age, but these responses largely dominate the behavioral repertoire of normal monkeys 9 months of age, whether living with peers only or with peers and some maternal object.

Before repetitive separation the infant peers showed a perfectly normal behavioral repertoire, a repertoire of behaviors appropriate for 90-day-old monkeys. The level of self-mouthing and self-clinging was relatively high and the level of exploration and play very low. After 20 separations were completed and 270 days had passed, the multiply separated peers when not subjected to further separation possessed their 90-day-old behavioral repertoire and nothing else. They sucked and clung at an infantile level, showed no interest in exploration, and bypassed any attempts at play. They were oral-erotic, mutually clinging robots, uninterested in exploring the other world or engaging in social interactions, particularly play. It was as if their behavioral repertoires were frozen at 90 days of age when the multiple separations began. This complete behavioral arrest was more complete and far more dramatic than any similar phenomenon previously observed, even in animals under total social isolation. Furthermore, the multiply separated peers always had potential playmates for almost half the days between the 90- and 270-day period. Adequate potentialities for socialization existed, but they had not and could not be used. Baby monkeys raised with peers only are somewhat delayed in forming bonds of play and passion, but they are all essentially normal at 6–9 months of age. It is possible that all of Suomi's infant monkeys had inadvertently walked through Ponce de Leon's behavioral fountain of youth, but this is unlikely.

The paradigm for anaclitic depression was mother-infant separation until Suomi created the complementary paradigm of age mate-infant separation. These data indicate that the concept of anaclitic depression should be broadened to include the loss of the beloved social object, whether it be mother or peer. In both cases depression is occasioned by social loss, and the kind of love lost is probably not an important variable.

Intense nonsocial depression in monkeys was achieved by Harlow and Suomi (18) using vertical chambers large enough to allow free movement in all three planes. These vertical chambers were stainless steel troughs sloping downward and inward to a rounded bottom covered by a platform of hardware cloth. Chambering is a severe deprivation condition, but other variables are doubtlessly operating.

Although there was little reason to believe that the vertical chambers would produce depression more precisely, more quickly, and more permanently than the technique of our time-honored total social isolation chamber, the facts totally belied the thoughts. One group of monkeys raised in partial social isolation until approximately 1 year of age and another group with limited social experience that had been pitted for 45 days antecedent to 90 days of age showed deep and persistent depression in terms of the high frequency of self-clutch and rocking behaviors and the loss of locomotion and environmental exploration behaviors. Furthermore, after the first group of monkeys had been removed from the vertical chambers and tested for 8 consecutive weeks, they showed no indication of recovery whatsoever as measured by each and all of the behavioral tests. Actually many of the depression measures are surprisingly persistent, lasting for months rather than days or weeks.

It is surprising, indeed, that the vertical chamber technique, which as so far used involves apparently other variables than merely those of social loss, remains the most potent, pervasive, and persistent of all our depression devices. At the present time we are analyzing the physical qualities of the vertical chambers in terms of depression-production efficiency, and we plan to measure social variables incorporated within these chambers.

The similarities and differences between anaclitic adolescent and adult depression remain in large part a matter of conjecture. A group of four subadult monkeys were subjected to repetitive separations, and another group was placed in large vertical chambers. After both multiple separation and chambering the experimental group showed some significant behavioral differences from members of control groups, but the results were far less striking than the results obtained on the infants. The primary differentiating measure was that the chambered subadult monkey demonstrated an abnormal pattern of sitting quietly near, but not contacting, social partners. These must be regarded as merely exploratory studies, giving only incomplete clues concerning the nature of reactive depression in mature animals.

Our present information on the induction of depression in subhuman primate forms ranges from data that are merely descriptive to data that are clearly definitive. Yet all of these give information and ideas concerning the most appropriate research roads to be followed. We can only hope that one or more of the roads will lead to the perfect palace where all depressions are domiciled. One hopeful aspect of depression research is that it can never fail. Someone will become depressed. If the subjects become depressed, the experimenter will be elated, if the subjects remain elated, the experimenter will become depressed. Unfortunately, the two end states are not equally desirable.

PERSPECTIVES: PAST, PRESENT, AND FUTURE

The primary goal of psychopathology is the description of abnormal syndromes, the determination of underlying variables (behavioral and biochemical), and the creation of effective treatment conditions. Obviously the animal of primary choice to meet these goals is man. However, there are many advantages in using nonhuman animals, particularly nonhuman primates, in determining and assessing the variables producing each and all disease entities. Furthermore, once disease entities analogous to those of man have been delineated and described in simian and subsimian forms and identical or similar consecutive agencies determined, these subhuman animals offer advantages in testing and even determining the relative efficacy of therapeutic agents, both behavioral and biochemical.

Subhuman subjects can be maintained under completely controlled conditions—behavioral, physiological, and neurological. Furthermore, treatments both delicate and drastic may be employed without fear of personal disaster in subhuman animals, but not in man. Men are not monkeys and monkeys are not men. Neither men nor monkeys are dogs, cats, or rodents. Choosing from the myriad of mammals, the court of last resort for psychopathological research must, of course, be a court composed of men. It is to be hoped that those techniques which are ruinous will be lost before men become the subjects.

At Wisconsin we have conducted multiple researches on privation and deprivation, and our data give clarity and classification to the earlier clinical efforts. Here the monkey data are definitive. We have initiated researches on the acquisition and analysis of fears and phobias. Phobias are easily produced, and once produced, they persist. Our own data, however, show little situational generality, and the mechanisms generating or inhibiting fear generality remain to be investigated.

We are in the midst of a major program of the induction of various forms of depression in rhesus monkeys, and by various techniques we can now induce profound and prolonged depression in them. We have been most successful in the induction of anaclitic or childhood depression, but we believe that variations of our techniques and the control and manipulation of early physical and social variables will enable us to surmount any age-range barriers that presently exist. We have achieved unexpected success in the behavioral rehabilitation of monkeys apparently socially destroyed by prolonged periods of social privation, and we have initiated researches designed to rehabilitate monkeys depressed by other means.

We are interested in simulating psychopathic states other than depression in simian subjects. Work by others (13) suggests that we may have inadvertently produced sociopathic animals, but further research is needed. We have inadvertently produced schizophrenia-like behavior in individual monkeys, and we are initiating research designed to produce such states under deliberate defined and definitive conditions. In other words, we are seeking to exhaust the monkeys' psychopathic capabilities, so that we know where simian insanity ends and human hopelessness begins and how and where they overlap.

REFERENCES

1. L. S. Kubie. *In:* M. Heiman (ed.). Psychoanalysis and social work, p. 3. New York: International Universities Press, 1953.
2. D. Premack. *In:* A. M. Schrier and F. Stollnitz (eds.). Behavior of nonhuman primates, vol. 4, p. 185. New York: Academic Press, 1971.
3. B. T. Gardner and R. A. Gardner. *In:* A. M. Schrier and F. Stollnitz (eds.). Behavior of nonhuman primates, vol. 4, p. 117. New York: Academic Press, 1971.
4. W. T. McKinney and W. E. Bunney. *Arch. Gen. Psychiat., 21*:240, 1969.
5. J. L. Gewirtz. *In:* B. M. Foss (ed.). Determinants of infant behavior, vol. 1, p. 213. London: Methuen, 1961.
6. G. L. Rowland. The effects of total social isolation upon learning and social behavior in rhesus monkeys. Unpublished Ph.D. diss., Univ. Wisconsin, 1964.
7. G. A. Griffin and H. F. Harlow. *Child Develop., 37*:533, 1966.
8. S. J. Suomi and H. F. Harlow. *Develop. Psychol., 6*:487, 1972.
9. M. A. Novak. Submitted for publication.
10. W. A. Mason and P. C. Green. *J. Comp. Physiol. Psychol., 55*:363, 1962.
11. W. D. Joslyn. Behavior of socially experienced juvenile rhesus monkeys after eight months of late social isolation and maternal-offspring relations and maternal separation in juvenile rhesus monkeys. Unpublished Ph.D., diss., Univ. Wisconsin, 1967.
12. D. L. Clark. Immediate and late effects of early, intermediate and late social isolation in the rhesus monkey. Unpublished Ph.D. diss., Univ. Wisconsin, 1968.
13. W. R. Beavers and J. M. Lewis. Personal communication, 1972.
14. R. A. Spitz. *Psychoanal. Stud. Child, 2*:313, 1946.
15. J. Bowlby. *Psychoanal. Stud. Child, 15*:9, 1960.
16. S. J. Suomi, H. F. Harlow, and C. J. Domek. *J. Abnorm. Psychol., 76*:161, 1970.
17. H. F. Harlow and M. K. Harlow. *In:* A. M. Schrier, H. F. Harlow, and F. Stollnitz (eds.). Behavior of nonhuman primates, vol. 2, p. 287. New York: Academic Press, 1965.
18. H. F. Harlow and S. J. Suomi. *J. Child Aut. Schiz., 1*:246, 1971.

NOTE

University of Wisconsin Primate Laboratory, 22 North Charter Street, Madison, Wisconsin 53706. This research was supported by U.S. Public Health Service grants MH-11894, MH-18070, and RR-00167 from the National Institutes of Health to the University of Wisconsin Primate Laboratory and Regional Primate Research Center, respectively.

Index